MONETARY POLICY IN A CONVERGING EUROPE

FINANCIAL AND MONETARY POLICY STUDIES

Volume 31

The titles published in this series are listed at the end of this volume.

MONETARY POLICY IN A CONVERGING EUROPE

Papers and Proceedings of an International Workshop organised by De Nederlandsche Bank and the Limburg Institute of Financial Economics

Edited by

KOOS ALDERS
De Nederlandsche Bank, Amsterdam, The Netherlands

KEES KOEDIJK
Limburg Institute of Financial Economics, University of Limburg, Maastricht, The Netherlands

CLEMENS KOOL
Limburg Institute of Financial Economics, University of Limburg, Maastricht, The Netherlands

CARLO WINDER
De Nederlandsche Bank, Amsterdam, The Netherlands

Kluwer Academic Publishers
Dordrecht / Boston / London

Library of Congress Cataloging-in-Publication Data

Monetary policy in a converging Europe : papers and proceedings of an international workshop organised by De Nederlandsche Bank and the Limburg Institute of Financial Economics / edited by Koos Alders ... [et al.].

p. cm. -- (Financial and monetary policy studies ; v. 31)

ISBN-13: 978-1-4612-8532-8 e-ISBN-13: 978-1-4613-1249-9

DOI: 10.1007/978-1-4613-1249-9

1. Monetary policy--European Union countries--Congresses. 2. Monetary policy--Congresses. I. Alders, Koos. II. Nederlandsche Bank (Amsterdam, Netherlands) III. Limburg Institute of Financial Economics. IV. Series.

HG925.M659 1996

332.4'94--dc20 95-35840

Published by Kluwer Academic Publishers,
P.O. Box 17, 3300 AA Dordrecht, The Netherlands.

Kluwer Academic Publishers incorporates the publishing programmes of D. Reidel, Martinus Nijhoff, Dr W. Junk and MTP Press.

Sold and distributed in the U.S.A. and Canada
by Kluwer Academic Publishers,
101 Philip Drive, Norwell, MA 02061, U.S.A.

In all other countries, sold and distributed
by Kluwer Academic Publishers Group,
P.O. Box 322, 3300 AH Dordrecht, The Netherlands.

Printed on acid-free paper

Table of Contents

Preface

This book contains the papers and proceedings of an international workshop organised by De Nederlandsche Bank NV and the Limburg Institute of Financial Economics of the University of Limburg (LIFE) in February 1995. It covers the most important monetary issues in the transition process towards an Economic and Monetary Union in Europe, and contains contributions of reputed experts in the respective research and policy areas: Bayoumi (IMF), Borio (BIS), Dueker (Federal Reserve Bank of St. Louis), Fischer (Schweizerische Nationalbank), Groeneveld (De Nederlandsche Bank), Koedijk (LIFE), Kool (LIFE) and Monticelli (Banca d'Italia). The various contributions discuss among other things the scope for inflation targetting, the P-star approach, monetary interdependencies between the "core" ERM countries, policy consequences of money demand (in)stability in Europe, differences between the monetary transmission mechanisms in various industrial countries, and the preferred exchange rate policy during the remainder of Stage Two of EMU. Finally, De Grauwe (Catholic University of Leuven), Hogeweg (European Monetary Institute), Bakker (De Nederlandsche Bank) and Thygesen (Institute of Economics at the Copenhagen Business School), in a panel discussion, review the main topics and debate "The Best Way to EMU".

The editors would like to express their gratitude to all the contributors to this volume. Special thanks to Cobie Hogewoning-Visscher and Kasper van Veen for invaluable assistance in editing the final version of the book. They also thank the other participants of the workshop and the organising committee.[1] We hope – and believe – the book provides an informative overview of current issues for anyone interested in monetary policy in a converging Europe.

Amsterdam/Maastricht
June 1995

Koos Alders
Kees Koedijk
Clemens Kool
Carlo Winder

[1]The organising committee was made up of Jansen, Koedijk and Kool of LIFE and Alders, Groeneveld, Haan, Hoogduin, Weeling and Winder of De Nederlandsche Bank.

Monetary Policy in a Converging Europe: Overview of the Issues and Summary of the Discussion

KOOS ALDERS,[1] KEES KOEDIJK,[2] CLEMENS KOOL[2]
AND CARLO WINDER[1]

[1]*De Nederlandsche Bank, Amsterdam, The Netherlands*
[2]*Limburg Institute of Financial Economics, University of Limburg, Maastricht, The Netherlands*

1. Introduction

With the date of the start of Stage Three of Economic and Monetary Union (EMU) rapidly approaching, the interest of central bankers and academics in various topics related to monetary policy in a converging Europe is increasing strongly. This book contains contributions from experts on subjects such as experiences of countries which have recently adopted a monetary policy strategy of direct-inflation-targeting, increasing monetary interdependencies in ERM countries, money demand (in)stability and the possible consequences for monetary policy co-ordination in Europe, credit characteristics and the monetary policy transmission mechanism in various industrialised countries, and finally the issue of which exchange rate policy to pursue in the run-up to the start of Stage Three.

This introductory chapter contains an overview of these issues. Following a summary of each of the five studies, the main points from the discussion at the Workshop are highlighted with particular focus on the contributions from a number of discussants. The panel discussion which concluded the Workshop, is summarised in the chapter "The Best Way to EMU: Summary of the Panel Discussion".

2. Dueker and Fischer on Inflation Targets

In the recent past, some industrial countries have started to formulate monetary policy in terms of explicit inflation targets. Principal objective of the public announcements of such targets of course is to influence market expectations. Although these countries in general have achieved their goal of reducing inflation, it is unclear what the contribution of the inflation targets has been. Inflation has also been reduced in countries without explicit targets. In the paper of Dueker and Fischer, presented at the workshop by Fischer from the Swiss National Bank, the authors investigate to what extent explicit inflation targets as currently used by a number of developed countries have indeed been instrumental in lowering the expected (baseline) rate of inflation in these countries. To this end, three countries with explicit inflation targets viz.

Koos Alders, Kees Koedijk, Clemens Kool and Carlo Winder (eds.), Monetary Policy in a Converging Europe, pp. 1–19.

New Zealand, Canada, and the United Kingdom, are matched with three neighbouring countries without inflation targets: Australia, the United States, and Germany, respectively. A pairwise quantitative comparison is performed using a sophisticated estimation technique. The empirical analysis is based on the estimation of a switching model with three state variables that together characterise the economy. The first state variable equals one when the economy is in the low inflation state and zero when it is in the high inflation state. The second state variable is equal to one when the central bank cares about the level of the exchange rate and zero when it does not, while the third state variable is unity when the noise in the system (the variance of the residual) is high and zero when it is low.

The short-run nominal interest rate is assumed to be the central bank's policy instrument and as such to reveal the central bank's inflation preferences. Therefore, the dependent variable in the switching regression is the change in the nominal interest rate minus an exogenous time-series forecast of the change in the nominal interest rate divided by the price level. Equivalently, the dependent variable may be seen as the sum of the one period-ahead expected inflation plus the unpredicted part of the nominal interest rate change. This variable is labeled "intended" inflation by the authors and is regressed on an intercept and two feedback terms, reflecting deviations of the actual price level and exchange rate from their targeted levels respectively. An actual price level or exchange rate in excess of the target may lead the central bank to allow for higher inflation (and nominal interest rates) in the short-run. All regression parameters are state-dependent. The results show a marked difference between the inflation target for the high and low states respectively. Both inflation states are highly persistent. The hypothesised feedback mechanisms are insignificant in most cases. For each country, the baseline inflation target path is derived by summing across states the product of the probability of being in the low (high) inflation state with the inflation target estimate of the low (high) state. In general, the results show abrupt swings in the baseline path.

A comparison of inflation performance in Australia and New Zealand shows that in both countries actual as well as baseline inflation fell sharply to unprecedentedly low levels in the late eighties and remained low in the nineties, suggesting that both countries in recent years have acted as if they were placing increased emphasis on zero inflation. Although the fall in New Zealand's rate led the Australian events, the results do not suggest that New Zealand has made considerable gains relative to Australia because of its explicit inflation targets. The Canadian baseline inflation rate shifted to the low inflation state in 1992. Although this is consistent with the announcement of inflation targets in early 1991, some problems remain. Firstly, baseline inflation of just below 4 percent in the low state is well above the announced target range of 1–3 percent and above actual inflation. Secondly, the United States went to a comparable low inflation state much earlier without explicit targets. British monetary policy has changed continuously over the last two decades, leading to extremely volatile interest and inflation patterns. The empirical estimates for the

United Kingdom find that the baseline shifts with actual inflation. In 1992, actual inflation appears to lead the shift in the baseline and, thus, in preferences. For Germany, the baseline inflation target has been constant at 2 percent since 1985, consistent with the Bundesbank's informal target. Overall, the paper provides little if any empirical support for the hypothesis that explicit inflation targets have contributed to reducing baseline inflation. All countries appear to have settled on low inflation paths in the late eighties and early nineties. Without the help of formal inflation targets, the United States and Germany, however, have shifted earlier and to a lower path than their neighbours with inflation targets.

The first discussant, Briault (Bank of England), objected to the exclusion of real factors from the analysis. In his view, the domestic and worldwide cyclical conditions in the late eighties may have contributed considerably in the reduction of inflation and as such should have been used as information variables. He also questioned the paper's focus on current inflation instead of expectations of future inflation. Referring to the long and variable lags generally found between a change in monetary policy and subsequent inflationary developments, he argued against the use of the short-term interest rate in response to current inflation. Moreover, due to this transmission lag of perhaps two years, the decline of actual inflation in the United Kingdom in the early 1990s must be the result of contractionary policy in the late 1980s, before the switch to inflation targets. The already very short sample becomes therefore even shorter and it seems hardly possible to draw conclusions from the current evidence. Briault asked also for confidence intervals around the baseline point estimates to get some feeling for the uncertainty surrounding the estimates. He also admitted to be confused by the definition of the baseline inflation path and the various terms that refer to it, such as the policy-implied, cyclical or typical inflation. He wondered whether the empirical test was about absolute shifts in the baseline, shifts in actual inflation relative to an unchanged baseline or simultaneous shifts in actual and baseline inflation in one country relative to another. In addition, he pointed to the strong assumption of stable reaction functions. Finally, Briault used the strong relation between forward-looking bond yields and average inflation performance in the past to argue that credibility in general cannot be acquired by merely announcing inflation targets but need to be bought by low inflation performance. In his view, for a better test, we need to wait at least a substantial period.

The second discussant, Neumann (University of Bonn), started with the statement that perceived instability in money demand functions by itself does not make inflation targeting a superior monetary policy. He also pointed out the danger of credibility losses for a central bank using inflation targets when inflation picks up again. Secondly, he objected to the causality implied by the paper between targets and inflation preferences. In his view, (changes in) inflation targets follow from and signal (changes in) central bank preferences, not the other way round. According to Neumann, a more appropriate discriminatory test about central bank's preferences would be to estimate reaction functions over different periods and test for their equality. Neumann also supported Briault's claim that real factors and their consequences such as the accommodation of oil price shocks in the 1970s should be taken into account. On a more detailed level, Neumann criticised the construction of the dependent variable and its dependancy on the magnitude and volatility of unexpected interest rate shocks which if dominant could significantly influence the results. Also, Neumann noted that over the long-run, baseline and actual inflation should be equal on average, which is not always the case in the paper. Overall, Neumann was unconvinced of the appropriateness of the applied method and the results.

In the general discussion, support was expressed for the positions of Neumann and Briault. Additionally, Bayoumi directed attention to the influence of explicit inflation targets on the sacrifice ratios of deflation. Schotman suggested to make the state probabilities an explicit function of macroeconomic driving forces. Pikkarainen argued that a switch from indirect exchange rate targets to direct inflation targets may have little to do with a shift in central bank preferences, but more with a change in strategy and control technique. Icard pointed out that a potential credibility gain of inflation targeting may come from explicit government commitment to the central bank's objectives, as has been the case in New Zealand. In response, Fischer acknowledged the difficulty of focusing on actual versus expected inflation. He also noted, though, that expectations are generally unobserved and that the use of forward rates or longer-term bond yields leads to other problems, including the presence of unobservable risk premia. At the least, inflation targets provide a nominal anchor for the checklists that central banks normally use to evaluate current conditions, according to Fischer. As such, inflation reports contribute to better information and communication about short-run monetary policy.

3. Groeneveld, Koedijk and Kool on the P-Star Approach and ERM "Core" Countries

One of the consequences of the rapidly proceeding economic and financial integration within the European Union is that the impact of international monetary developments on domestic inflation has strongly increased. Insight in these monetary interdependencies is of crucial importance for monetary authorities in conducting their policy and plays for instance a prominent role in the discussions on policy coordination between the member states of the European Union. Obviously, these discussions are important for Stage Three of EMU, but they may also be relevant in Stage Two if empirical evidence would for instance indicate that German inflation is strongly influenced by European monetary conditions. The contribution of Groeneveld of De Nederlandsche Bank, Koedijk and Kool, both from the University of Limburg, presented at the workshop by the first author, addresses these issues by analysing the price developments in Germany, France, Belgium and the Netherlands using the P*-approach.

The P*-model of inflation is in the spirit of the traditional quantity theory of money and states that the equilibrium price level P* changes proportionally with the money stock, provided that the velocity of money and real output are at their equilibrium values. The differential between actual and equilibrium price levels – the so-called price gap – yields information on and serves as a summary statistic of inflationary prospects. In the traditional P*-approach it is assumed that the equilibrium price level is ultimately determined by domestic monetary aggregates. In view of the close interdependencies between European countries this rather heroic assumption is likely to be violated. Groeneveld et al. consider therefore also an extension of the standard P*-model, which takes into account monetary spill-over effects between the "core" ERM countries. To this end, they use the P*-framework to construct the price gap on an area-wide level. For the respective countries various forms of the P*-model – using both domestic and area-wide price gap variables – are analysed using data for the sample period 1973–1992. The analysis enables the authors to compare the impact of domestic and area-wide price gaps. Furthermore, by considering various subsamples they can appraise the evolution over time of the significance of the alternative price gaps.

The empirical evidence obtained for the traditional P*-model, which uses the price gaps based on domestic variables, shows that the significance of these gaps has strongly decreased after 1979 for Belgium, France and The Netherlands, and has even become negligible since the mid 1980s. For Germany, on the other hand, the domestic price gap has a stable and significant impact on German inflation. The finding that the relationship between domestic prices and monetary aggregates has deteriorated for Belgium, the Netherlands and France can be attributed to the growing commitment to the exchange rate objective within the European Monetary System for the conduct of monetary policy. In order to achieve a credible peg of the respective currencies to the Deutsche Mark, the influence of foreign – viz. German – monetary conditions has obviously increased. The finding that for Germany the domestic price gap has a significant influence on German inflation for all sample periods considered, is supportive for this hypothesis.

The results for the extended P*-model which includes also the price gap at an area-wide level as explanatory variable, indicate that for all countries the impact of the area-wide price gap has increased over time, reflecting the intensivation of monetary interdependencies between the ERM-countries considered. With respect to the relative importance of both gaps for explaining domestic inflation, the evidence shows that, for Belgium and the Netherlands, the area-wide price gap has strongly gained importance at the cost of the influence of the domestic gap. Since the late 1970s, it is actually only the area-wide gap that contains information on inflationary prospects in these countries. For France this shift in relative importance is also present, but it is less pronounced compared to Belgium and the Netherlands. The findings for Germany indicate that both the domestic and the area-wide price gap have an impact on German inflation, though the domestic gap is still more significant. These results show that also for Germany foreign monetary conditions, summarised in the area-wide price gap, exert an influence on the domestic inflation process.

Examination of the P*-model using only the area-wide price gap, shows that this overall measure serves as a satisfactory indicator of inflationary prospects in the individual countries. Groeneveld et al. consider also the P*-model for the "core" ERM countries as a whole. In line with the above findings, this analysis yields supportive evidence too. These empirical results strongly corroborate the hypothesis that domestic inflation in the "core" ERM countries has become more sensitive to area-wide monetary conditions over time and that an area-wide monetary aggregate could be useful as an additional indicator of future inflation in the countries considered. Groeneveld et al. conclude therefore that implicit targeting of an area-wide monetary aggregate in addition to explicitly targeting the German money supply may become necessary to achieve and maintain price stability in Europe in the near future.

Herrmann (Bundesbank) was the first discussant and considered the contribution of Groeneveld et al. as an interesting application of the P*-approach. Incorporating monetary spill-over effects to make the model applicable to small countries is a welcome extension of the traditional model. The analysis is also of interest because it includes a proposal to take a European dimension of monetary policy more explicitly into account. The P*-approach is successfully tested for Germany and the Bundesbank considers it as a possible and helpful illustration of the relationship between monetary growth and price developments, though this concept is of course not the only theoretical and empirical base of monetary policy in Germany. Herrmann made it also clear that the Bundesbank prefers a strategy in Stage Three of EMU, which uses monetary targets and the P*-approach is to be taken seriously in the discussions on possible European monetary strategies. An application of this approach in Stage Two of EMU, when monetary policy is still the responsibility of the domestic monetary authorities, is in his opinion, however, less appropriate. A strategy of monetary targeting has its advantages for a central bank, not least owing to its transparency and as a method of increasing the credibility of monetary policy and with a view to assigning responsibilities in the economic decision-making process. These aspects are important if one wants to understand why the Bundesbank does not prefer a strategy based on European variables before Stage Three, which would blur the responsibilities of the national central banks. The empirical evidence presented by Groeneveld et al. is in this respect also not supportive for those who advocate a European monetary targeting approach in Stage Two already. Comparing the results for German inflation using either the German or the area-wide price gap shows that no indication exists that the latter may contribute to German inflation beyond the German price gap. Moreover, in the equations for the European price developments the influence of the area-wide gap seems less significant than the price gap in the national German case.

The contribution of Groeneveld et al. may be useful to identify the most appropriate monetary strategy for Stage Three of EMU, but the analysis leaves open several questions. One may for example ask how convincing the main assertion is that a particular area-wide money supply explains price developments in the "core" ERM countries. In the P*-approach one has to show that the price gap is the result of both the output gap and the velocity gap. On an area-wide level the question arises whether it is the depreciation of the domestic currency, the output gap or the velocity gap which is responsible for area-wide price developments. Groeneveld et al. do not address this issue in their paper. Herrmann emphasised also that it is of importance to formulate the relationship between inflation and its determinants carefully. Inclusion of a constant term as Groeneveld et al. do, makes no sense, as it would imply a permanent change in the price level even if there is no price gap. Instead, a term for the change in the equilibrium price has to be included as an explanatory variable. A final point raised by Herrmann concerned the development of the German price gap, as calculated by Groeneveld et al. The development of this gap does not accord with the traditional interpretation of monetary policy in Germany during the last two decades. The absence of large price gaps in the second half of the 1970s and the 1980s is in contrast with the fact that in those periods the Bundesbank observed overshooting of the monetary targets and an acceleration of inflation later on. This observation suggests that a closer look at the appropriateness of the methodology applied by Groeneveld et al. may be necessary.

Poret (OECD) was the second discussant and noted that the results obtained by Groeneveld et al. are consistent with the standard small open economy model under which, with fixed exchange rates and free capital mobility, domestic money supply is endogenous and prices are determined by foreign prices. The results are in particular consistent with the timing of the phasing out of capital controls in European countries. The role of free capital mobility was also stressed in a study by Hoeller and Poret, cited by Groeneveld et al., which showed that an OECD-wide P*-model outperformed an EU-wide P*-equation. This result suggests that co-ordination of monetary policy within a broader area than the European Union may be as important for European inflation as co-ordination confined to European countries. Poret raised also a question about the robustness of the empirical results. Groeneveld et al. mention the problem of multicollinearity between the domestic and area-wide price gap. Poret suggested as a solution to introduce in the model the difference between the two price gaps, in addition to the domestic price gap variable. Extending the sample period beyond 1992 to cover the period of currency turbulence within the EMS would also be a feasible procedure to test the robustness of the P*-model. In the above-mentioned study it was found that the predictive power of the P*-model was not better than rival and more standard price models, including a random walk model. This throws some doubt on the appropriateness of the P*-methodology. In this regard, Poret also stressed that it is worth noting that the US Federal Reserve, after a period of apparent enthusiasm for the P*-approach, seems to have reassessed the practical usefulness of the P*-indicator. It may be useful to take the lessons from the US past experience with the P*-approach into account, if such an indicator should be more actively considered by monetary policy-makers in Europe.

During the general discussion several participants raised questions about the appropriateness of the methodology used by Groeneveld et al. Monticelli addressed the issue that P*-models are basically reduced-form equations. He prefers analyses based on money demand equations, since these offer the opportunity to incorporate information from economic theory. Bomhoff among others doubted the reliability of the area-wide price gap as calculated by Groeneveld et al. The applied statistical methods are valid if the real exchange rate would follow a random walk. Since the authors consider a period which is characterised by fixed nominal exchange rates combined with sudden parity adjustments, this assumption is likely to be violated. Therefore, additional tests would in his opinion be highly desirable.

4. Monticelli on Money Demand (In)Stability: Monetary Policy Co-ordination in Europe

Under the Maastricht Treaty, the member states of the European Union have agreed upon the establishment of the Economic and Monetary Union in 1999 at the latest provided certain conditions are fulfilled. Because of the far-reaching nature of this commitment, it is not surprising that in recent years the demand for money within the European Union has been a major research topic. The emphasis in this research area is put on establishing the properties of area-wide demand for money, whereby in particular the stability of area-wide vis-à-vis national money demand is a prominent issue. As a result of the predominantly empirical focus, the theoretical and methodological issues have received somewhat less attention. The contribution of Monticelli of the Banca d'Italia aims to fill this shortage by analysing at a theoretical level the implications of (in)stability of national and area-wide demand for money for the co-ordination of monetary policies by countries committed to an exchange rate agreement. Because of this last condition the analysis applies particularly to Stage Two of EMU.

As the conceptual framework serves a stylised two-country rational expectations model, containing for each country a demand for money relationship and two equations describing the demand and supply of output. The economies are liable to real and monetary shocks, which are modelled by adding stochastic disturbance terms to the equations. The country blocks are connected by two relationships, describing the linkages between the domestic and foreign interest rates and prices. With respect to the former the uncovered interest parity condition is assumed to be valid, while for the latter a stochastic version of purchasing power parity is maintained, the random disturbance accounting for stochastic shocks to the real exchange rate. Money supply is determined by a policy rule, for which a formulation is chosen that encompasses both money targeting and interest rate pegging as special cases. The policy rules reflect the objectives of the monetary authorities, amounting to the pursuit of price stability. A nice feature of the model is that a country will not necessarily pursue only its domestic objectives, but may also take into account the objectives of the other country. This is what Monticelli calls the degree of symmetry and the framework enables to distinguish various degrees of symmetry. Using this analytical set-up, Monticelli considers two alternative schemes of monetary co-ordination between the countries which are committed to an exchange rate agreement.

According to the first scheme, roughly corresponding to the actual situation for the countries participating in the Exchange Rate Mechanism of the EMS, exchange rate stability is in the two country set-up ensured by one country, the non-anchor country. Its money supply will be endogenous and adjusted in the presence of shocks in order to maintain a stable exchange rate. The anchor country is able to use its money supply to pursue the objective of price stability. The model has two important implications. Firstly, monetary shocks in the non-anchor country do not affect the price level in both countries, irrespective of the degree of symmetry in the objectives for the anchor country. This result indicates that if monetary shocks in one country constitute the main source of instability, it is beneficial for both countries that it will take the responsibility to maintain the stable exchange rate. Secondly, shocks to the real exchange rate will have opposite effects on the price level in both countries, and the degree of symmetry between domestic and foreign objectives has influence on the optimal mix of money targeting and interest rate pegging: the larger the degree of symmetry, the larger will be the weight of interest rate pegging in the policy rule. If the importance attached to the objectives of the non-anchor country is high, money supply targets are interpreted more flexibly by the anchor country, resulting in a higher degree of accomodation of shifts in money demand, in order to dampen the international transmission of instability to the non-anchor country.

The second co-ordination scheme analysed by Monticelli is based on the assumption that total area-wide money supply is jointly controlled, whereas in the former case the anchor country managed its national money supply. The money supply rule is now determined by a combination policy encompassing area-wide money targeting and interest rate pegging at the area level as special cases. The alternative assumptions imply that monetary shocks in both countries have an impact on the price level in each country. However, area-wide monetary control is preferable to a national policy if the variance of shocks to area-wide money demand is smaller than the variance of the perturbations in the individual countries. As in the former scheme, shocks to the real exchange rate affect both countries in an opposite direction, but in this case the optimal mix between money targeting and interest rate pegging is independent of the degree of symmetry between domestic and foreign objectives. Monetary policy is again unable to reduce the total impact of the shock to the real exchange rate, but as a result of the area-wide monetary control, it is also impossible to distribute the impact among the two countries. In that respect, the issue of the optimal degree of symmetry of the exchange rate agreement becomes non-existent.

The theoretical results derived for both co-ordination scenarios lead to a number of important policy implications, the content of which depend on the stability of national and area-wide demand for money. If the demand for money in both the individual countries and the area as a whole is stable, there is no principal variance in terms of stabilisation performance between the situation that an anchor country pursues a national monetary policy, while the other country pegs the exchange rate, and the one in which an area-wide policy is followed. The choice between both options is in this case of a political and institutional nature. If the demand for money in one country is more stable than in the other and in the area as a whole, that country should be the anchor. If demand for money is unstable both in the individual countries and at an area-wide level, monetary targeting should be abandoned and a set of alternative monetary indicators needs to be monitored. In the final case that area-wide money demand is stable, while the demand for money in the individual countries in unstable, it becomes beneficial for all countries if monetary policy will be conducted at an area-wide level, taking into account the monetary conditions of the area as a whole rather than the national conditions.

Fase (De Nederlandsche Bank) acted as the first discussant and complimented Monticelli with his interesting and challenging contribution. He had, however, two principal comments. The first one was that from a theoretical point of view the model needs analytical elaboration before the firm policy conclusions on monetary co-ordination within the European Union are warranted. The theoretical framework used by Monticelli is extremely simple and Fase suggested several possible ways to extend the model. Introduction of dynamic optimalization to circumvent time inconsistency problems and a more coherent analysis of money supply processes are in his opinion desirable to make the analytical framework more appropriate to appraise the merits of the alternative co-ordination scenarios. In his second comment, Fase went further into the relationship between the theoretical analysis and the policy implications. He wondered whether the conclusions were maybe drawn overhastily. The issues which are crucial to the decision on the optimal scheme of monetary co-ordination are principally of an empirical nature and there are several ways of conceiving these issues. An illustrative example concerns the stability of the demand for money. In the literature several definitions of stability have been put forward and the specific choice will have a great impact on the final conclusions.

Arnold (Nijenrode University), the second discussant, raised a fundamental point concerning the stabilization objectives of the future European Central Bank. Price stability in all individual countries will, given fixed exchange rates, lead to a stable area-wide price level. The reverse is however not true. Due to the covariances between national prices, it is possible to have a stable area-wide price level without price stability at the national levels. If the European Central Bank aims at stabilising all national price levels, it is doubtful whether a stable European money demand function would provide sufficient guidance for monetary policy in Europe. In his view the practical usefulness of a stable European demand for money has therefore still to be established.

During the discussion, other participants noticed, following Fase's argument, the need to extend the analytical framework used by Monticelli. Bomhoff noted the restrictive set-up of a one-period model in which the most important source of uncertainty is a temporary shock to the real exchange rate. For an appraisal of the risks of a monetary union, an analysis using a richer menu of uncertainties, including unpredictable trends in the velocity of money and in the real exchange rate, is needed. Weber argued that a more comprehensive description of the supply-side of the model is desirable and that a more realistic and sophisticated model of producer's behaviour will probably have an impact on the final conclusions. Obviously, extensions of the model will make the analyses more complicated, but having an easier analysis is not always an excuse for ignoring relevant aspects. While admitting the highly stylised nature of his model, Monticelli proved, however, to be quite confident about the robustness of his findings. He expressed his expectation that extensions of the model would probably not alter the conclusions concerning the optimal monetary co-ordination and policy mix.

5. Borio on Credit and Monetary Transmission

Recent events have highlighted the relevance of the credit structure and other aspects of the financial structure for the transmission mechanism of monetary policy. E.g. the ERM crisis in 1992 and 1993 revealed hitherto largely unnoticed cross-country differences in the speed and intensity of responses of market interest rates to increases in central bank rates. This, together with differences in private sector indebtedness, caused a marked divergence in the ability of authorities to sustain exchange rate commitments.

The paper by Borio (BIS) provides a large amount of information on the various characteristics of credit to the non-government sector in fourteen industrialised countries. The paper, which is based on answers provided by national central banks to a detailed questionnaire by the BIS, provides a unique overview of the structure of credit to the private sector in different countries. Borio explained that his paper forms only part of a more broad research project carried out by the BIS on differences in financial structures and the transmission mechanism of monetary policy.

In presenting the main findings of this study, Borio makes use of the popular classification in Anglo-Saxon countries (the United States, the United Kingdom, Canada and New-Zealand) versus other countries. This distinction appears appropriate in a number of aspects of credit to the non-government sector, although there are some exceptions. Notably, the ratio of total credit of the non-government sector to GDP ranges typically from about 80 to about 130 percent. In this respect, the Anglo-Saxon economies all fall in this middle range. The classification is valid, however, for the ratio of household credit to total credit, which is typically important for monetary policy due to the sensitivity of housing expenditures to interest rate changes. The paper shows that the household sector accounts for less than half the total credit outstanding in almost all countries. In Anglo-Saxon countries the share is generally higher than in other countries.

Another distinction is that between credit provided to intermediaries (such as banks) and through the money and capital markets. This distinction is important as there is no full substitutability between banking lending and security financing. In particular in securities markets, interest rates typically adjust faster than bank loan rates and investors in securities are generally less willing or able to insulate borrowers, at least temporarily, from adverse changes in market conditions. On both counts, the impact of monetary policy may be expected to be stronger. The BIS-figures confirm the widely-held view that securities generally make up a larger share of credit in Anglo-Saxon countries than elsewhere (for example close to 20 percent in the US and the UK versus less than 2 percent in Austria). Borio cannot identify any marked tendency towards convergence between Anglo-Saxon and other countries. The often-heard claims of a pronounced generalised trend towards disintermediation do not appear to be justified. With respect to the distinction between banks and other financial intermediaries, the data show that the banks' share of credit is considerably smaller in the Anglo-Saxon countries, Japan and Sweden than in countries such as Germany, Switzerland, Austria and the Netherlands which have a long-standing universal banking tradition. Also in this field there is no clear tendency towards convergence.

Also, and even of more immediate interest for the transmission mechanism is the maturity breakdown of credit and the degree of adjustability of interest rates on debt contracts. Firstly, on the maturity breakdown, it is interesting to note Borio's finding that the share of medium and long-term credit is especially high in countries having a long-standing universal banking tradition which are also those where lower inflation rates have historically been enjoyed. Secondly, the larger the share of variable rate financing (defined as debt on which interest rates are reviewable within one year and in relation to short-term rates), the faster the response of market interest rates to changes in central bank rates and the stronger the cash flow and income effects of monetary impulses. Borio finds that the differences between the two groups of countries are also relevant in this field. On average, Anglo-Saxon countries appear to have higher shares of short-term and variable rate credit, especially for households. In all of them, the share of household credit at variable rates appears to be roughly as high as that of the business sector whilst it is even considerably higher in the UK and Canada. The major exception seems to be the US but the relatively high share of long-term financing in this country appears to be overstated due to the ease with which agents can switch between variable and fixed-rate debt. Among the other countries, Italy is a significant exception with its high share of variable rate credit.

The above characteristics of credit in Anglo-Saxon countries tend to amplify the impact of monetary policy. Borio also referred to the results of other parts of the BIS central bank project on transmission, namely an examination of the whole balance sheets of households and businesses and of the adjustment of the short-term bank loan rates to changes in policy rates. This evidence tends to point in the same direction. Due to, on balance, a financial structure that tends to amplify income/cash-flow and valuation effects and/or to speed up the adjustment of interest rates, the impact of monetary policy would be expected to be stronger in the UK, Canada, Australia and the US, and also in Japan, Italy and Sweden. On the other hand, in most other continental European countries, the effects of changes in central bank rates on economic activity would be expected to be less pronounced and rapid. This ranking is broadly borne out by simulations with national central bank monetary models and more simple statistical exercises examining the response of lending to policy rates. All these findings are evidence of the importance of financial structures for the transmission of monetary policy, even though information is far from complete yet.

The discussants with respect to Borio's paper at the workshop were Boeschoten and Swank (De Nederlandsche Bank), and Viñals (Banco de España). They all expressed their appreciation for the work presented in the paper calling it a unique and comparative overview of the structure of credit to the private sector which had not been available to date in such a systematic way. Boeschoten underlined that there are two ways of looking at the results. One way is to start from the proposition that the economic structure determines the financial structure. This kind of fundamental analysis would cast light on the extent to which countries' financial structures differ relating to specific economic characteristics, and to what extent certain elements are likely to persist or change over time. However, in Borio's paper, a less ambitious line of approach is followed starting from the financial structure, in particular the structure of credit, and to study its potential relevance for the transmission of monetary policy. As a drawback of this approach, Boeschoten stated that a clear framework is missing which hardens the interpretation of the findings. He then commented on a couple of more specific issues. If credit rationing no longer plays an important role in a macro-economic sense, then what is left over from the credit channel are merely the cash-flow effects stemming from changes in interest rates. However, recent model simulations by national central banks in conjunction with the BIS show that the ultimate cash-flow effect of interest rate increases on the economy is rather limited and even positive. This stems from the fact that the negative cash-flow effects via credit are more than offset in most cases by higher revenues on asset holdings. Boeschoten therefore stressed the need for a more complete picture of the effect of financial structure on monetary transmission by simultaneously focusing on credit and assets. He also questioned the strong focus of Borio's paper on the effects of short-term interest rates given the limited size, in his opinion, of cash-flow effects. The main effects must run through the cost of capital channel and the wealth channel. However, for these channels, the long-term interest rate plays a crucial role. Therefore, besides the financial structure, it is particularly the persistence of interest rate changes and the effects on long-term rates which really matter. Referring to the model simulations, Boeschoten underlined that also here the assumptions made with respect to the yield curve play a crucial role.

The second discussant, Swank, raised some questions on the possible policy implications. As an example, Swank mentioned the discussion of whether the ECB should pursue a strategy of monetary targeting. This calls for a stable demand-for-money function. If this condition is satisfied, Swank doubted whether it would really be necessary to worry about cross-country differences in the structure of credit. On the other hand, he admitted that with large differences, the burden of monetary policy measures could be distributed so unevenly that it would threaten the political cohesion amongst Monetary Union members. This, in turn, could hamper the decisiveness of the ECB. According to Borio's findings, the UK and Italy may pose problems in this respect because of their substantial short-term debt compared to other European countries. However, Swank was not convinced that such differences would disqualify the UK and Italy from the third stage of EMU. Borio's evidence of only slowly, or not at all, converging financial structures of European countries was noted as an important observation. However, Swank also questioned whether economies should really be highly financially integrated to form a viable monetary union. Finally, Swank mentioned VAR-analyses which, in contrast to the simulations with national central bank models, seemed to indicate that cross-country differences in monetary transmission are less pronounced than one would expect on the basis of comparisons between financial structures. Swank wondered whether this suggested that certain differences in financial structures tend to offset other differences in their influence on the transmission.

Viñals, the third discussant, said that Borio's paper was a reflection of the changing nature of the research on monetary transmission which shows increased interest in the role of credit compared to the traditional, monetarist view. He mentioned some limitations of research of this kind, namely problems with differences in national definitions (e.g. banks in the UK) and the limited amount of years to assess convergence (only 1983 and 1993 figures). Viñals said that the paper answers the question as to whether Anglo-Saxon countries differ in terms of their credit structures from other countries and whether there is convergence or not, but the question of the implications of these differences remains largely unanswered. Thus he appreciated the incredible amount of evidence found but felt that an overall assessment of how the tables fit together was missing and what the implications of differences in the credit structure are for the transmission mechanism and for monetary policy.

During the general discussion, many participants also focused on the question of the implications of monetary policy. Herrmann spoke of a project full of puzzles with the observation that the UK is an outlier compared to financial structures and monetary transmissions in other countries as the only clear conclusion. He confirmed that the countries with high inflation in the past are also those countries with a high share of adjustable-rate credit; however, he also noted that countries such as Spain and Sweden, with more or less similar shares of adjustable-rate credit in total private sector credit compared to Germany, had much higher inflation in the past than Germany. Lastly Herrmann wondered how central banks can pursue monetary policy at all if their knowledge of the transmission mechanism is so poor. Neumann commented on the evidence of slow convergence in financial structures in Borio's paper. He said that convergence might now occur much more rapidly due to the single market and the possible speedy adjustment of banks during the remainder of Stage Two. Briault, however, doubted whether convergence would take place and he mentioned that unlike in the 1970s and 1980s, the UK had a low inflation rate in the 1950s and 1960s but with the same mortgage and other credit structure characteristics. To him this showed that the differences in financial structures are much more related to taste and culture, thus doubting the prospects of quick further convergence. In his final reply to the various speakers, Borio again referred to other parts of the BIS project on monetary transmission. Reacting to Swank's question as to whether the differences are a reason to worry or not in the light of the future European monetary policy, his answer was positive since the different effects of a single monetary policy by the ECB in different participating countries can be seen as a potential economic cost of the EMU. However, he stressed that in his view potential economic costs involved would in all probability be overshadowed by others and hence not represent a decisive factor in the decision of whether or not to move to Stage Three. In reply to Herrmann's cry on how central banks could pursue monetary policy at all with such limited knowledge of the transmission mechanism, Borio referred to the example of a car driver: even without a detailed knowledge of how exactly the engine works, every car driver can handle a car quite well by instinctively knowing how much to step on the gas and how much to put on the brake.

6. Bayoumi on Exchange Rate Policy in the Run-up to EMU

In his paper, Bayoumi (IMF) discusses which countries are likely to benefit from participation in an EMU and which exchange rate policies should be pursued by countries in the move towards EMU.

The guiding principle for the debate on the suitability of EMU for potential participants has been the theory of optimum currency areas. Bayoumi underlines that the empirical literature on the potential costs has come to fairly consistent conclusions. Firstly, the costs of participating in the EMU, which are related to the loss of monetary sovereignty, are higher, the less similar underlying economic shocks are. Bayoumi argues that the current so-called "core" countries of the EU (Germany, the Netherlands, Belgium, Luxembourg, France, Denmark, Austria "and possibly Sweden") face relatively similar economic disturbances and are therefore relatively good candidates for EMU. By contrast, other countries face relatively dissimilar disturbances and are therefore probably less well suited for a single currency area. Secondly, non-monetary mechanisms such as labour mobility or federal fiscal transfers are too limited in Europe to lessen the impact of dissimilar shocks. Other factors even tend to reinforce the distinction between the core countries in the EMU and its periphery, like intra-regional trade which is highest within the "core" countries. It is more difficult to assess the potential benefits arising from EMU. Apart from estimates of lower transaction costs, there is uncertainty about the economic gains to be made due to other more indirect benefits. This makes it very difficult to assess which countries benefit on balance from membership to the EMU. Due to these uncertainties, Bayoumi thinks it could well be the case that social and political factors play a more important role in the decision whether or not to join the single currency area.

On the second question of which exchange-rate policies to follow prior to the start of Stage Three, Bayoumi first describes how the Maastricht Treaty envisaged quite a gradual transformation from the then-existing ERM arrangement with narrow margins to a single European currency. This original plan was jeopardised by the exchange rate turbulences experienced in 1992 and 1993, resulting finally in a widening of the intervention bands (apart from the case of the Netherlands vis-à-vis Germany). Although the ERM currencies have generally remained reasonably close to the central parities, Bayoumi stresses the fact that the current exchange rate system is significantly different from the earlier one in the sense that in essence the ERM moved back to a system in which exchange rates are determined by market forces.

He does not believe that the main causes of the exchange rate problems experienced in 1992 and 1993 were the high capital mobility and the disruptive effects of capital movements. Instead, the main cause was the tension as perceived by financial markets between the external and domestic requirements of monetary policies in ERM-countries, following the rise in interest rates in reunified Germany. Bayoumi notes that the exchange rates which came under most pressure during these years were clearly those where doubts existed concerning the willingness of governments to raise interest rates. Bayoumi admits that market behaviour can involve elements of herd behaviour, thereby making it very difficult to predict when a currency will come under pressure, but he says that this is very different from saying that financial markets were wrong and that doubts about policies in the affected countries were unfounded.

He then turns his attention to what he calls a "striking example" of a successful fixed exchange rate regime in an environment of high capital mobility, namely the pre-1914 gold standard. The key to the success of that system was the full convertibility of the currency into gold albeit with well-defined escape clauses. In that system, investors retained the belief that the value of their investment was secure in the long run, even in countries where gold convertibility had been temporarily suspended (e.g. the United States in 1862 soon after the start of the Civil War). Because governments were expected to come back to the system at the original gold parity, there was no reason for market participants to put pressure on the currency. Therefore, private capital flows generally tended to be stabilising, according to Bayoumi. In contrast to this, the Bretton Woods system and the ERM were systems of fixed but adjustable exchange rates pegs. Governments try to stabilise exchange rate movements around the parities, but retain the right to change those parities under certain circumstances. Such revisions, however, can imply large and permanent losses for private investors. In case of an increasing likelihood of devaluations, private market flows can become destabilising.

From this analysis, Bayoumi draws direct implications for the exchange rate policy in the transition period to EMU. He describes the Maastricht Treaty as a badly written book ("There was a beginning and a middle, but no well defined end") since it gives no guidance regarding future parities. A lesson from history could be that eventual exchange rate parities at which the different currencies enter the third stage of EMU should be announced in advance. In this respect, Bayoumi mentions the Resumption Act of 1875 in the United States in which the authorities laid down a date four years later on which gold convertibility was to be restored at the pre-Civil War parity. Bayoumi makes it clear that any announcement of future exchange rate parities can only be credible if the national governments involved commit themselves to implementing the necessary policies. In the context of the EMU, such a new exchange rate commitment would complement and strengthen the effects of the already-agreed convergence criteria.

Acting as a first discussant, Icard (Banque de France) firstly pointed out that the debate on the costs and benefits of the Union is only of concern for the UK and Denmark with their opting-out clauses. For other EU countries the decision to move to EMU will be primarily a political one to be made by the Council on the basis of the convergence criteria listed in the Treaty. Supposing that only countries for which benefits outweigh costs are able to join the EMU, this would in fact add a kind of new criterion to the Treaty which is impossible according to Icard. He was fairly critical about Bayoumi's second issue on exchange rate policy in the ERM. He stressed that the current ERM is not that much different from the former system of narrow margins. Icard did not believe that the system is currently more unstable than it used to be, on the contrary. Monetary policies are still geared towards maintaining exchange rate stability and the convergence criterion which requires that a currency should not experience severe tensions during the two years before the decision to move to Stage Three is still fully applicable even in the current system of widened bands.

Icard shared Bayoumi's concern that the period up to the start of Stage Three might give rise to uncertainty and exchange rate tensions. A lesson from the study of the functioning of the pre-1914 gold standard regime would be that a clear dedication of economic policies towards the objective of fixed exchange rates should help to stabilise market expectations. Icard stressed that part of Bayoumi's concern is already addressed, at least partly, by the formulation of the convergence criteria in the Treaty, especially those related to exchange rate stability and sustainable public finances. Bayoumi's idea that the rates at which currencies would enter the EMU should be pre-announced provoked critical remarks by Icard. Pre-announcing conversion rates might bring about more volatility in the period prior to the announcement if markets suspect such a decision was to take place. He thought that a very early announcement would be unrealistic because it would present the risk of asymmetric shocks occurring in a period in which convergence was not yet sufficient. An early announcement could also raise legal problems with respect to the Treaty provisions on the external value of the ecu. Icard concluded that although he shared Bayoumi's concern to some extent about the need to announce as early as possible the rates at which national currencies enter EMU, he could not see how this might be feasible before the Council has taken its political decision to move to EMU and with which countries. Only then it will be conceivable and useful to peg the parities and to set up powerful measures to defend them until Stage Three has actually started.

The second discussant, Gros (Centre for European Policy Studies), stressed that the basic reason for problems with measuring net benefits is that the nature of benefits and the nature of costs are so different: costs are of a macro-economic nature and cannot be precisely measured exactly whereas benefits are of a micro-economic nature and can be measured more precisely. Turning to Bayoumi's list of the likely net beneficiaries, Gros doubted whether one can exclude all the other remaining EU member countries. His own research has led him to the conclusion that there are only four really "peripheral" countries, namely Greece, Portugal, Ireland and Finland, because of very different economic structures. The UK might be added on account of its strikingly different macro-economic reactions. Gros pointed towards some recent developments in the literature on the optimum currency area, in particular on the dynamic labour market adjustment patterns at a regional level in the US compared to the European Union. Recent studies show that unemployment rates adjust at a similar speed to shocks in the US and the European Union but that the adjustment of the rates are geared to two different mechanisms: people tend to move across regional frontiers in the US (migration) and in and out of the labour force in the European Union (participation rate). Gros raised the question whether one could say that one mechanism is obviously better than the other.

Turning to the possible pre-announcement of conversion rates favoured by Bayoumi, Gros found this idea attractive but not without problems. Announcements of this type are inherently not credible. The standard "time inconsistency" approach makes clear that when the "final" day comes, all governments will have an incentive to renege and engineer a last time devaluation. The reluctance to convert to such surprise devaluations in the ERM in the past might well have been caused by the fact that countries were often faced with a price in the form of higher interest rates caused by the expected further devaluations. Since this would not be possible once the EMU has started, the incentive could be stronger than in the past (the so-called "end-game problem"). Gros had serious doubts about Bayoumi's idea of a credible commitment as to the future value of a currency. He pointed out the difficulties involved in achieving credibility in the ERM: "If markets did not believe the ERM with its system of mutual support and fixed limits of intervention, how should they believe a mere announcement as to what the future conversion rates would be? It seems that the core of the problem has been assumed away". Instead of announcing conversion rates, Gros stressed that governments should concentrate on preparing a credible path for fiscal consolidation. He raised doubts about what he called "vague intentions" to achieve the 3 percent deficit criterion. Improvements on this front would be a more powerful stabiliser for financial markets than announcements of central rates.

The general discussion also mainly focused on Bayoumi's idea of pre-announcement and the surrounding credibility problems. How can financial markets be convinced of the pre-announced rates so long as there is insufficient convergence in various areas, e.g. government finances? De Grauwe and Neumann paid further attention to the comparison of the period up to the ERM and the pre-1914 gold standard. While the "end-game problem" did not exist in the latter period due to the fact that everything could be repeated, they stressed that in the current period it is an important problem: now there is a real incentive for individual countries to "play the game" of pre-announcing convergence rates but to take advantage of a last time devaluation, after which the exchange rates are fixed for eternity. Herrmann and Hochreiter, among others, doubted whether a pre-announcement would lead to financial markets' behaviour being stabilising. Instead, monetary policies would probably have to do the hard job. Furthermore, in their view, experiences in Austria before the entry into the ERM and in Switzerland show that convergence in fundamentals and appropriate policies are more important for exchange rate stability than institutional arrangements, including the pre-announcing of rates. Monticelli raised the problem of responsibility for monetary policy in the period between pre-announcing and the start of EMU: "Who runs monetary policy in the meantime?" According to him, pre-announcement would in fact mean that a single monetary policy already has to be pursued. This point was picked up by Viñals who stressed the legal problems involved with this set-up since national monetary policies during Stage Two would still be independent. He concluded that the only real credible commitment of exchange rate parities would be the immediate start of Stage Three by a group of core countries.

Do Inflation Targets Redefine Central Bank Inflation Preferences? Results from an Indicator Model*

MICHAEL J. DUEKER[1] AND ANDREAS M. FISCHER[2]
[1]*Federal Reserve Bank of St. Louis*
[2]*Swiss National Bank*

ABSTRACT

This paper examines whether inflation targets have been instrumental in reducing the policy-implied, short-term trend rate of inflation, which is defined as the baseline inflation rate. To investigate whether announced targets have generated distinct benefits in terms of reductions in the baseline inflation rate to date, the authors compare the baseline inflation rates in three inflation-targeting countries with those in neighboring non-inflation-targeting countries. The study matches New Zealand with Australia; Canada with the United States; and the United Kingdom with Germany.

The comparative analysis stemming from an indicator model using a Markov-switching process suggests that inflation targets have brought about a change in inflation preferences in the 1990s. This statement needs to be qualified however, because the inflation-targeting countries generally followed a non-inflation-targeting neighbor in reducing their baseline inflation rates. The United States and Germany shifted to a low baseline path prior to similar shifts by their inflation-targeting neighbors. Given that the neighboring countries moved first and appear to have settled on a lower baseline inflation rate, it is difficult to determine how instrumental the targets were in bringing about the shift in preferences.

1. INTRODUCTION

Several central banks have recently made policy declarations in the form of explicit inflation targets that give increased emphasis to price stability. The countries include New Zealand (announced in 1990), Canada (1991), the United Kingdom (1992), Sweden (1993), Finland (1993) and Spain (1994). The broad aim of inflation targets is to define a nominal anchor for monetary policy and influence market expectations. Although the first three countries achieved their announced targets ahead of sched-

*The authors would like to thank Clive Briault, Clemens Kool, Manfred Neumann and Mathias Zurlinden for helpful comments. Rita Meier provided valuable assistance in preparing this manuscript.

Koos Alders, Kees Koedijk, Clemens Kool and Carlo Winder (eds.), Monetary Policy in a Converging Europe, pp. 21–37.

ule, inflation targeting is still viewed with scepticism, largely because the 1990s have seen a marked disinflation in countries with and without inflation targets alike.

In this article we examine whether announced inflation targets have been instrumental in reducing the policy-implied, short-term trend rate of inflation, which we define as the baseline inflation rate. To investigate whether announced targets have generated distinct benefits in terms of reductions in the baseline inflation rate to date, we compare the baseline inflation rates in three inflation-targeting countries with those in neighboring non-inflation-targeting countries. Our study matches New Zealand with Australia; Canada with the United States; and the United Kingdom with Germany. Throughout the analysis, we concentrate on reductions in the inflation trend to date, rather than potential reductions in future expected inflation brought by inflation targeting, since proponents of inflation-targeting have cited the already accrued disinflation as a key benefit of explicit inflation targets.

The empirical methodology is to estimate a Markov-switching model to uncover high and low states representing baseline rates of inflation. We can think of the high and low bands as estimates of the high and low points of a typical inflation cycle for that country. Because the states are unobserved and only inferred probabilistically, the points between the high and low inflation states represent points between the peak and trough. The baseline inflation path is then derived by multiplying the probability of being in the low (high) inflation state times the estimate of the low (high) inflation state.

The first part of the empirical analysis centers on comparing the model-implied trough rate of inflation with actual inflation in the 1990s. Permanent shifts in the baseline path represent changes in the central bank's inflation preferences. The second stage of the analysis is to compare the inflation-targeting country with a neighboring non-inflation-targeting country and examine whether the neighbor has undergone a similar change in inflation preferences without the aid of announced inflation targets. If the profile of the baseline inflation path is similar in the two countries, then the hypothesis that the announcement of inflation targets provides distinct benefits is rejected.

We use the indicator model from Dueker and Fischer (1994a), which extends McCallum's (1987) nominal targeting rule to a small open economy by allowing feedback from the gap between the exchange rate and its implicit target. Instead of setting parameters in a McCallum-type targeting rule and simulating, the parameters are estimated using a Markov-switching model. Such a model, which allows discrete parameter changes to occur, should be adept at capturing changes in the implicit baseline path for inflation.

The paper is organized as follows. The first section presents a brief overview of OECD inflation and discusses how the behavior of actual inflation may provide information for baseline inflation and the role of inflation targets. The section thereafter presents the indicator model. The model depicts an implicit inflation targeting rule that allows for time-varying feedback from the exchange rate and the inflation rate. This is fol-

Table 1. Consumer prices in the OECD area. Percentage changes from previous period, not seasonally adjusted (Source OECD).

	Year-end annual rates						At actual rate	
	1972–81 (Average)	1981–90 (Average)	1990	1991	1992	1993	12 months to latest month available (August 1994)	Inflation target
Countries with inflation targets:								
United Kingdom	14.7	6.0	6.1	5.9	3.7	1.6	2.4	1–4 (at least until 1997)
Canada	9.5	5.2	5.0	5.6	1.5	1.8	0.2	1–3 (1995)
Finland	12.3	6.2	4.9	4.3	2.9	2.2	1.9	2 (1995)
New Zealand	13.7	10.2	5.0	2.6	1.0	1.3	1.7[d]	0–2 (continuously)
Spain	16.8	8.7	6.5	5.9	5.9	4.6	4.8	1–3 (1997)
Sweden	10.1	7.1	10.9	9.3	2.3	4.6	2.6	1–3 (1995)
Countries without formal targets:								
United States	9.0	4.1	6.1	4.2	3.0	3.0	2.9	
Japan	9.3	1.7	3.8	3.3	1.7	1.3	0.0	
Germany[a]	5.2	2.2	2.7	3.5	4.0	4.1	3.0	
France	10.9	5.5	2.8	3.2	2.4	2.1	1.7	
Italy[b]	16.6	8.7	6.3	6.5	5.3	4.2	3.7	
Austria	6.5	3.2	3.5	3.3	4.0	3.6	3.2	
Belgium	7.9	4.2	3.4	3.2	2.4	2.8	2.4	
Denmark	10.9	5.3	2.7	2.4	2.1	1.3	2.2	
Greece	17.9	18.4	22.9	19.5	15.9	14.4	11.1	
Iceland[c]	41.2	31.7	7.2	6.8	3.7	4.1	0.8	
Ireland	15.5	6.4	3.1	3.2	3.1	1.4	2.7[d]	
Luxembourg	7.2	4.0	3.7	3.1	3.2	3.6	2.1[f]	
Netherlands	7.2	2.0	2.6	3.7	3.2	2.6	2.6	
Norway	9.3	7.0	4.4	3.4	2.3	2.3	1.6	
Portugal[c]	21.1	16.8	13.7	11.4	8.9	6.5	4.8	
Switzerland	4.8	3.1	5.3	5.8	4.0	3.3	0.5	
Turkey[e]	35.8	46.7	60.4	66.0	70.1	66.1	107.5	
Australia	11.3	7.9	6.6	3.2	1.0	1.8	1.7[d]	

[a]Western Germany.

[b]Index for households and salary earners.

[c]Excluding rent.

[d]Since consumer prices are available only on a quarterly basis, the figures shown for the rates of change over 12 and 6 months are calculated as the rate of change over 4 and 2 quarters respectively to the last quarter available. The monthly rate is calculated as the change between the two most recent quarterly indices, expressed at a monthly rate and centered at the mid-month of the quarter.

[e]1971–1981: Istanbul index (154 items); from 1982, Turkish index.

[f]To the latest month available.

lowed by estimation results. The exercise identifies specific periods when price stability was the primary policy objective and seeks to answer the question whether countries with formal targets have been more rigorous in pursuing a policy of zero inflation.

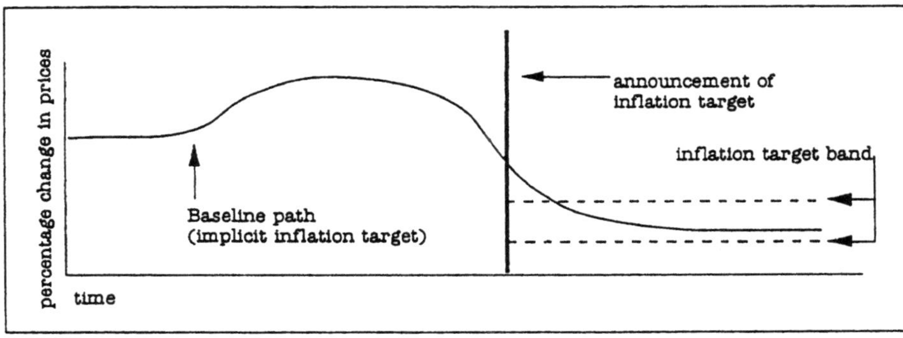

Figure 1. Changes in inflation preferences and baseline inflation.

2. Changes in Inflation Preferences

The inflation record for OECD countries and the announced inflation targets for the United Kingdom, Canada, Finland, New Zealand, Spain and Sweden are summarized in Table 1. All inflation rates are measured by the CPI (unless indicated otherwise). The inflation targets are expressed in terms of the CPI except for Finland and the United Kingdom. Finland's inflation target of 2 percent for 1995 is based on a modified CPI index excluding indirect taxes, subsidies and housing related capital costs, while the United Kingdom's target refers to the retail price index excluding mortgage interest payments.[1] Table 1 shows that New Zealand, the United Kingdom have met their targets, Canada will most likely meet its target for 1995 and it remains unclear as to whether Finland, Sweden and Spain will achieve their targets. However, inflation in the 1990s has been low in the OECD area. Table 1 also shows that inflation in OECD countries (excluding Greece and Turkey), which averaged 4.7 percent for the 1981–1990 period, amounted to just 2.5 percent for the first half of 1994. Moreover, countries such as Iceland, Australia, Ireland, and Norway, which experienced annual average inflation of more than 6 percent during the 1980s, are currently enjoying low inflation without the announcement of formal targets. As a result, the current inflation trend for the OECD area is consistent with the targets set by all inflation targeting countries, except New Zealand, whose target is 0 to 2 percent. From the evidence on recent price behavior alone, it is difficult to determine whether the improved inflation performance over the last two years is due to a change in preferences captured most clearly in the announcement of inflation targets or due to a global absence of inflationary pressures.

The principal hypothesis we consider attributes the improved inflation performance to a permanent shift in the central bank's baseline inflation rate. Shifts in the baseline inflation rate are interpreted as shifts in the inflation preferences of the central bank. Although central banks often make reference to price stability as being their primary objective, rarely however is it defined quantitatively. Our term central bank inflation preferences refers to "revealed" preferences based on monetary settings, which are measured through interest rate changes in our indicator model discussed in the next section. Figure 1 shows how the baseline inflation path moves to an unprecedentedly low level following the announcement of the inflation targets and falls within the bands set by the central bank. The alternative hypothesis is that the recent disinflation has taken place with no change in inflation preferences. Under the alternative, the baseline inflation path does not move to a new state during the disinflation phase and, the reduction in inflation if any, is attributed to non-policy forces such as the fall in oil prices or a global recession.[2] One means of testing the change in inflation preferences hypothesis is to identify a baseline inflation path for several OECD countries and compare its behavior with actual inflation. A desired characteristic of the identified baseline inflation path is that it should represent policy-driven changes in the trend rate of inflation. Essentially the test of inflation preferences is a graphical analysis, plotting the behavior of baseline and actual inflation. The next section outlines the indicator model used to estimate the baseline path for six OECD countries.

3. Description of the Empirical Model

We begin with a general empirical model and show which features and parameters are relevant for an empirical characterization of an inflation targeting policy.[3] The model takes the quarterly change in the 3-month interest rate as the policy instrument and adds a forecast of the relationship between the policy instrument and inflation to derive the current quarter's "intended" inflation rate.

Assuming that the short-term interest rate is the policy instrument and that our forecasts mirror the general consensus at the time, our "intended" inflation variable should reflect the central bank's policy intentions. Our empirical model can explain fluctuations in intended inflation from three distinct sources: the first source is variation in the baseline inflation path; the second source is intended inflation above or below the long-run target rate in the short run to maintain a price level target; the third source recognizes that, in a small open economy, the central bank may intervene to keep the exchange rate within a comfort zone.

The following equations incorporate these three potential motives for modifying short-run intended inflation. Several parameters are assumed to be subject to discrete changes, because, for example, the central bank may choose to intervene periodically on behalf of the exchange rate. Also, the extent to which the central bank targets a path for the price level, as opposed to targeting a rate of inflation period-by-period, may be subject to change. Finally, the target rate of inflation might also vary across time. In equations (1)–(4) below, i stands for the 3-month interest rate, P for the price level, $\hat{P}$ is the target price level conditional on the values of the Markov state variables, and $\tilde{P}$ is the expected target level, not conditional on the values of the state variables. Similarly, ê is the baseline exchange rate (in logs) conditional on the values of the state variables, and $\tilde{e}$ is the baseline rate not conditional on the values of the state variables.

We allow for three state variables subject to Markov switching: S1 for parameters related to inflation and/or price level targeting, S2 for parameters related to exchange-rate intervention, and S3 for parameters related to the variance.[4] In equations (1–4), parameter α(Si) indicates that parameter α is subject to Markov switching governed by state variable Si. In equations (3), (5) and (6), Y_t denotes available information through time t.

$$\text{Interest rate changes } \Delta ln(1+i_t) = \lambda_0(S1_t) + \Delta ln({}^{1+i}/_{P})_{t/t-1} - \lambda_1(S1_t)\left[ln\tilde{P} - lnP\right]_{t-1}$$
$$-\lambda_2(S2_t)\left[ln\tilde{e} - lne\right]_{t-1} + \hat{u}(S1_t, S2_t)$$
$$\text{var}\left[\hat{u}(S1_t, S2_t)\right] = \sigma^2(S3_t)\tfrac{n}{n-2}$$
$$\hat{u}(S1_t, S2_t) \approx \text{student-}t \quad (1)$$

$$\text{Target Price Level: } ln\hat{P}_t(S1_t) = \lambda_0(S1_t) + \delta_1(S1_t)ln\tilde{P}_{t-1} + (1-\delta_1(S1_t))lnP_{t-1} \quad (2)$$

$$\text{Expected Target: } ln\tilde{P}_t = \sum_{i=0}^{1} Prob\,(S1_t = i|Y_t)ln\hat{P}\,(S1_t = 1) \quad (3)$$

$$\text{Baseline Exch. Rate: } ln\hat{e}(S2_t) = \delta_2(S2_t)ln\tilde{e}_{t-1} + (1-\delta_2(S2_t))lne_{t-1} \quad (4)$$

$$\text{Expected Baseline: } ln\tilde{e}_t = \sum_{j=0}^{1} Prob\,(S2_t = j|Y_t)ln\hat{e}(S2_t = j) \quad (5)$$

$$\text{Prob}(S1_t = i, S2_t = j, S3_t = k|Y_{t-1}) = \text{Prob}\,(S1_{t-1} = i|Y)\text{Prob}\,(S2_t = j|Y_{t-1})$$
$$\text{Prob}\,(S3_t = k|Y_{t-1})$$
$$P(S1_t = 1|S1_{t-1} = 1) = p_1$$
$$P(S1_t = 0|S1_{t-1} = 0) = q_1$$
$$P(S2_t = 1|S2_{t-1} = 1) = p_2$$
$$P(S2_t = 0|S2_{t-1} = 0) = q_2$$
$$P(S3_t = 1|S3_{t-1} = 1) = p_3$$
$$P(S3_t = 0|S3_{t-1} = 0) = q_3 \quad (6)$$

An important feature of the indicator model is the forecast for $\Delta\ln({}^{1+i}/_{P})_{t/t-1}$.[5] Equation (1) implies that *intended* inflation (interest rate changes minus the forecasted change in $\Delta\ln({}^{1+i}/_{P})_{t/t-1}$) in any given quarter equals the baseline inflation path (λ_0) plus possible adjustments due to the gap between the target and actual price levels and to the gap between the actual and baseline exchange rates. The size of the feedback coefficients $\lambda_1(S1)$ and $\lambda_2(S2_t)$ determines the rate at which one tries to close the respective

Table 2. Parameter estimates for the indicator model.

Parameter	NZ	AUS	CAN	USA	UK	Germany
$\lambda_0(S1 = 0)$	14.93	9.39	8.38	6.72	4.77	5.50
	(1.21)	(.470)	(.366)	(.603)	(.420)	(.371)
$\lambda_0(S1 = 1)$	0.73	2.67	3.81	3.67	14.26	2.40
	(.050)	(.453)	(.314)	(.420)	(.957)	(.553)
$\lambda_1(S1 = 0)$	0	0	0	0	0	0
$\lambda_1(S1 = 1)$	0	.169	0	0	0	0
		(.069)				
$\delta_1(S1 = 0)$	n.a.	1	n.a.	n.a.	n.a.	n.a.
$\delta_1(S1 = 1)$	n.a.	0	n.a.	n.a.	n.a.	n.a.
$\lambda_2(S2 = 0)$	.263	.055	0	.206	0	0
	(.042)	(.016)		(.078)		
$\lambda_2(S2 = 1)$	.079	.055	0	0	0	0
	(.023)	(.016)				
$\delta_2(S2 = 0)$	.341	.252	n.a.	1	n.a.	n.a.
	(.192)	(.205)				
$\delta_2(S2 = 1)$	.785	.252	n.a.	0	n.a.	n.a.
	(.106)	(.205)				
$\sigma^2(S2 = 0)$	.980	.132	.191	.229	.161	.189
	(.204)	(.069)	(.039)	(.074)	(.095)	(.043)
$\sigma^2(S2 = 1)$	.980	1.58	4.66	6.37	3.95	2.93
	(.204)	(.542)	(1.54)	(3.03)	(1.16)	(.836)
p_1	.880	.941	.918	.947	.946	.969
	(.053)	(.034)	(.045)	(.050)	(.037)	(.034)
q_1	.900	.882	.931	.984	.881	.969
	(.049)	(.078)	(.044)	(.019)	(.064)	(.034)
p_2	.357	n.a.	n.a.	.994	n.a.	.895
	(.245)			(.018)		(.080)
q_2	.629	n.a.	n.a.	.893	n.a.	n.a.
	(.155)			(.20)		
p_3	1	.978	.898	.958	.423	n.a.
		(.033)	(.046)	(.035)	(.271)	
q_3	0	.983	.699	.865	.562	.968
		(.021)	(.123)	(.095)	(.128)	(.024)
1/n	0	.149	0	.196	0	0
		(.132)		(.153)		
No. of parameters	12	12	8	12	8	8
Log-likelihood	−143.9	−122.4	−138.1	−133.2	−187.9	−111.3

Note: Standard errors are given in parentheses, if no standard error appears for a coefficient this implies that the coefficient was set at a boundary value and not estimated. The source for the interest rate and exchange rates is BIS, and the consumer price indexes were taken from the OECD databank. All series are quarterly averages of monthly data.

gaps through policy actions. A low feedback coefficient implies that the central bank prefers gradualism as opposed to rapid adjustment to the target path. Equation (2) permits this period's price level target to be a weighted average of last period's actual and target levels plus trend growth. Such rebasing of the targets occurs for values of $\delta_1 < 1$. Consequently, shifts in the target price level are gradually accommodated. As δ_1 decreases from one, the rate of accommodation increases. McCallum (1993) used a similar weighting scheme, however in his model δ_1 remains constant.

With respect to exchange-rate intervention, we normalize the Markov state variable S2 to equal zero in states when the central bank does not consider the exchange rate when setting interest rates: $\lambda_2(S2_t = 0) = 0, \delta_2(S2_t = 0) = 1$, which implies that the implicit comfort zone or baseline exchange rate is unchanging when the central bank is choosing not to conduct unsterilized exchange rate intervention. Equations (4) and (5) are analogous to equations (2) and (3), but generate an implicit baseline exchange rate, rather than the price level.

Because of the autoregressive nature of equations (2) and (4), inferences of the state at time t would depend on the entire history of past realizations of the state variables if it were not for the collapsing procedure of equations (3) and (5). Kim (1994) provides the justification for the collapsing procedure and he notes that its use generally introduces a small approximation to the estimation of a Markov switching model. He shows that the approximation to the evaluation of the likelihood function does not affect the parameter estimates, however.

An independence assumption in equation (6) for the state variables reduces the number of parameters needed for the transition probabilities. With k state variables, each taking on two values, one would need to estimate $(2^k)^2 - (2^k)$ transition probabilities. Whereas with the independence assumption, there are only 2k estimated parameters. In our model with three state variables, the reduction due to the independence assumption is from 56 to 6 estimated parameters.

Maximum-likelihood estimates of the parameters are obtained by maximizing the log of the expected likelihood or

$$\sum_{t=1}^{T} \ln\left(\sum_{i=0}^{1} \sum_{j=0}^{1} \sum_{k=0}^{1} \text{Prob}\,.(S1_t = i,\ S2_t = j,\ S3_t = k|Y_{t-1}) L_t^{(i,j,k)} \right) \tag{7}$$

where the student-*t* densities are

$$\begin{aligned} \ln L_t^{(i,j,k)} &= \ln\Gamma(.5(n+1)) - \ln\Gamma(.5n) - .5\ln(\pi\sigma^2(S3_t = k)) \\ &\quad -.5(n+1)\ln\left(1 + \frac{\hat{e}\,(S1_t = i,\ S2_t = j)_t^2}{n\sigma^2(S3_t = k)}\right) \end{aligned} \tag{8}$$

and Γ is the gamma function.

4. Estimation Results and Interpretation

The indicator model is used to estimate (baseline) policy-implied inflation rates for six countries: the United States, Australia, Canada, Germany, New Zealand and the United Kingdom. Three non-inflation targeting countries, the United States, Germany and Australia are included for comparative purposes. The sample frequency is quarterly for all countries. The interest rate is a 3-month domestic rate, prices are measured by the consumer price index, and the exchange rate is the domestic/US dollar rate except for the United Kingdom where the domestic/German mark rate is used.[6] For the United States the exchange rate is replaced with an interest rate spread that represents the slope of the yield curve. The availability of 3-month market rates has forced us to work with a non-uniform sample period.

The parameter estimates in Table 2 correspond to the model's equations (1)–(6). The parameter estimates in Table 2 and the nature of the state switching suggest that monetary policy in the six countries can be described as a policy of inflation targeting with occasional periods of exchange-rate intervention. The time-varying variance governed by the S3 variable is an important determinant for the instrument settings for all countries. A striking feature for all countries is the observed regime shift in the level of the implicit long-run inflation target (λ_0).[7] The implicit long-run inflation targets are characterized as having persistent low and high states. Evidence of persistence is found in Table 2 where $p_1 + q_1$ is close to two for all countries.

Table 2 shows that in some cases we reduced the number of estimated parameters if preliminary estimates of the full model suggested that some of the parameters lie on the boundary of the parameter space. In general, the indicator model is able to explain the interest rate changes fairly well, particularly over the second half of the sample. In some countries where interest rate changes are volatile, the information value of the instrument may be questioned. Australia and the United Kingdom in particular have noisy interest rate changes. In both countries, the interest rate moved more than 600 basis points (in absolute terms) within two quar-

Table 3. Summary of the main results.

	Annual inflation when		Probability of being in high inflation state when inflation targets were announced	Feedback significant			
	S1 = low state	S1 = high state		Price (S1 = 0)	S1 = 1	Exchange rate (S2 = 0)	S2 = 1
USA	3.7	6.7		No	No		
Australia	2.7	9.4		No	Yes	Yes	Yes
Germany	2.4	5.5		No	No	No	No
Canada	3.8	8.4	100	No	No	No	No
New Zealand	1.0	14.4	0.0	No	No	Yes	Yes
United Kingdom	4.8	14.2	0.10	No	No	No	No

ters, making inferences about the underlying policy objectives difficult.

Table 3 summarizes the key empirical results. The first two columns record the high and low point estimates of the baseline inflation targets. An unsettling feature of the baseline estimates for the United Kingdom and Canada is that the estimate for the low inflation state exceeds that of its paired neighbour and exceeds the respective upper ranges of the announced inflation targets. The next subsections comment on the plausibility of these estimates. The last four columns of Table 3 note whether or not the feedback mechanism was significant in the high and low inflation state. The estimates of the feedback parameters suggest that the price feedback parameter is insignificant in most countries, whereas the exchange rate feedback is important only for the smaller countries: Australia and New Zealand.

The profile of the baseline inflation target path tends to be subject to abrupt swings in all countries. In our view, this feature does not reflect hasty changes in inflation preferences on the part of policymakers. Nor does it mean that central bankers prefer "cold turkey" to "gradualism". Rather, permanent shifts in the baseline inflation path provide information regarding the timing as to when the changes in preferences took place. For example, Table 3 (column three) reports evidence that the United Kingdom and New Zealand had changed their inflation preferences well before the announcement of the inflation targets. The estimated probability of being in the high inflation state is close to zero for these two countries.

New Zealand Versus Australia

Australia and New Zealand are often regarded as commodity-exporting countries linked by a free trade agreement.[8] The major difference in structure reflects that Australia is mineral rich and New Zealand is not. As can be seen from Table 1, the inflation profile for the two countries has been similar. From 1981 to 1990 inflation averaged 7.9 and 10.2 percent in Australia and New Zealand respectively. Since 1992 inflation has been consistently below 2 percent in both countries.

The framework for Australian and New Zealand monetary policy differs in two respects.[9] First, in contrast to New Zealand, where the Reserve Bank objective of the 0 to 2 inflation target is underpinned by the Reserve Bank Act of 1989, the long-run objective of Australian monetary policy is loosely defined as keeping inflation at levels comparable with those of its major trading partners. Second, the Policy Targets Agreement between the Reserve Bank of New Zealand Governor and the Minister of Finance defines a precise target framework for inflation. Time frame, escape clauses, policy reports and sanctions are clearly specified within the Reserve Bank Act. On the other hand the Reserve Bank of Australia does not follow such a targetry framework.

It is difficult to say that New Zealand has made considerable gains relative to Australia based on the results from our indicator model. The change in inflation preferences hypothesis is supported by the data for both countries, implying that inflation targets are not necessarily key for price stability. Figure 2 plots the implicit inflation target (baseline) with actual inflation (annual moving average). Figure 2a for New Zealand shows that both actual inflation and the baseline fell sharply to unprecedentedly low levels in early 1988, a result consistent with the change in

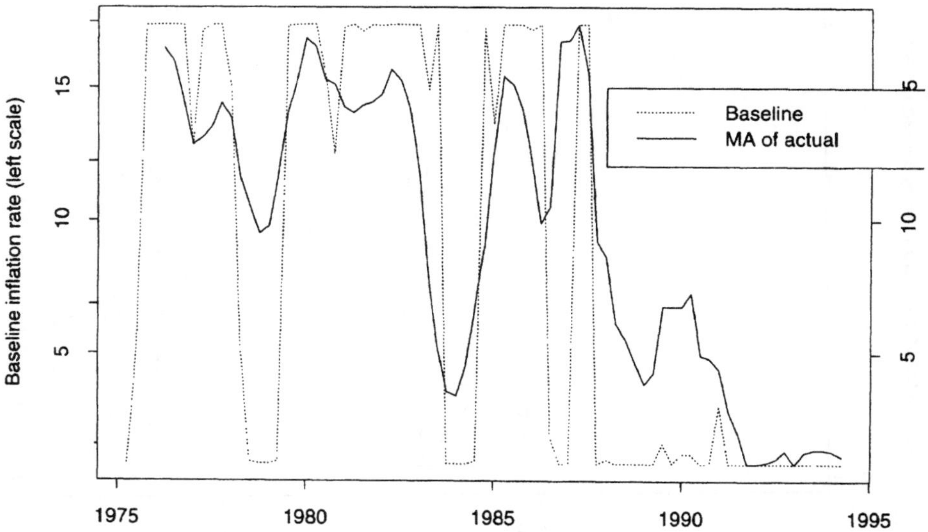

Figure 2a. Baseline inflation rate for New Zealand.

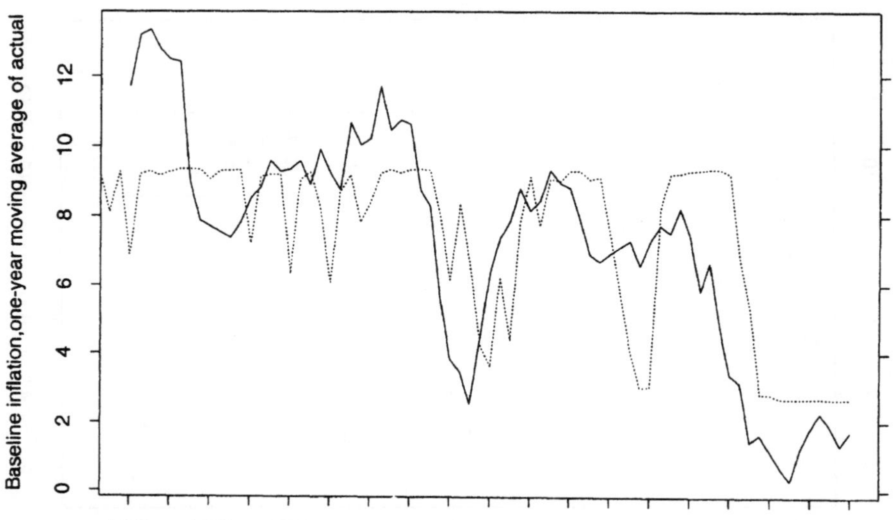

Figure 2b. Baseline inflation rate for Australia.

preferences hypothesis. The permanent fall in New Zealand's baseline rate to a level of near zero percent is consistent with the 0–2 percent inflation targets announced first in 1990. A similar baseline path is observed in Figure 2b for Australia. However, it is important to note that Australia's baseline rate fell after New Zealand's

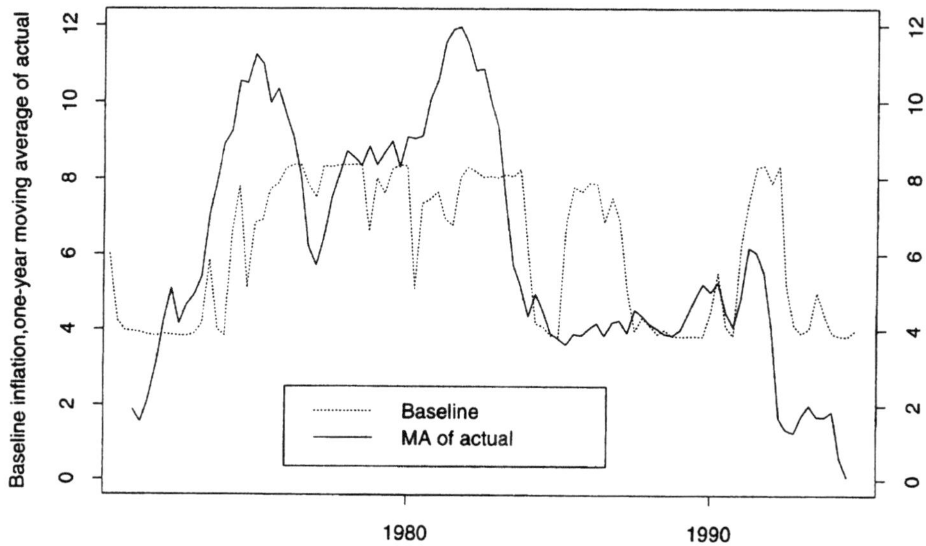

Figure 2c. Baseline inflation rate for Canada.

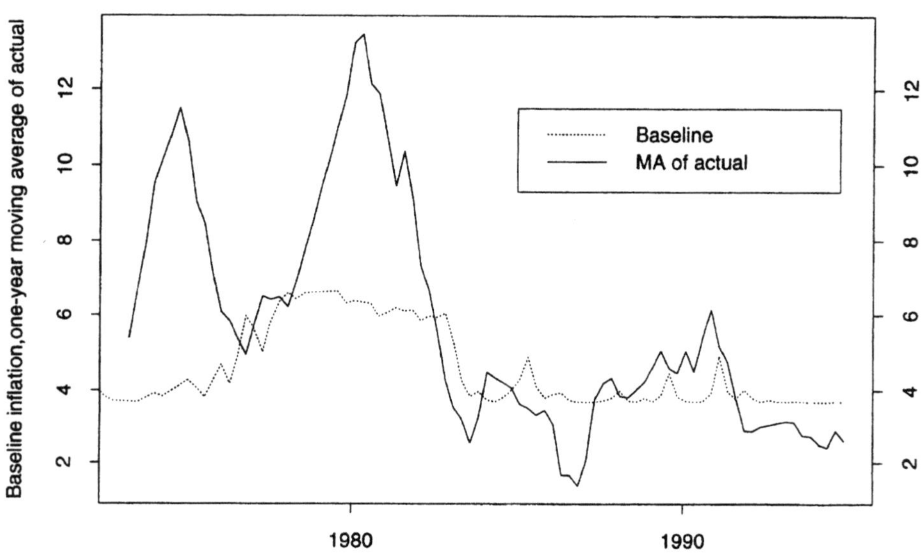

Figure 2d. Baseline inflation rate for the U.S.

baseline shift. We conclude that both Australia and New Zealand have acted in the 1990s as if they were placing increased emphasis on zero inflation.

Canada Versus the United States

Although the United States and Canada underwent similar disinflationary cycles, Canadian inflation has been above United States inflation since the collapse of the Bretton Woods system. In recent years, however, the inflation gap between the two countries has narrowed. Since the mid-1980s the two inflation rates have hovered around the 4 to 5 percent level. After the Bank of Canada's announcement of inflation targets in February 1991, Canadian inflation measured by the CPI dipped below United States' inflation for the first time since 1970 and has remained in the 0 to 2 percent range, which is consistently below the inflation rate in the United States.

A key reason why the Bank of Canada opposed an exchange rate target was that United States' monetary policy was viewed to be too growth oriented and the implicit inflation objective in the United States of three percent was regarded as too high. Freedman (1995) mentions that a further motive for announcing the inflation target was to signal to the public that the Bank of Canada was serious about its objective of price stability. Indirectly, the target to reduce inflation to 1 to 3 percent by 1995 was also signalling that it wanted to do better than the United States in terms of inflation performance. Thus if the change in inflation preferences hypothesis is correct for Canada, one would expect (1) a downward movement of the baseline inflation rate around February 1991, the date of the target announcement; and (2) a lower implicit inflation target in Canada than in the United States.

The empirical results from the indicator model find weak evidence for the change in inflationary preferences hypothesis for Canada. Figure 2c shows that the Canadian baseline inflation rate shifted to the low inflation state in 1992, albeit at a level just under 4 percent – well outside the Bank of Canada's target range of 1 to 3 percent. The spike behavior of inflation and the baseline in 1991 is explained by the newly introduced Goods and Services tax. The relative high estimate of 3.8 percent during the 1990s for the Canadian baseline rate is surprising, particularly since actual inflation has been near the bottom half of the 1 to 3 percent target range. Our baseline result is dictated by the fact that there is no evidence of a feedback mechanism for prices of the exchange rate. Consequently, the good inflation performance of the 1990s is not reflected in the instrument settings.

Figure 2d for the United States shows evidence of a shift in inflation preferences occurring in the mid-1980s. The baseline inflation path rises steadily from 3 to 7 percent from the late 1970s to the mid-1980s. Since the mid-1980s there appears to be a break with past policy, because the near-constant baseline rate of three percent can be interpreted as a shift to a new inflation environment. Hence, a change in inflation preferences appears to have arisen after the 1979–1983 disinflationary cycle.

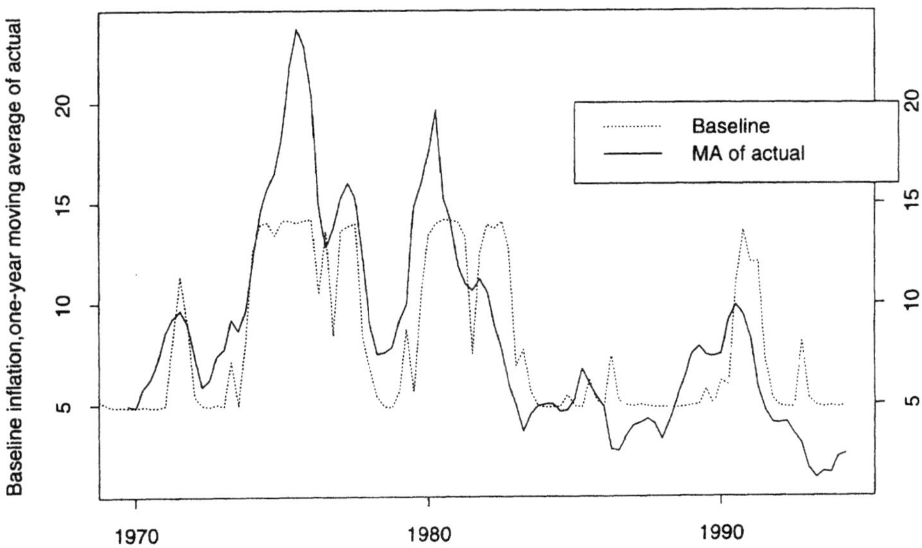

Figure 2e. Baseline inflation rate for the United Kingdom.

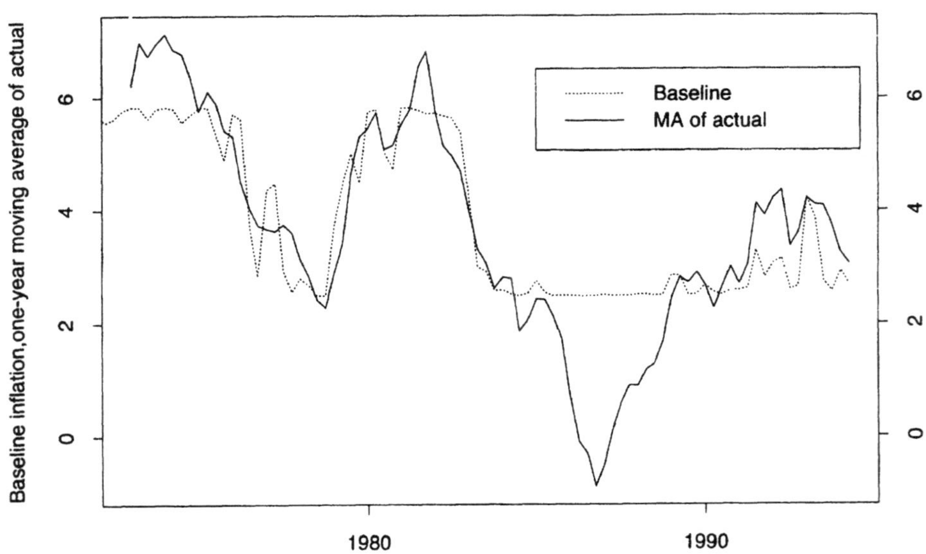

Figure 2f. Baseline inflation rate for Germany.

The United Kingdom Versus Germany

The actual and the baseline inflation paths for the United Kingdom and Germany, which are depicted in Figures 2e and 2f, show that British inflation, which has the higher historical average, has also been more volatile. The different inflation records reflect the different targeting strategies of the two countries. The strategy of British monetary policy has changed continuously over the last two decades. The Bank of England pursued a policy of monetary targeting during the mid 1970s to early 1980s. The Bank shifted emphasis to the exchange rate prior to its entry into the EMS in 1990, which it left in 1992. Since then it has followed a strategy of inflation targeting.[10] The Bundesbank has, in contrast, maintained the same nominal anchor in the form of monetary targets since 1975.

The estimates for the United Kingdom find that the baseline rate fluctuates with actual inflation. There is evidence of a shift in inflation preferences after the introduction of inflation targets in 1992, however only after actual inflation fell. The baseline path hovers near the lower band for the greater part of the sample after 1984. The estimated baseline path of more than 4 percent is not necessarily inconsistent with the Bank of England's inflation target of 1–4 percent. Our baseline estimates are in terms of the consumer price index, whereas the Bank of England's inflation targets are measured by the 12-month price rise in retail price index excluding mortgage interest payments.

Table 4. Informal inflation targets for Germany.

Year	Unavoidable inflation %
1975	4.5
1976	4.5
1977	3.5 'less than four'
1978	3
1979	3 'no new inflation'
1980	4
1981	3.8
1982	3.5
1983	3.5
1984	3
1985	2.5
1986–1994	2.0

Source: Von Hagen (1994).

The estimates of the baseline inflation path in Germany follow the Bundesbank's informal inflation targets, which are documented in Von Hagen (1994) and reproduced in Table 4. From 1975 to 1985, the Bundesbank referred to a varying informal target as unavoidable inflation. Since 1986 the Bundesbank has pursued a fixed, unconditional inflation target of 0–2 percent. As can be seen from Figure 2f, the German baseline inflation rate lacks persistence, jumping between the high and low states before 1985. Thereafter, a clear shift in the baseline path can be detected. The baseline has remained constant since 1985 at 2 percent, consistent with the Bundesbank's informal target.

5. Conclusion

Our indicator model, which uses a Markov-switching process to estimate the implicit inflation target (baseline) path, is set-up to reflect the extreme position that price stability is the sole objective of monetary policy. Output considerations were intentionally excluded from our indicator model on the grounds that we were interested in determining whether previous and current monetary settings are consistent with a policy of inflation targeting. Since our model allows for accommodation of past policy mistakes, considerations for output stabilization can be easily included in our modelling framework by adding an additional feedback mechanism for real output.

The comparative analysis stemming from our indicator model suggests that inflation targets have brought about a change in inflation preferences in the 1990s. This statement needs to be qualified however, because the inflation-targeting countries generally followed a non-inflation-targeting neighbor in reducing their baseline inflation rates. The United States and Germany shifted to a low baseline path prior to similar shifts by their inflation-targeting neighbors. Given that the neighboring countries moved first and appear to have settled on a lower baseline inflation rate, it is difficult to determine how instrumental the targets were in bringing about the shift in preferences.

One area of future research is to consider the role of forward rates in our indicator model. Because, the decision making process with inflation targets tends to be forward looking, policy decisions are usually based on forecasts and on a range of leading indicators rather than actual inflation. This feature is not incorporated in the indicator model. By considering forward exchange rates and proxy measures for expected price changes in the feedback mechanism, such an option could overcome the problem of lag adjustment implicitly built in the indicator model.

Notes

1. For further details about the Finnish inflation targets see Pikkarainen and Tyräinen (1993).
2. The alternative hypothesis is consistent with the view that inflation cycles are highly correlated across countries, implying that central banks are responding to global inflationary pressures. Ball's (1993) work on sacrifice ratios finds that the starting dates of the disinflationary cycles are similar across countries, although stark differences in the durations exist.
3. Dueker and Fischer (1994b) provide a non-technical survey of how the indicator model fits closely with the models of McCallum.
4. The basic filtering and smoothing algorithms for a Markov-switching model are discussed in Hamilton (1988, 1989).
5. The forecasts stem from a Kalman filter which allows time-varying changes in the variance. The forecast model is presented in Dueker and Fischer (1994a).
6. In some countries an alternative price index may have been preferable. For example, the Bank of Canada and the Reserve Bank of New Zealand base their policy decisions on a modified CPI index (although the inflation targets are defined in terms of the CPI).
7. This result is contrary to the findings in Dueker and Fischer (1994a) for Switzerland. The Swiss

model, which uses the monetary base as the control instrument, finds evidence of a single long-run inflation target.

8. The two countries can be viewed as a single trading block because the Australia-New Zealand Closer Economic Relationship Trade Agreement removed all tariffs and quantitative restriction/quotas on merchandise trade between the two countries since July 1, 1990.
9. See Fischer (1995) for a discussion of New Zealand's experience with inflation targets.
10. Bowen (1994) outlines the Bank of England's targetry strategy.

References

Ball, L. (1993), "What Determines the Sacrifice Ratio?", *NBER Working Paper* #4306.

Bowen, A. (1994), "British Experience with Inflation Targetry", paper presented at the CEPR Workshop on Inflation Targets, Milan 25/26 November 1994, forthcoming in L. Leiderman and L. Svensson, CEPR (eds.), *Inflation Targets*.

Dueker, M.J. and A.M. Fischer (1994a), "Inflation Targeting in a Small Open Economy: Empirical Results for Switzerland", *SNB mimeo*.

Dueker, M.J. and A.M. Fischer (1994b), "A Guide to Nominal Feedback Rules and their Use for Monetary Policy", Swiss National Bank, *Geld, Währung und Konjunktur*, 327–335.

Fischer, A.M. (1995), "New Zealand's Experience with Inflation Targets", forthcoming in L. Leiderman and L. Svensson, CEPR (eds.), *Inflation Targets*.

Freedman, C. (1995), "The Canadian Experience with Targets for Reducing and Controlling Inflation", forthcoming in L. Leiderman and L. Svensson, CEPR (eds.), *Inflation Targets*.

Hagen, J. von, (1994) "Inflation Target in Germany ...?" paper presented at the CEPR Workshop on Inflation Targets, Milan 25/26 November 1994, forthcoming in L. Leiderman and L. Svensson, CEPR (eds.), *Inflation Targets*.

Hamilton, J. (1988), "Rational Expectations Econometric Analysis of Changes in Regimes: An Investigation of the Term Structure of Interest Rates", *Journal of Economic Dynamics and Control*, 12, 385–432.

Hamilton, J. (1989), "A New Approach to the Economic Analysis of Nonstationary Time Series and the Business Cycle", *Econometrica*, 57, 357–384.

Kim, C.-J. (1994), "Dynamic Linear Models with Markov Switching", *Journal of Econometrics*, 1–22, Elsevier, Amsterdam.

McCallum, B.T. (1987), "The Case for Rules in the Conduct of Monetary Policy: A Concrete Example", Federal Reserve Bank of Richmond, *Economic Review*, 10–18.

McCallum, B.T. (1993), "Specification and Analysis of a Monetary Policy Rule for Japan", Bank of Japan, *Monetary and Economic Studies*, 11, No. 2, 1–45.

Pikkarainen, P. and T. Tyräinen (1993), "The Bank of Finland's Inflation Target and the Outlook for Inflation over the next few Years", Bank of Finland, *Bulletin June–July*, 8–12.

Monetary Interdependencies in the "Core" ERM Countries: The P-Star Approach*

HANS GROENEVELD,[1] KEES KOEDIJK[2] AND CLEMENS KOOL[2]
[1]*De Nederlandsche Bank*
[2]*University of Limburg and LIFE*

ABSTRACT

Two versions of the P-star model (P*) of inflation are tested for Belgium, France, Germany and the Netherlands for the period 1973.I–1992.IV. In the first, conventional version the statistical links between national monetary aggregates and domestic inflation are examined. Conversely, the chosen set up in the second version allows for symmetric monetary spill-over effects between these countries. The estimates suggest that inflation in Belgium and the Netherlands is nowadays fully determined by the European price gap and not by domestic monetary conditions, while the relative importance of the European price gap is increasing in the case of France and Germany. All in all the European price gap provides an accurate indicator for future inflationary tendencies in all four countries. Moreover, we find that the European inflation equation is stable over the sample period. Taken together these results suggest that (implicit) targeting of a European monetary aggregate in addition to explicitly targeting the German money supply may become necessary to achieve and maintain price stability in Europe in the near future.

1. INTRODUCTION

The quantity theory of money and its equation of exchange have been extensively used to empirically analyze the relevance of money in an economy. However, in the 1980s doubts have arisen about the existence of stable relationships between money, prices and output, which prompted several countries to abandon or downgrade the practice of monetary targeting (Goodhart 1989). Recently, Hallman, Porter and Small (1989) – henceforth HPS – have drawn renewed attention to the quantity theory of money in the so-called P^*-approach. In this model, the equilibrium price level, or P^*, is assumed to change proportionally with the money stock, provided that the velocity of this monetary aggregate and real output are at their "equilibrium" levels. The

*The views expressed in this paper are personal and do not necessarily reflect those of the Nederlandsche Bank.

Koos Alders, Kees Koedijk, Clemens Kool and Carlo Winder (eds.), Monetary Policy in a Converging Europe, pp. 39–60.

essence of this conceptual framework is that deviations between the actual and equilibrium price level – the price gap – convey information for the short run dynamics of inflation.

HPS (1989) apply the P^*-approach for the U.S. and conclude that the model is supported by the data. Soon the validity of this concept was also empirically tested for other countries (Bank of Japan 1990, Hoeller and Poret 1991, Kole and Leahy 1991, Reimers and Tödter 1994 among others). Generally speaking, the results of these studies are encouraging: only for relatively small countries the P^*-model tends to be rejected in some instances. As Kool and Tatom (1994) point out, this last finding could stem from the neglect of cross-country spill-over effects in the case of small open economies with fixed exchange rates. By including a price gap based on monetary conditions in Germany in inflation equations for Austria, Belgium, Denmark, Luxemburg and the Netherlands, they find strong evidence that the domestic price level in the latter countries is largely determined by monetary developments in Germany.

In the existing P^*-literature hardly any attention is paid to the impact of economic integration on the relationship between international monetary developments and changes in domestic prices over time. This issue is especially relevant for the countries currently participating in the ERM and may also have direct policy implications. Firstly, national economic policies in these countries have been increasingly oriented towards the exchange rate objective and thus have facilitated a growing convergence in prices, costs and monetary aggregates in the course of time (see, for instance, Caporale and Pittis 1993, Giavazzi and Giovannini 1989). This convergence may in turn have led to a gradual erosion of the German leadership role.[1] Hence, German monetary policy has possibly become more and more subject to feedback (symmetric spill-over effects) from other ERM countries, whereby German dominance has been gradually replaced by policy coordination (Fratianni and von Hagen 1992). Secondly, the European Monetary Institute (EMI) is currently preparing an adequate monetary framework for the European System of Central Banks ESCB) in the third stage of Economic and Monetary Union (EMU). One of the questions in this respect is whether intermediate targets in general and monetary targets in particular will be useful for the conduct of future monetary policy (Monticelli and Viñals 1993). Even in the present second stage of EMU, where monetary policy is still the responsibility of domestic monetary authorities, evidence that German inflation is influenced by European monetary conditions may call for an informal amendment of the monetary strategy in the anchor country of the ERM.[2] Such a modification could in principle facilitate the transition from stage 2 to 3 to some extent if the ESCB would also predominantly base its policy decisions on the medium-term development of European monetary aggregates.

In order to gain insights into the aspects mentioned above, we shall extend the conventional P^*-approach in the spirit of McKinnon (1982) by examining to what extent inflation behaviour in four core ERM countries (Germany, France, Belgium and the Netherlands) is determined by domestic and European monetary conditions, respectively, over the period 1973.I–1992.IV. To this end, we first calculate "European" aggregates for money, real output and prices. Subsequently, we compute a European price gap reflecting the average monetary conditions in these four countries and investigate its impact on price trends in each country. Hence, this extension of the P^*-approach allows for a simple and straightforward test whether domestic or European price gaps are an accurate indicator for inflationary threats in the "core" ERM countries.

The way the paper proceeds is as follows. In Section 2 we outline the theoretical background of the P^*-approach and the incorporation of symmetric monetary spillover effects. Section 3 contains the empirical results, both for domestic and European price gaps. Section 4 draws the results together in a brief concluding section.

2. Theoretical Underpinnings

2.1. The P^*-Methodology

The P^*-approach – developed by HPS (1989) – combines two long-standing propositions in economics: the quantity theory of money and the lagged adjustment of prices. In the P^*-framework, a gap between the actual and equilibrium price level causes a change in inflation which in turn restores the equilibrium between actual and equilibrium prices over time. The basis of the P^*-model is Fisher's well-known equation of exchange identity:[3]

$$P = M(V/Y) \tag{1}$$

where P denotes the price level, M the domestic stock of money, Y real output and V velocity of money. Without further elaboration, no testable hypothesis can be derived from equation (1), since it simply pins down actual velocity for given observations on P, M and Y. HPS (1989), however, hypothesize the following long-run equilibrium version of equation (1):

$$P^* = M(V^* / Y^*) \tag{2}$$

where P^* equals the equilibrium price level to which actual prices converge in the long run, and V^* and Y^* are equilibrium levels of the income velocity of money and potential real output, respectively. Assuming that V^* and Y^* can be determined independently, and that both are independent of the money stock, equation (2) shows that the equilibrium price level moves proportionally with the stock of money. The combination of equations (1) and (2) results in the so called price gap:

$$GAP = (p - p^*) = (v - v^*) + (y - y^*). \tag{3}$$

The price gap (p-p^*) represents a combination of the velocity gap (v-v^*) and the output gap (y-y*). However, equation (3) does not provide insights into the dynamics of the equilibrating mechanism following a monetary disturbance, when p becomes unequal to p*. In order to deal with these considerations we have opted for the following dynamic adjustment equation:

$$\Delta p_t = \alpha_0 + \alpha_1(p - p^*)_{t-1} + \sum_{j=1}^{n} \beta_j \Delta p_{t-j} + \varepsilon_t \tag{4}$$

where the inflation lags are introduced to account for short-run dynamics and ε_t is the random error term.[4] The P*-model hypothesises that in equilibrium the price gap, has a value of zero. The theory predicts that changes in the actual price level vary inversely with the price gap and hence that α_1 is negative. Nonstationarity of inflation (Δp) may lead to econometric problems in estimating equation (4). To circumvent these potential problems equation (4) can be rewritten without loss of generality as:

$$\Delta \pi_t = \alpha_0 + \alpha_1(p - p^*)_{t-1} + \sum_{j=1}^{n-1} \delta_j \Delta \pi_{t-j} + \delta_0 \pi_{t-1} + \varepsilon_t \tag{5}$$

where π now denotes inflation. If inflation is stationary, δ_0 is (significantly) negative, otherwise, δ_0 in equation (5) has a theoretical value of zero and may be omitted.

In the existing P*-literature hardly any attention is paid to the relationship between international monetary developments and changes in domestic prices over time. In the next step we lay-out the framework to integrate international monetary developments and the P*-model.

2.2. An Extension of the Conventional P-Framework*

The view underlying the traditional P*-framework that purely domestic monetary aggregates eventually determine the equilibrium price level in individual countries had already implicitly been challenged by McKinnon in 1982, though in completely different context. He found empirical evidence that the national (convertible) monies of an inner group of industrial countries were highly substitutable in demand according to anticipated exchange rate movements. This international currency substitution destabilised national money demands, which in turn led to a breakdown of the relationship between national inflation rates and the growth rates of national money supplies. However, national price movements appeared to be satisfactorily explicable by considering the growth of a crude index of a global monetary aggregate (comprising the money stocks for countries with convertible currencies in the 1970s).

The currencies of the core ERM countries may have become even closer substitutes for one another in the course of time than those of the group of industrial countries in which McKinnon was interested more than a decade ago (Bayoumi and Kenen 1993).[5] This could be associated with the burgeoning economic integration in the early 1980s, which eventually became firmly embedded in Europe. Lane and Poloz (1992) have empirically shown that currency substitution may indeed play an important role in money demand in countries currently participating in the ERM.

To cope with the above considerations we have extended the closed economy version of the P*-concept discussed in Section 2.1 to a similar monetary framework that is empirically applicable in a situation where symmetric monetary spill-over effects between the core ERM countries may occur. To be more precise, we assume that European equivalents of equations (1) and (2) can be formulated. Note that our strategy presupposes that a stable demand for an ERM monetary aggregate exists.[6, 7]

In this case the following equations result:

$$P_{eur} = M_{eur}(V_{eur}/Y_{eur}) \tag{6}$$

and

$$P^*_{eur} = M_{eur}(V^*_{eur}/Y^*_{eur}) \tag{7}$$

where M_{eur}, P_{eur}, Y_{eur}, and V_{eur} are the European money, price, output and velocity aggregates, respectively. The way in which these aggregates are constructed is explained in the next section. It is easy to see that combining equation (6) with equation (7) yields an expression analogous to equation (3).

Theoretically, the ERM-wide money supply does not only determine the equilibrium European price level, but also pins down the equilibrium price level in each of the core ERM countries (P^{d*}) through the exchange rate constraint, or in symbols:

$$P^{d*} = EP^*_{eur}/ER^*, \tag{8}$$

where E is the fixed nominal exchange rate, equal to the number of equilibrium domestic currency units per unit of foreign currency in which the European aggregates are expressed, and ER^* is the corresponding equilibrium real exchange rate.

The extended model has important theoretical implications for the short-run price dynamics in each country. Firstly, P^* in expression (3) must be replaced by P^{d*} as defined in equation (8) so that the following European price gap results:

$$GAP^f = [p - (p^*_{eur} + e - er^*)], \tag{9}$$

This price gap is now expected to influence the future path of inflation in each country. When the domestic price level exceeds the European equilibrium price level (corrected for permanent real exchange rate changes), we hypothesise that downward pressure on domestic inflation results. The amount of pressure this gap actually exerts on current domestic inflation and the speed of adjustment toward equilibrium depend on the extent of arbitrage in goods and capital markets, and the degree to which the economies are integrated.

Secondly, the effect of the domestic price gap on domestic inflation developments is expected to decrease with higher European integration and increased goods and capital mobility.[8]

Both hypotheses are tested in Section 4. In a first test, we replace the domestic gap by an aggregate European gap. In a second test, we include both gaps simultaneously in the estimation equation so that the appropriate equilibrium gap measure is a weighted average of the domestic gap in equation (3) and the European gap in equation (9):

$$(1-w)GAP^{d} + w\ GAP^{f} \tag{10}$$

where w is the weight attached to a fixed exchange rate regime. For a closed economy or a floating exchange rate regime, w equals zero and the appropriate equilibrium price level and gap measures are the conventional, domestically determined ones defined in equations (1) – (3). If there is a credible fixed exchange rate regime, then w equals one and the domestic equilibrium price level is determined by the overall European monetary conditions. In this case, the appropriate P^* and its related gap measure are determined as a weighted European average. An important element in constructing the European price gaps concerns the computation of variables on a European scale. In the next section we turn to this issue.

2.3. Aggregation Issues

In the literature, various methods have been used to convert domestic variables into one currency in order to obtain cross-country aggregates. Monticelli and Strauss-Kahn (1991), for instance, use actual nominal exchange rates for the conversion, whereas Bekx and Tullio (1989) and Artis et al. (1993) take base-period exchange rates and Kremers and Lane (1990) employ purchasing power parity (PPP) exchange rates. Bayoumi and Kenen (1993) finally sum the weighted rates of change of economic variables across countries and abstract from aggregating levels of variables.

Since all methods have conceptual drawbacks, we more or less arbitrarity present results obtained using current exchange rates, whereby the Deutsche mark functions as a benchmark.[9] Thus, all European aggregates have been computed by converting domestic variables expressed in national currency into German marks, after which they are summed. For money,[10] nominal and real output respectively, the European aggregates, therefore, may be expressed as:

$$M_{eur} = \sum_i (M_i/E_i) \tag{11}$$

$$Y^n_{eur} = \sum_i (Y^n_i/E_i) \tag{12}$$

and

$$Y_{eur} = \sum_i (Y_i/E_i) \tag{13}$$

where all exchange rates are defined as the number of units of domestic currency per unit of German marks. From the above expression, a European aggregate price level can be derived:

$$P_{eur} = \frac{Y^n_{eur}}{Y_{eur}} = \Sigma_i \left[\frac{(Y^n_i / E_i)}{\Sigma_i(Y_i / E_i)}\right] = \Sigma_i \left[\frac{(Y_i / E_i)P_i}{\Sigma_i(Y_i / E_i)}\right]. \tag{14}$$

Thus, the price level is a weighted average of national price indices. The weights are the shares of real output in individual countries in the European aggregate. To assess the sensitivity of our results for the aggregation method chosen, we carried out the same empirical analysis using base year (1985) exchange rates. Reassuringly, the results were qualitatively similar, albeit somewhat less strong in terms of significance in a few instances. The Bayoumi and Kenen aggregation method was not employed because the use of levels in aggregation is required within the context of the P*-model. Nevertheless, the European inflation rates resulting from the Bayoumi and Kenen aggregation method are almost identical to the inflation rates computed with either current or benchmark exchange rates.

Table 1. Statistical characteristics of inflation, real output growth and the growth of M3 (sample period 1973.I–1992.IV).

	P				Y				M3			
	M	Std	Sk	K	M	Std	Sk	K	M	Std	Sk	K
Belgium	1.3	0.9	1.3	5.4	0.4	2.1	–0.2	3.0	2.1	1.1	0.0	2.6
France	1.8	1.0	0.1	1.9	0.6	0.6	–0.7	3.5	2.6	1.0	0.7	3.1
Germany	0.9	0.6	0.7	4.4	0.5	1.1	0.1	3.1	1.8	0.7	0.6	2.9
Netherlands	1.0	1.2	–0.1	2.8	0.5	1.6	0.1	5.0	2.1	1.0	0.1	2.6
Core ERM	1.4	0.7	0.5	2.8	0.1	1.4	–0.1	3.6	1.8	1.2	0.3	4.7

Note: M = mean; Std = standard deviation; Sk = skewness; K = kurtosis.

2.4. Estimating Long-Run Trends

The crucial step in making the P*-framework operational as an indicator for inflationary trends is to determine the long-run velocity of money and potential real output (V^* and Y^*, respectively). Previous P*-studies have used different methods to give these equilibrium variables empirical content. For instance, estimates of these concepts have been based on simple linear time trends (Bank of Japan 1990, Christiano 1989), structural models (HPS 1989, 1991, Ebrill and Fries 1991) or the Hodrick-Prescott filter technique (Hoeller and Poret 1991, Kool and Tatom 1994). In the investigation of the validity of the P*-model for several countries belonging to the core ERM group, we shall however employ another method to generate the equilibrium variables. We shall use the Multi State Kalman Filter (MSKF) which has never been used in the P*-literature so far.[11]

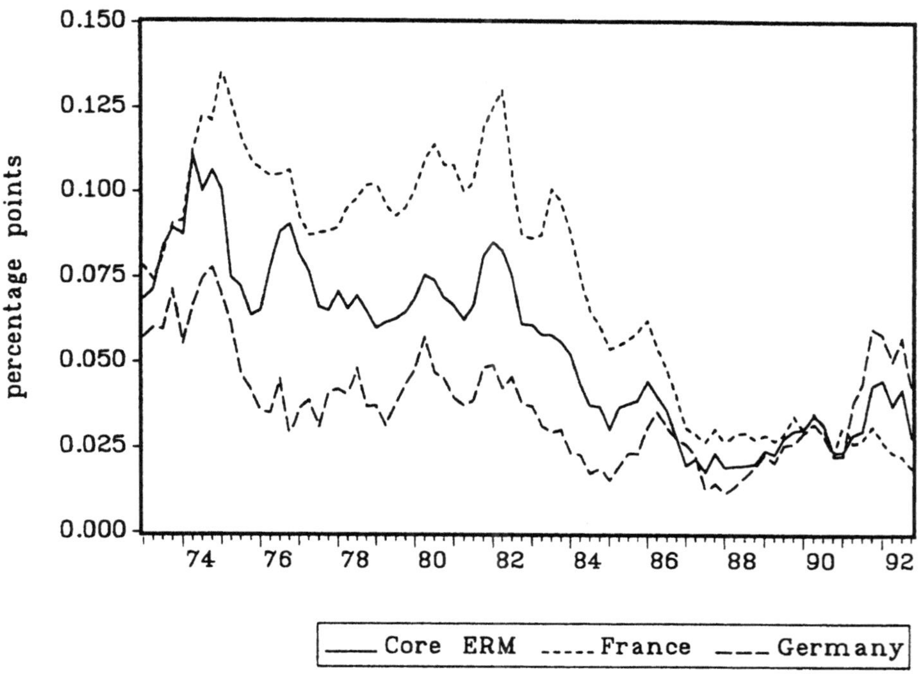

Figure 1. Annual inflation rates.

Table 2. ADF unit root results (growth rates).

Country	P	Y	M3	V3
Belgium	–4.0	–3.4	–5.2	–3.0
	(t,4)	(c,5)	(c,0)	(c,6)
France	–2.8	–3.2	–8.2	–5.8
	(t,4)	(c,3)	(t,0)	(c,3)
Germany	–2.2	–3.2	–8.5	–4.6
	(c,3)	(c,3)	(c,0)	(c,4)
Netherlands	–3.0	–3.5	–3.5	–9.2
	(t,4)	(c,7)	(c,1)	(c,1)
Core ERM	–2.6	–3.6	–4.5	–9.4
	(t,1)	(n,2)	(c,3)	(c,0)

Note: The entries show the relevant test statistic; the information in parentheses indicates the use of constant only, C, or a constant and trend, T, followed by the number of lagged dependent variables included. For the longest sample period used, the 5 percent significance level critical values are –3.56 and –2.96, with and without the inclusion of a trend, respectively.

3. The Empirical Results

3.1. Data Description

The quarterly data used in this paper are seasonally adjusted. Apart from the data on M3 which are obtained from the respective national central banks, all data have been collected from the BIS-databank. The income variables are, depending on the availability, GNP or GDP. The real income data are in 1985 prices. Only for Belgium the real and nominal income data are interpolated according to the quarterly pattern of industrial production.

Table 3. ADF unit root results (log levels).

Country	P	Y	M3	V3
Belgium	–2.1	–2.4	–2.4	2.1
	(t,5)	(t,4)	(n,4)	(n,4)
France	0.5	–2.7	–8.3	2.2
	(t,1)	(t,2)	(c,0)	(n,4)
Germany	–3.1	–2.2	–1.9	–2.9
	(t,2)	(t,4)	(t,0)	(t,0)
Netherlands	5.5	–2.9	–2.8	–2.8
	(c,0)	(t,0)	(t,8)	(t,2)
Core ERM	–4.4	0.4	3.7	–2.8
	(c,2)	(n,3)	(n,4)	(t,0)

Note: The entries show the relevant test statistic; the information in parentheses indicates the use of a constant only, C, or a constant and trend, T, followed by the number of lagged dependent variables included. For the longest sample period used, the 5 percent significance level critical values are –3.56 and –2.96, with and without the inclusion of a trend, respectively.

Table 1 documents some basic statistical indicators of inflation, output and money growth for Belgium, France, Germany, the Netherlands and these core countries as a group for the period 1973–1992. The variables on a European scale are constructed as outlined in Section 2.2. From this table it is apparent that inflation and monetary expansion were highest in France during this period and lowest in Germany, while real output growth was almost identical for the four countries in this time span. Figure 1 visualises the path of inflation in Germany, France and the core ERM group as a whole. The chart illustrates that inflation reached its highest level in the mid 1970s. However, the first five years of the EMS were also a period of quite rapidly rising prices. In this time span, European prices were on average increasing by 1.5 percentage point per quarter. This period was, however, characterised by frequent and relatively large adjustments in exchange rate parities. Thereafter, the average inflation rate in the core group came down to about 0.7 percentage point and the inflation differentials were markedly reduced.

An important issue for the correct specification of the price equation is the (non)-

stationarity of the variables involved. Tables 2 and 3 report results of standard Augmented Dickey-Fuller (ADF) tests for both the log levels and growth rates of prices, output and broad money and the corresponding velocity in the individual countries and the core group as a whole. In these tables we report the t-statistic on the lagged level of the preferred specification. This specification is given below the t-statistic. Significance at the 5 percent level is indicated and implies rejection of non-stationarity.

Table 4. ADF unit root results domestic and European price gaps.

Country	Domestic price gap	European price gap
Belgium	–6.6	–6.2
	(n,0)	(n,5)
France	–6.3	–5.1
	(n,3)	(n,3)
Germany	–7.1	–5.9
	(n,0)	(n,3)
Netherlands	–4.3	–6.6
	(n,4)	(n,1)

Note: The entries show the relevant test statistic; the information in parentheses indicates the use of a constant only, C, or a constant and trend, T, followed by the number of lagged dependent variables included. For the longest sample period used, the 5 percent significance level critical values are –3.56 and –2.96, with and without the inclusion of a trend, respectively.

The results reported in Table 2 indicate that the growth rate of output, broad money and velocity are stationary, were as the price level appears to be integrated of order two. The ADF test for the log levels of the former variables suggest that non-stationarity can not be rejected. Consequently, computation of the equilibrium values of velocity and real output by means of a deterministic trend is incorrect. The implication of these findings is that a procedure capable of handling stochastic trends is required to generate the equilibrium levels. As explained in the previous section, we use the Multi-State Kalman Filter to calculate equilibrium velocity and potential real output.

Before implementing the P*-model, we first have to verify whether the price gaps are stationary. In the P*-framework, short-run inflation dynamics are theoretically assumed to be influenced by the equilibrium price gap because of the existence of an underlying equilibrating adjustment process. If actual prices do not converge to these equilibrium prices, as is the case with non-stationary price gaps, either the P*-hypothesis is rejected or the method used to compute the price gaps is inappropriate. As can be concluded from Table 4 both the domestic and European price gaps satisfy the critical assumption of the P*-framework and are stationary in all instances.

The stationarity of the price gaps is also visible in Figure 2 where both the European and domestic price gaps are displayed: both variables fluctuate around zero. On the whole, the gaps do not always move closely together. Moreover, differences in the magnitude of local and European disturbances at a particular date are more a

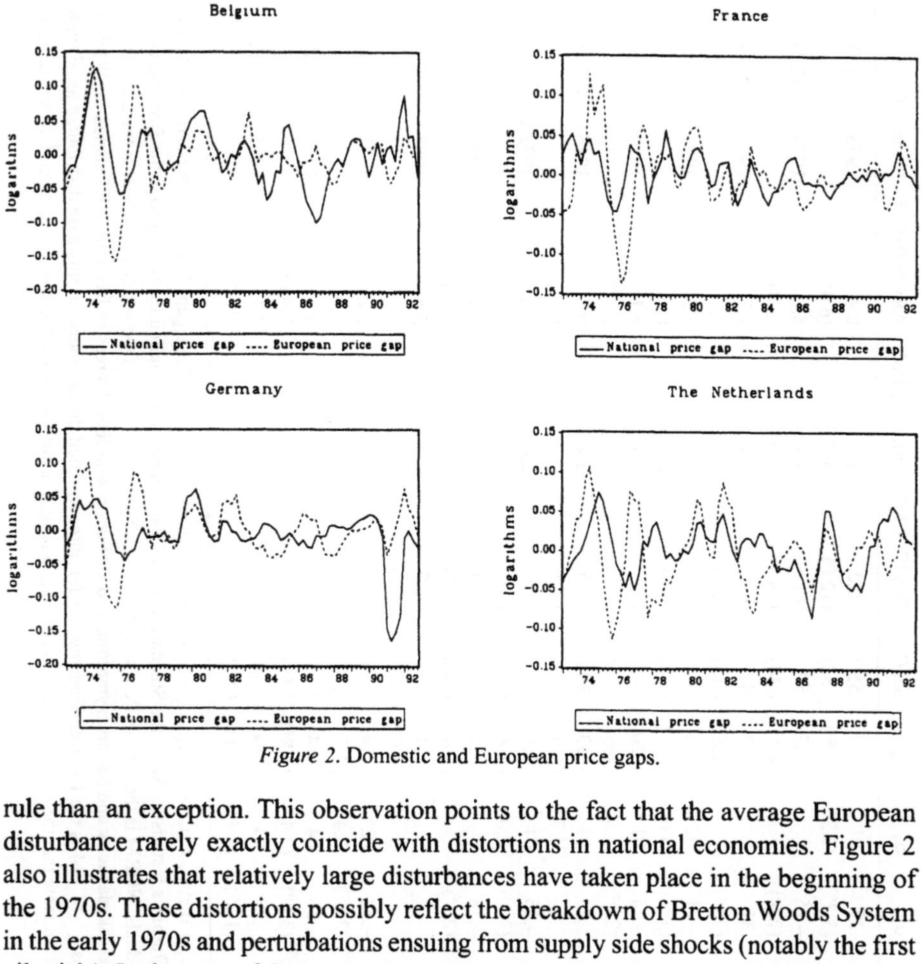

Figure 2. Domestic and European price gaps.

rule than an exception. This observation points to the fact that the average European disturbance rarely exactly coincide with distortions in national economies. Figure 2 also illustrates that relatively large disturbances have taken place in the beginning of the 1970s. These distortions possibly reflect the breakdown of Bretton Woods System in the early 1970s and perturbations ensuing from supply side shocks (notably the first oil crisis). In the case of Germany, the extreme negative price gap around 1991 can of course be connected with the German monetary unification. Around this date, bank deposits of East German residence were made elligible for conversion into DM. Immediately after conversion, East German M3 amounted to aproximately 15% of West German M3. In contrast, monetary union added an estimated 8.8% real output to the currency area (von Hagen, 1993). As a result actual velocity suddenly fell in relation to equilibrium velocity. The Bundesbank repeatedly argued that the excess supply of money created by monetary union implied a potential for a price level increase and acted accordingly. Interestingly, the results for the MSKF model indicate that this shock to velocity was almost completely perceived as a permanent shift in the level without affecting its growth rate. This finding seems to corroborate recent findings by Gerlach (1994) and Mayer and Fels (1994) who show that German demand for M3 has remained remarkably stable in the wake of unification.

Table 5. Regression results with domestic price gaps based on M3.

	α_0	α_1	α_2	α_3	α_4	α_5	α_6	SE (R^2)	D-h (SCLM)	Q(8) (NORM)	ARCH (HET)	SAMPLE
Belgium	–.00	–.33		–.18	.29	.01	–.07	.55	–0.2	8.8	0.4	1973.I–1992.IV
	(0.7)	(3.2")		(2.1')	(3.3")	(2.3')	(2.5')	(.32)	(12.0)	(4.2)	(6.9)	
Belgium	–.00	–.60	–.47	–.40	–.25		–.03	.50	0.1	4.8	5.6	1979.I–1992.IV
	(0.3)	(4.0")	(2.9")	(3.5")	(2.5')		(1.3)	(.44)	(18.7)	(1.9)	(8.4)	
Belgium	–.00		–.30		.31		–.03	.42	0.0	3.1	2.7	1985.I–1992.IV
	(0.3)		(1.9°)		(2.0')		(0.8)	(.15)	(9.6)	(0.4)	(16.3)	
France	–.00	–.72	–.52	–.27	–.21	.02	–.16	.50	0.0	2.7	3.2	1973.I–1992.IV
	(1.8°)	(5.6")	(5.2")	(1.9°)	(1.9°)	(4.0")	(2.2')	(.38)	(6.8)	(0.2)	(7.6)	
France	–.00	–.63	–.47	–.32	–.24	.01	–.20	.46	0.1	3.9	4.1	1979.I–1992.IV
	(1.6)	(4.5")	(4.3")	(2.1')	(2.0°)	(3.8")	(1.6)	(.36)	(5.3)	(0.6)	(14.2)	
France	–.00	–1.05	–.48			.01	–.13	.30	–2.3	3.4	9.3	1985.I–1992.IV
	(0.9)	(5.7")	(2.8")			(4.7")	(1.6)	(.62)	(6.0)	(1.3)	(7.7)	
Germany	–.00	–.93	–.58	–.42	–.15	.01	–.10	.56	1.3	5.0	1.8	1973.I–1992.IV
	(0.5)	(11.4")	(4.9")	(3.5")	(2.3')	(2.0')	(4.8")	(.60)	(9.6)	(0.2)	(11.5)	
Germany	–.00	–.85	–.43	–.41	–.18		–.11	.48	–0.3	3.0	1.7	1979.I–1992.IV
	(0.2)	(10.7")	(3.7")	(3.4")	(2.1')		(5.6")	(.64)	(7.2)	(1.3)	(7.9)	
Germany	–.00	–.86	–.57	–.27			–.11	.49	–1.0	2.5	5.4	1985.I–1992.IV
	(0.2)	(5.9")	(3.4")	(1.5)			(5.9")	(.47)	(5.6)	(0.5)	(5.1)	
Netherlands	–.00	–.83	–.66	–.49	–.32	.02	–.14	1.06	–1.0	4.1	2.2	1973.I–1992.IV
	(0.9)	(7.4")	(4.1")	(4.2")	(3.3")	(2.4')	(2.4')	(.49)	(8.0)	(0.2)	(20.9°)	
Netherlands	–.00	–.78	–.67	–.48	–.35	.04	–.14	1.08	–0.1	3.0	3.4	1979.I–1992.IV
	(0.3)	(6.3")	(3.7")	(3.7")	(3.0")	(3.4")	(1.8°)	(.51)	(9.3)	(0.2)	(19.0°)	
Netherlands	.00	–.80	–.62	–.40	–.29	.04	–.14	1.10	–2.2	6.1	7.1	1985.I–1992.IV
	(0.1)	(4.3")	(2.1')	(2.4')	(1.9°)	(3.4")	(1.4)	(.50)	(10.8)	(1.5)	(20.7°)	

Note: The following equation is estimated: $\Delta\pi = \alpha_0 + \alpha_1\Delta\pi_{-1} + \alpha_2\Delta\pi_{-2} + \alpha_3\Delta\pi_{-3} + \alpha_4\Delta\pi_{-4} + \alpha_5\,\Delta$ energy prices $+ \alpha_6$ Price gap. The absolute t-ratios are below the estimated coefficients in parentheses. D-h is Durbin's h statistic. SE is the Standard Error of the regression multiplied by 100. Q(8) is the Box-Pierce Q-statistic for testing for serial correlation in the residuals. NORM is the Jarque-Bera statistic for testing the normality of the residuals. ARCH is the test statistic for fourth order Auto Regressive Conditional Heteroskedasticity and has an asymptotic χ^2 distribution with four degrees of freedom. HET stands for White's statistic for heteroskedasticity and is distributed as χ^2. SCLM is the Breusch-Godfrey test for autocorrelated disturbances, in this case distributed as χ^2 with eight degrees of freedom. The symbols °, and ' and " denote that the statistic under consideration is significantly different from zero at the ten, five and one per cent level, respectively.

3.2. *Testing the P*-Model*

Having established that the rate of inflation is non-stationary, we explicitly test the P^*-framework for the four European countries on the basis of expression (5). We first consider the relevance of domestically determined price gaps for inflation developments in each country. Subsequently, we include aggregate or European price gaps in the equations. In the most general specification, four lags of the dependent variable have been included along with the equilibrium (domestic and/or European) price gap and a constant. Following Ebrill and Fries (1991) and Reimers and Tödter (1994), we have also included an extra variable to account for supply shocks. To this end, we have incorporated changes in energy prices as a proxy variable for "imported" price shocks. In the presented estimation results insignificant lagged dependent variables have been dropped to save degrees of freedom. In addition to showing results for the whole sample, we also report sub-sample results for the periods 1979.I –1992.IV and 1985.I–1992.IV. In this way we can identify the relative impact of the domestic and European price gap on actual inflation over time.

The estimations with the domestic price gaps are presented in Table 5. A glance at this table reveals several noteworthy things. Firstly, the usefulness of these gaps as an indicator for future domestic price movements is beyond question in the entire time span in all cases. The coefficients of the gaps are significant and carry the theoretically expected negative sign. A second remarkable finding concerns the mixed results in the shorter sub-samples. On the one hand, we have Germany where the national price gap exerts a significant and stable influence on domestic inflation of about –.11 percentage point. On the other hand, the explanatory power of the domestic price gap in the case of Belgium, France and the Netherlands decreases after 1979 and becomes negligible since the mid 1980s. In a sense these empirical findings buttress the (theoretical) notion that Belgium, France and the Netherlands by deliberately chosing to anchor their currencies to the Deutsche mark not only "automatically" import Germany's low inflation through the exchange rate constraint but also have to adopt the same monetary policy stance of the Bundesbank in order to ensure a smooth operation of the European Monetary System. Viewed in this light, it should not come as a great surprise that the long-run relationship between domestic money measures and domestic price trends has – almost completely – disappeared in the time span covering the EMS period in the non-anchor ERM countries.

On the basis of the above findings a logical extension of the traditional P^*-framework seems to insert the German price gaps in the inflation equations for Belgium, France and the Netherlands (see Kool and Tatom 1994). However, we do not opt for this strategy because it ignores the possibility that the increased degree of inflation and interest convergence in Europe in the past decade (see, for instance, Bini Smaghi 1994, Collins 1988 and Ungerer et al. 1986) may also have had implications for the dynamics of inflation in Germany. In this respect Germany may have become more and more subject to monetary spill-over effects from other core ERM countries.

Table 6. Regression results with European price gaps based on M3.

	α_0	α_1	α_2	α_3	α_4	α_5	α_6	SE (R^2)	D-h (SCLM)	Q(8) (NORM)	ARCH (HET)	SAMPLE
Belgium	–.00	–.33		–.16	.33	.01	–.05	.55	–0.2	5.1	1.7	1973.I–1992.IV
	(0.9)	(3.0")		(1.8°)	(3.1")	(2.0')	(1.3)	(.30)	(6.1)	(2.9)	(5.9)	
Belgium	–.00	–.60	–.40	–.34	–.30		–.11	.48	0.3	3.5	3.9	1979.I–1992.IV
	(0.5)	(4.3")	(2.3')	(2.8")	(2.5')		(2.1')	(.48)	(11.0)	(2.1)	(7.0)	
Belgium	–.00				–.43		–.16	.39	1.0	6.0	6.6	1985.I–1992.IV
	(1.1)				(2.6")		(3.5")	(.23)	(7.1)	(0.2)	(3.9)	
France	–.00	–.65	–.51	–.38	–.25	.02	–.03	.52	1.2	3.4	1.0	1973.I–1992.IV
	(1.6)	(5.2")	(5.1")	(2.9")	(1.7°)	(3.8")	(1.0)	(.32)	(6.6)	(2.1)	(15.7)	
France	–.00	–.63	–.44	–.43	–.34	.01	–.08	.47	0.0	3.8	2.7	1979.I–1992.IV
	(1.8°)	(4.6")	(4.0")	(3.0")	(2.1')	(4.1")	(1.7°)	(.35)	(6.5)	(4.7°)	(11.7)	
France	–.00	–.99	–.37			.01	–.05	.30	–0.4	2.4	10.0'	1985.I–1992.IV
	(1.0)	(5.3")	(2.6")			(4.6")	(2.6')	(.61)	(3.7)	(0.7)	(6.7)	
Germany	–.00	–.96	–.60	–.43	–.12	–.01	–.00	.59	0.8	4.0	0.4	1973.I–1992.IV
	(0.2)	(8.9")	(4.3")	(3.3")	(2.0°)	(1.5)	(0.1)	(.56)	(8.6)	(1.4)	(28.5')	
Germany	–.00	–.77	–.36	–.40	–.17		–.14	.51	1.2	1.7	0.9	1979.I–1992.IV
	(0.3)	(6.2")	(2.5')	(3.2")	(1.8°)		(1.7°)	(.59)	(4.3)	(0.6)	(9.9)	
Germany	–.00	–.43			–.30		–.28	.49	0.4	6.6	2.6	1985.I–1992.IV
	(0.1)	(2.9")			(2.5')		(3.6")	(.46)	(7.5)	(0.6)	(5.0)	
Netherlands	–.00	–.84	–.64	–.47	–.27	.02	–.16	1.07	–2.2	4.0	7.0	1973.I–1992.IV
	(1.1)	(7.1")	(4.0")	(4.0")	(2.7")	(3.1")	(2.2')	(.48)	(11.0)	(0.9)	(16.0)	
Netherlands	–.00	–.81	–.59	–.40	–.25	.04	–.28	1.05	–2.2	3.4	6.0	1979.I–1992.IV
	(0.6)	(6.1")	(3.3")	(3.0")	(2.2')	(3.9")	(3.3")	(.54)	(9.8)	(0.3)	(20.6°)	
Netherlands	–.00	–.64				.04	–.48	1.20	–1.4	10.9	4.4	1985.I–1992.IV
	(0.0)	(3.3")				(4.1")	(2.1')	(.40)	(12.8)	(2.5)	(1.9)	

Note: The following equation is estimated: $\Delta\pi = \alpha_0 + \alpha_1\Delta\pi_{-1} + \alpha_2\Delta\pi_{-2} + \alpha_3\Delta\pi_{-3} + \alpha_4\Delta\pi_{-4} + \alpha_5\,\Delta$ energy prices $+ \alpha_6$ Price gap. The absolute t-ratios are below the estimated coefficients in parentheses. D-h is Durbin's h statistic. SE is the Standard Error of the regression multiplied by 100. Q(8) is the Box-Pierce Q-statistic for testing for serial correlation in the residuals. NORM is the Jarque-Bera statistic for testing the normality of the residuals. ARCH is the test statistic for fourth order Auto Regressive Conditional Heteroskedasticity and has an asymptotic χ^2 distribution with four degrees of freedom. HET stands for White's statistic for heteroskedasticity and is distributed as χ^2. SCLM is the Breusch-Godfrey test for autocorrelated disturbances, in this case distributed as χ^2 with eight degrees of freedom. The symbols °, and ' and " denote that the statistic under consideration is significantly different from zero at the ten, five and one per cent level, respectively.

Table 7. Regression results with domestic and European price gaps based on M3.

	α_0	α_1	α_2	α_3	α_4	α_5	α_6	α_7	SE (R^2)	D-h (SCLM)	Q(8) (NORM)	ARCH (HET)	SAMPLE
Belgium	–.00	–.33		–.16	.31	.01	–.06	–0.3	.55	0.1	5.2	1.3	1973.I–1992.IV
	(0.8)	(3.2")		(1.8°)	(3.1")	(2.3')	(2.2')	(1.0)	(.32)	(5.8)	(4.1)	(8.6)	
Belgium	–.00	–.58	–.39	–.34	–.29		–.02	–.10	.48	0.0	3.5	4.0	1979.I–1992.IV
	(0.5)	(4.2")	(2.3')	(3.0")	(2.5')		(0.7)	(2.0°)	(.48)	(11.0)	(1.7)	(9.0)	
Belgium	–.00				–.42		–.01	.16	.39	0.3	7.3	4.4	1985.I–1992.IV
	(1.1)				(2.5")		(0.2)	(2.9")	(.20)	(8.3)	(0.4)	(4.8)	
France	–.00	–.64	–.42			.02	–.22	–.03	.51	0.5	4.2	2.7	1973.I–1992.IV
	(1.4)	(5.3")	(4.3")			(4.0")	(2.8")	(1.1)	(.35)	(6.0)	(1.5)	(10.3)	
France	–.00	–.65	–.46	–.30	–.25	.01	–.16	.06	.46	0.1	3.2	3.3	1979.I–1992.IV
	(1.6)	(4.6")	(4.3")	(2.0°)	(2.0')	(4.1")	(1.1)	(1.0)	(.36)	(6.0)	(1.9)	(20.4)	
France	–.00	–1.03	–.45			.01	–.11	–.04	.30	–2.6	3.3	9.6'	1985.I–1992.IV
	(1.0)	(5.7")	(2.7")			(4.6")	(1.2)	(1.5)	(.61)	(7.2)	(1.1)	(17.9)	
Germany	–.00	–.95	–.61	–.44	–.15	–.01	–.11	.04	.56	0.5	3.4	0.4	1973.I–1992.IV
	(0.5)	(13.0")	(5.4")	(3.4")	(2.2')	(1.9°)	(4.2")	(0.7)	(.60)	(8.0)	(0.4)	(15.5)	
Germany	–.00	–.82	–.42	–.40	–.19		–.10	.04	.48	–0.3	3.4	1.8	1979.I–1992.IV
	(0.1)	(9.4")	(3.4")	(3.3")	(2.1')		(3.5")	(0.6)	(.63)	(7.8)	(1.2)	(10.3)	
Germany	–.00	–.62	–.21		–.24		–.07	–.16	.49	1.0	10.4	3.2	1985.I–1992.IV
	(0.1)	(3.7")	(1.7°)		(1.9°)		(2.1')	(1.5)	(.47)	(17.0°)	(0.7)	(6.1)	
Netherlands	–.00	–.85	–.56	–.41	–.26	.03	–.12	–.14	1.04	0.9	3.4	4.8	1973.I–1992.IV
	(1.1)	(7.5")	(3.4")	(3.3")	(2.8")	(3.3")	(2.1')	(2.0')	(.50)	(11.6)	(0.1)	(19.3)	
Netherlands	–.00	–.81	–.55	–.37	–.25	.04	–.10	–.24	1.04	–1.9	3.6	5.8	1979.I–1992.IV
	(0.5)	(6.5")	(3.1")	(2.8")	(2.2')	(3.7")	(1.2)	(2.7")	(.54)	(10.2)	(0.3)	(20.0)	
Netherlands	–.00	–.68				.04	–.21	–.37	1.16	–1.3	10.8	5.4	1985.I–1992.IV
	(0.3)	(3.7")				(3.9")	(1.9°)	(2.1')	(.43)	(11.4)	(3.4)	(3.0)	

Note: The following equation is estimated: $\Delta\pi = \alpha_0 + \alpha_1\Delta\pi_{-1} + \alpha_2\Delta\pi_{-2} + \alpha_3\Delta\pi_{-3} + \alpha_4\Delta\pi_{-4} + \alpha_5\,\Delta$ energy prices $+ \alpha_6$ domestic price gap $+ \alpha_7$ European price gap. The absolute t-ratios are below the estimated coefficients in parentheses. D-h is Durbin's h statistic. SE is the Standard Error of the regression multiplied by 100. Q(8) is the Box-Pierce Q-statistic for testing for serial correlation in the residuals. NORM is the Jarque-Bera statistic for testing the normality of the residuals. ARCH is the test statistic for fourth order Auto Regressive Conditional Heteroskedasticity and has an asymptotic χ^2 distribution with four degrees of freedom. HET stands for White's statistic for heteroskedasticity and is distributed as χ^2. SCLM is the Breusch-Godfrey test for autocorrelated disturbances, in this case distributed as χ^2 with eight degrees of freedom. The symbols °, and ' and " denote that the statistic under consideration is significantly different from zero at the ten, five and one per cent level, respectively.

Consequently, German dominance could have been gradually replaced by policy coordination (Fratianni and von Hagen 1992).

In order to shed more light on these issues, we explicitly investigate the extent to which the inflation experience in the four countries can be explained by European monetary conditions in the course of time. To this end, we have estimated two specifications. In the first one we have replaced the domestic price gap by the European price gap, which can be interpreted as a summary measure of the average monetary circumstances in the core ERM group. In the second specification the domestic and European price gap are included simultaneously in the equations. An examination of the correlation between European and domestic price gaps shows that both gaps have become more correlated over time (not reported here). This means that the second alternative could introduce some multicollinearity in the regressions and hence that the results with both gaps included should be interpreted with some care. The outcomes with the European price gaps are recorded in Table 6, while the estimations with both the domestic and European gap are documented in Table 7.

As can be inferred from Table 6, no causal relation between the European price gap and price developments in Belgium is found over the whole sample. In this period the European price gap has a coefficient of –0.05 and a t-statistic of only –1.3. The explanatory power of the European price gap however clearly improves in the sub-periods 1979.I–1992.IV and 1985.I–1992.IV. In the former sub-sample the coefficient of the European price gap and its corresponding t-statistic have risen to –0.11 and –2.1, respectively, whereas the impact and significance of this gap have increased further in the latter time span to –0.16 and –3.5, respectively. Hence, the predictive value of the European price gap for inflationary pressure in Belgium has considerably increased over time. Interestingly, an opposite pattern is observable for the Belgian results with the domestic price gaps reported in Table 5. Here we found that the impact of the domestic price gap has eroded with the passage of time. These developments are presumably set in motion by stronger macroeconomic policy coordination in Europe associated with the establishment of the EMS.

The estimations for France, Germany and the Netherlands presented in Table 6 show a quite similar pattern. For each of these countries inflation has become more sensitive to disturbances on a European scale over time. In every country the European price gap exercises a significant impact on domestic inflation at the 10% and 5% level after 1979 and 1985, respectively. Taken on its own, this is an important observation since it implies that price movements in the country that is widely acknowledged as the de-facto anchor of the ERM are also less insulated from monetary factors in other core ERM countries than a decade ago. It should be emphasised however that Germany remains the only country where the domestic price gap still possesses explanatory power after the inception of the EMS. National price gaps have – almost completely – lost their informative value for the future course of inflation in the other countries under investigation. Another remarkable aspect concerns the results for the Netherlands. In this case, the results suggest that the Euro-

Table 8. Regression results with the (weighted) European price level.

	α_0	α_1	α_2	α_3	α_4	α_5	α_6	SE (R^2)	D-h (SCLM)	Q(8) (NORM)	ARCH (HET)	SAMPLE
Core ERM	–.00	–.80	–.37	–.37	–.24	.01	–.12	.47	–1.2	3.3	9.0°	1973.I–1992.IV
	(1.0)	(7.4")	(2.8")	(2.7")	(2.3')	(2.1')	(3.8")	(.47)	(8.8)	(0.5)	(32.5")	
Core ERM	–.00	–.80	–.39	–.52	–.29	.01	–.15	.39	–2.8	3.7	1.2	1979.I–1992.IV
	(1.4)	(6.0")	(2.5')	(3.2")	(2.2')	(2.0')	(3.1")	(.45)	(7.9)	(0.3)	(8.9)	
Core ERM	–.00	–.82	–.33			.01	–.12	.37	0.2	4.9	2.2	1985.I-1992.IV
	(0.7)	(4.7")	(2.6')			(1.7°)	(2.7')	(.47)	(12.0)	(1.4)	(5.9)	

Note: The following equation is estimated: $\Delta\pi = \alpha_0 + \alpha_1\Delta\pi_{-1} + \alpha_2\Delta\pi_{-2} + \alpha_3\Delta\pi_{-3} + \alpha_4\Delta\pi_{-4} + \alpha_5 \Delta$ energy prices $+ \alpha_6$ Price gap. The absolute t-ratios are below the estimated coefficients in parentheses. D-h is Durbin's h statistic. SE is the Standard Error of the regression multiplied by 100. Q(8) is the Box-Pierce Q-statistic for testing for serial correlation in the residuals. NORM is the Jarque-Bera statistic for testing the normality of the residuals. ARCH is the test statistic for fourth order Auto Regressive Conditional Heteroskedasticity and has an asymptotic χ^2 distribution with four degrees of freedom. HET stands for White's statistic for heteroskedasticity and is distributed as χ^2. SCLM is the Breusch-Godfrey test for autocorrelated disturbances, in this case distributed as χ^2 with eight degrees of freedom. The symbols °, and ' and " denote that the statistic under consideration is significantly different from zero at the ten, five and one per cent level, respectively.

pean price gap significantly influences inflation over the full sample as well as over the sub-periods.

The results with both the domestic and European price gaps reported in Table 7 accord with the estimations where both variables are included separately. Indeed, the results in Table 7 also point to a shift in relative importance from domestic to European price gaps for accurately predicting inflationary trends in individual countries over the years. The extent to which the European price gap provides a better indicator for inflationary risks differs however across countries. In the case of Belgium and the Netherlands we clearly find that the appropriateness of domestic price gaps for conducting inflation forecasts has sharply deteriorated, while the European price gap has remarkably gained in importance over the years. Since the late 1970s only the European gap contains relevant information for the future path of inflation in these countries. Conversely, the insertion of both gaps in the inflation equation for Germany reveals that the impact of the domestic price gap on price movements is still somewhat more significant, though the European gap has definitely become more relevant in terms of significance. France takes an intermediate position in some respects. Although the empirical evidence again supports the general conclusion that the relative importance of domestic versus European price gaps for predicting inflationary tendencies has shifted towards the latter in the course of time, this shift is less pronounced than in the case of Belgium and the Netherlands. However, the European price gap does give a more accurate signal of changes in domestic prices to come after 1985.

All in all, the results suggest that the process of economic convergence in Europe has rendered domestic inflation in the core ERM countries more sensitive to monetary conditions on a European level over time. This development is reflected in an opposite change of the impact and significance of the domestic and European price gaps; the relative usefulness of the latter variable for detecting potential inflationary risks in individual countries has clearly improved after 1979. The extent to which this is the case differs however across countries. For Belgium and the Netherlands the European price gap provides a better indicator for inflationary pressures, while the information content of the domestic gap is – still – at least as accurate as that of the European price gap in the case of Germany. The latter finding could be interpreted as a sign of the special position of Germany in the ERM. At any rate, the results with just the European price gap (see Table 6) demonstrate that this measure of the overall monetary conditions in the core ERM group can serve as an additional indicator supplementing the existing target for German M3 in the transition to Stage Three. As such, the growth of a European monetary aggregate might at times put a different perspective on monetary developments in Germany. In concrete, this option could imply that when monetary developments in Germany are distorted by identifiable transitory factors, while at the same time a European monetary aggregate is growing at an acceptable and satisfactory pace, more weight is placed on the latter variable in formulating and implementing monetary policy in the core countries.

In addition to the above analysis we have also tested the validity of the P*-framework for the core ERM group as a whole. In this constellation the aggregate European inflation derived from equation (14) acts as the dependent variable. The format of the estimation equation is identical to that of expression (5). The results of this exercise are summarised in Table 8. The most salient outcome is that a stable and significant long-run relationship between European inflation and the European price gap exists both in the entire period and in the sub-samples. Despite technical and practical difficulties attached to targeting a European monetary aggregate (Sardelis 1993), this observation at least suggests that some controllability over the average inflation in Europe may be retained through the coordination of monetary policies in the core ERM countries.

4. Conclusion

In this paper we have tested the P*-model of inflation for Belgium, France, Germany and the Netherlands for the period 1973 to 1992. The standard P*-model has been extended in order to take monetary interdependencies between these countries into account. In this way we are able to investigate to what extent inflation behaviour in four core EMU countries (Germany, France, Belgium and the Netherlands) has been determined by domestic and European monetary conditions over time. For this purpose a European price gap is calculated.

In the case of Belgium and the Netherlands the relative impact of the European price gap has become dominant over time, reflecting the almost complete loss of monetary autonomy in these countries as a result of pegging the exchange rate to the German mark. In the case of France and Germany, we find that in both countries the relative importance of the European price gap as an indicator of future inflationary pressures is increasing. Moreover, in all four countries the European price gap is an accurate indicator of future inflation.

In addition, we find that the P*-framework is also valid for inflation behaviour on a European level. Taken together, our results suggest that a European monetary aggregate could be used as an additional indicator for inflationary pressures in the core countries. Implicit targeting of a European monetary aggregate in addition to explicitly targeting the German money supply may become necessary to achieve and maintain price stability in Europe in the near future.

Obviously, the present analysis is a first step. In future work we would like to investigate the extent to which the framework holds if other countries, which have also pursued monetary policies primarily directed at achieving exchange rate stability against the Deutsche mark, are included.

Notes

1. Many studies are devoted to this subject e.g. De Grauwe (1989), Artis and Nachane (1990), Artus et al. (1991), Henry and Weidmann (1994), Herz and Röger (1992) and Gardner and Perraudin (1993).
2. The theoretical and empirical foundations of German monetary policy are discussed in Issing (1992).
3. Humphrey (1989) gives a review of the precursors of this approach and shows that a variant of the approach can be traced back to David Hume.
4. Here, as in the remainder of the paper, lower-case letters stand for the natural logs of their level counterparts, i.e. $p = \ln(P)$.
5. Giovannini and Turtelboom (1992) review the extensive theoretical and empirical literature on currency substitution.
6. For earlier work on the demand for money in European countries, see Den Butter and Fase (1981).
7. This hypothesis is generally accepted by recent empirical studies indicating that a European demand for money function is generally more stable than money demand in individual countries Bekx and Tullio (1989), Kremers and Lane (1990), Artis et al. (1993), Monticelli and Strauss-Kahn (1991), and Fase and Winder (1993). On the other hand, Arnold (1994) asserts that the existence of a stable European demand for money is a mere statistical artifact.
8. In the extreme case of a very small country, the domestic money supply becomes totally endogenous. Then, we are back in the standard version of the monetary approach to the balance of payments used by Kool and Tatom (1994).
9. Existing studies on money demand on a European scale mostly conclude that the results are fairly robust to different methods of adding up national variables Monticelli and Strauss-Kahn (1991) and Cassard et al. (1994).
10. We use harmonised domestic money measures that are roughly comparable across countries. Although cross border holdings are excluded from the European aggregate this way, the resulting measurement error appears to be acceptable. See Angeloni et al. (1991) and the Economic Unit (1993).
11. For an in-depth discussion of the technical and algebraic features of the Kalman filter method the reader is referred to Harvey (1991) and Kool (1989).

References

Angeloni, I., C. Cottarelli and A. Levy (1991), "Cross-Border Deposits and Monetary Aggregates in the Transition to EMU", *IMF Working Paper*, WP 91/114.

Arnold, I.J.M. (1994), "The Myth of a Stable European Money Demand", *Open Economies Review*, 5, 249–259.

Artis, M.J., R.C. Bladen-Hovell and W. Zhang (1993), "A European Money Demand", in P.R. Masson and M. Taylor (eds.), *Policy Issues in the Operation of Currency Unions*, Cambridge University Press, Cambridge.

Artis, M.J. and D. Nachane (1990), "Wages and Prices in Europe: A Test of the German Leadership Hypothesis", *Weltwirtschaftliches Archiv*, 126, 59–77.

Artus, P., S. Avouyi-Dovi, E. Bleuze and F. Lecointe (1991), "Transmission of U.S. Monetary policy to Europe and asymmetry in the European Monetary System", *European Economic Review*, 35, 1369–1384.

Bank of Japan (1990), "A Study of Potential Pressure on Prices: Application of P^* to the Japanese Economy", *Special Paper*, No. 186, February.

Bayoumi, T. and P.B. Kenen (1993), "How Useful is an EC-wide Monetary Aggregate as an Intermediate Target for Europe?", *Review of International Economics*, 1, 209–220.

Bekx, P. and G. Tullio (1989), "A Note on the European Monetary System and the Determination of the DM-Dollar Exchange Rate", *Cahiers economiques de Bruxelles*, 123, 329–343.

Bini Smaghi, L. (1994), "EMS Discipline: Did it Contribute to Inflation Convergence?", Banco *Nazionale del Lavoro Quarterly Review*, 189, June, 187–197.

Boughton, J.M. (1992), "International Comparisons of Money Demand: a Review Essay", *Open Economies Review*, 323–343.

Butter, F.A.G. den, and M.M.G. Fase (1981), "The demand for money in EEC-Countries", *Journal of Monetary Economics*, 8, 201–230.

Caporale, G.M. and N. Pittis (1993), "Common Stochastic Trends and Inflation Convergence in the EMS", *Weltwirtschaftliches Archiv*, 129, 207–215.

Cassard, M., T.D. Lane and P.R. Masson (1994), "ERM Money Supplies and the Transition to EMU", *IMF Working Paper*, WP 94/1.

Christiano, L.J. (1989), "P*: Not the Inflation Forecaster's Holy Grail", *Federal Reserve Bank of Minneapolis, Quarterly Review*, Fall 1989, 3–18.

Collins, S.M. (1998), "Inflation and the European Monetary System", in F. Giavazzi, S. Micossi and M. Miller (eds.), *The European Monetary System*, Cambridge University Press, Cambridge, 112–139.

Ebrill, L.P. and S.M. Fries (1991), "Broad Money Growth and Inflation in the United States", *IMF Staff Papers*, 38, 736–750.

Economic Unit (1991), "Report on Harmonisation of Broad Monetary Aggregation", *Committee of Governors of the Central Banks of the Member States of the European Economic Community*.

Economic Unit (1993), "Cross-border Holdings and EC-wide Monetary Relationships", *Committee of Governors of the Central Banks of the Member States of the European Economic Community*.

Fase, M.M.G. and C.C.A. Winder (1993), "The Demand for Money in the Netherlands and the other EC Countries", *De Economist*, 141, 471–496.

Fratianni, M. and J. von Hagen (1992), *The European Monetary System and European Monetary Union*, Westview Press, San Francisco/Oxford.

Gardner, E.H. and W.R.M. Perraudin (1993), "Asymmetry in the ERM: A Case Study of French and German Interest Rates Before and After German Unification", *IMF Staff Papers*, 40, 427–450.

Gerlach, S. (1994), "German Unification and the Demand for German M3", *BIS Working Paper*, 21.

Giavazzi, F. and A. Giovannini (1989), *Limiting Exchange Rate Flexibility: The European Monetary System*, MIT Press, Cambridge, Massachusetts.

Giovannini, A. and B. Turtelboom (1992), "Currency Substitution", *National Bureau of Economic Research, Working Paper*, 4232.

Grauwe, P. de (1989), "Is the European Monetary System a DM-Zone?", *CEPR Discussion paper*, 297.

Goodhart, C. (1989), "The Conduct of Monetary Policy", *The Economic Journal*, 99, 293–346.

Hagen, J. von (1993), "Monetary Union, Money Demand, and Money Supply: A review of the German Monetary Union", *European Economic Review*, 37, 803–836.

Hallman, J.J., R.D. Porter and D.H. Small (1989), "M2 per Unit of Potential GNP as an Anchor for the Price Level", *Board of Governors of the Federal Reserve System*, Washington D.C., April 1989.

Hallman, J.J., R.D. Porter and D.H. Small (1991), "Is the Price Level tied to the M2 Monetary Aggregate in the Long Run?", *The American Economic Review*, 81, 841–858.

Harvey, A.C. (1991), *Forecasting, Structural Time Series Models and the Kalman Filter*, Cambridge University Press, Cambridge.

Henry, J. and J. Weidmann (1994), "Asymmetry in the EMS Revisited: Evidence from the Causality Analysis of Daily Eurorates", *Rheinische Friedrich-Wilhelms-Universität Bonn, Discussion Paper*, B–280.

Herz, B. and W. Röger (1992), "The EMS is a Greater Deutsche Mark area", *European Economic Review*, 36, 1413–1425.

Hoeller, P. and P. Poret (1991),"Is P-star a Good Indicator of Inflationary Pressure in OECD Countries?", *OECD Economic Studies*, 17.

Humphrey, T.M. (1989), "Precursors of the P-star Model", *Federal Reserve Bank of Richmond Economic Review*, 75/4, 3–9.

Issing, O. (1992), "Theoretical and Empirical Foundations of the Deutsche Bundesbank's Monetary Targeting", *Intereconomics*, 289–300.

Kole, L.S. and M.F. Leahy (1991), "The Usefulness of P* Measures for Japan and Germany", Board of Governors of the Federal Reserve System, *International Financial Discussion Papers*, 414.

Kool, C.J.M. (1989), *Recursive Bayesian Forecasting in Economics: The Multi State Kalman Filter Method*, Thesis Erasmus University Rotterdam.

Kool, C.J.M. and J.A. Tatom (1994), "The P-star Model in Five Small Economies", *The Federal Reserve Bank of St. Louis Review*, 76, 11–29.

Kremers, J.J.M., and T.D. Lane (1990), "Economic and Monetary Integration and the Aggregate Demand for Money in the EMS", *IMF Staff Papers*, 37, 777–805.

Lane, T.D. and S.S. Poloz (1992), "Currency Substitution and Cross-Border Monetary Aggregation: Evidence form the G-7", *IMF Working Paper*, WP/92/81.

Mayer, T. and J. Fels (1994), "Bundesbank Adrift: German Economic Commentary", *Goldman Sachs*, 11th February 1994.

McKinnon, R.I. (1982), "Currency Substitution and Instability in the World Dollar Standard", *The American Economic Review*, Vol. 72, No. 3, 320–333.

Monticelli, C. and M.O. Strauss-Kahn (1991), "European Integration and the Demand for Broad Money", *Bis Working Papers*, No. 18.

Monticelli, C. (1993), "All the money in Europe?": An Investigation of the Economic Properties of EC-Wide Extended Monetary Aggregates", *Economic Unit of the Committee of Governors of EC Central Banks*, mimeo.

Monticelli, C. and J. Viñals (1993), "European Monetary Policy in Stage Three: What are the Issues?", *Centre for Economic Policy Research, Occassional Paper*, 12.

Reimers, H.E. and K.H. Tödter (1994), "P-Star as a Link Between Money and Prices in Germany", *Weltwirtschaftliches Archiv*, 130, 273–289.

Sardelis, C. (1993), "Targeting a European Monetary Aggregate: Review and Current Issues", *Commission of the European Communities, Economic Papers*, 102.

Ungerer, H., O. Evans, T. Mayer and P. Young (1986), "The European Monetary System: recent developments", *IMF Occasional Paper*, 48.

Policy Consequences of Money Demand (In)Stability: National vs. European*

CARLO MONTICELLI
Bank of Italy

ABSTRACT

This paper explores the implications of the (in)stability of national and area-wide money demand for the co-ordination of national monetary policies under an exchange rate agreement. If both national and area-wide money demands are stable and predictable, the symmetric and asymmetric schemes of monetary co-ordination are on an equal footing from the point of view of the stabilisation performance. If no money demand possesses the desirable properties, monetary targeting should be forsaken. If money demand in one country is significantly more stable than in the others and in the area as a whole, that country should be the anchor. If the area-wide money demand is the most stable, it is to the benefit of *all* countries to adopt the co-ordination scheme based on area-wide monetary control which, furthermore, automatically solves the issue of the symmetry of the system.

1. INTRODUCTION

The investigation of the properties of money demand functions defined for a group of EU countries as a whole is one of the novel strands in the empirical research on the demand for money. Following the path-breaking work of Bekx and Tullio (1989) and Kremers and Lane (1990), a number of authors – surveyed in detail by Van Riet (1992, 1993) and Monticelli and Papi (1995) – have estimated area-wide money demand equations for different definitions of the money stock and for different groups of EU countries, obtaining encouraging results.

On the policy front, several European countries – including Spain, France and Italy – have reduced the importance attached to developments in the quantity of money in their monetary policy strategy. This change in attitude towards monetary aggregates suggests that the information about the evolution of the final

*The opinions presented in this paper are personal and do not reflect those of the Bank of Italy. The author wishes to thank M.M.G. Fase and the other participants in the workshop for stimulating comments.

Koos Alders, Kees Koedijk, Clemens Kool and Carlo Winder (eds.), Monetary Policy in a Converging Europe, pp. 61–76.

variables conveyed by movements in the money stock is considered to be less reliable than in the recent past, presumably as a result of reduced stability and predictability of the money demand relationships.

This paper does not intend to survey the vast literature which has tried to appraise the properties of national and European money demands (for this see Fase 1993, and Monticelli and Papi 1995). Nor it intends to explore the implications of these studies for the future single monetary policy in EMU, given the uncertainty about the timing of Stage Three, the participants at its inception, the implications of such a major regime change for the key macroeconomic relationships (see Giovannini, 1991; Arnold, 1994). Rather, it aims at proposing a conceptual framework to assess the implications for the co-ordination of European monetary policies of the (in)stability of money demand relationships at the national and at the area level.

The paper is organised as follows. Section 2 briefly recalls the reasons why the (in)stability of money demand plays an important role in the conduct of monetary policy. Section 3 puts forward an analytical framework to assess the properties of two different schemes of monetary co-ordination under an exchange rate agreement. Section 4 investigates the first scheme which hinges on one country performing the role of nominal anchor while the other countries behave as exchange rate peggers. Section 5 turns to the second scheme of monetary co-ordination which is instead based on area-wide monetary control. Section 6 concludes discussing the policy implications of national and European money demand (in)stability.

2. Why is Money Demand (In)Stability so Important?

As the title bluntly reveals, the discussion in this section *takes for granted* that the assessment of the empirical properties of money demand functions is fraught with policy implications. This claim can be easily established by a revealed preference argument: unless economists are foolish enough to waste their efforts in irrelevant pursuits, the immense literature investigating the demand for money – with varying techniques, specifications, definitions of money and geographical aggregations – must reveal that the results of this inquiry are indeed important for the definition and implementation of policies.

In the world of Tinbergen (1952), where the structure of the economy is taken to be known, money demand, like all the other macroeconomic relationships, is assumed to be stable. Thus, econometric analysis of money demand "only" serves to gauge the relevant parameters which enable the setting of the n policy instruments consistent with the attainment of the n final goals. Unfortunately for policy makers, uncertainty is a feature of economic systems which is so pervasive that cannot be ignored in devising policies.

Uncertainty impinges on the functioning of the economy through countless channels. Several methods – some of which bafflingly sophisticated and complex – have been developed to study the role of uncertainty in the definition of economic policies. However, the policy importance of the (in)stability of money demand can be appreciated even by resorting to the heroic, simplifying assumption that the effects of uncertainty can be captured by adding stochastic disturbances to the otherwise traditional (log-) linear macroeconomic models. This is what Poole (1970) did in his path-breaking paper, where he showed that the instability of money demand – as expressed by the size of the variance of the disturbances to the money demand function relative to that of the shocks affecting the other macroeconomic relationships – is crucial to decide whether the stabilisation objectives are best pursued by controlling the money stock or by pegging the interest rate.

The fundamental insights of that paper have been confirmed by a vast literature which has extended the original set-up to consider the supply side and different types of expectations (Sargent and Wallace 1975, Parkin 1978); price and wage indexation (Gray 1976); the external sector (Boyer 1978, Turnovsky 1984); the market for bank reserves (Bryant 1983); the behaviour of financial intermediaries (Papademos and Modigliani 1983). Furthermore, this line of research has clarified the link between the properties of money demand and monetary policy: the more stable is money demand, the higher is the information content of movements in the quantity of money about the future (or current but unobservable) developments in the final variables (see e.g. LeRoy and Waud 1977, and Canzoneri et al. 1983).

However, as B. Friedman (1975, 1977) first pointed out, the stability of the demand for money per se is not sufficient to justify the adoption by monetary authorities of a two-step strategy based on the setting of an intermediate target defined in terms of quantity of money: since changes in money are not – except in trivial, unrealistic cases – a sufficient statistic for movements in income and prices, the reliance on an intermediate target leads the authorities to ignore the information about the final variables which is embodied in other indicators, such as interest rates.

While this logic is correct, it abstracts from several practical and behavioural considerations which underlie the use by central banks of intermediate targets – and of monetary aggregates in particular.

In fact, reliable intermediate targets not only convey information on the final variables but also have a "signalling" function in influencing the expectations of economic agents: by providing a clearly understandable nominal anchor – especially in an environment of diffuse structural uncertainty (Brunner 1980) – intermediate targets may help the co-ordination of price- and wage-setting decisions, thus avoiding that conflicts about income distribution lead to inflationary pressures (Courakis 1981, Woolley 1987, Bernanke and Mishkin 1992). Moreover, as Rogoff (1985) has shown among others, the adoption of intermediate targets may reduce the welfare loss arising from the time inconsistency of monetary policy, which has been first pointed out by Barro and Gordon (1983a, 1983b) and has then been investigated by several contributions surveyed by Blackburn and Christiansen (1989) and by Cukierman (1992).

Whether the setting of monetary targets is a desirable strategy for monetary policy is still an open question, as revealed both by the unresolved issues in the academic literature (see, for example, the review by B. Friedman 1990) and by the difference in central bank practices. Yet, whatever the answer, the assessment of the stability of money demand relationships is crucial for the conduct of monetary policy, since it makes it possible to pass a judgement on the reliability of the information content of money. And such a judgement, implicitly or explicitly, underlies the policy response to the crucial question central banks are confronted with daily: should changes in money demand be accommodated? If so, by how much?[1] Getting this answer right, or at least avoiding gross mistakes, improves the stabilising performance of monetary policy, and hence the terms of the trade-off between credibility and flexibility, irrespective of whether money is an intermediate target or an information variable and of whether movements in the quantity of money are viewed as reflecting, or instead as bringing about, changes in nominal income.

The arguments discussed so far are quite general and, duly amended, hold for small and large economies, for closed and open ones. However, they have particularly stringent policy implications when they are applied to a group of countries, like EU ones, which are so closely integrated from an economic and financial point of view to make it sensible to coordinate monetary policies through an exchange rate agreement. The next sections put forward a framework to explore these implications.

3. The Analytical Framework

This section sketches the framework underpinning the theoretical analysis of the policy implications of national vs. EU-wide money demand (in)stability. The reference model, which is taken from Monticelli and Papi (1995, Chapter 2), is a two-country, log-linear rational expectations set-up in which both economies are assumed to have the same size and economic structure, and are subject to real and nominal disturbances.

Each country block contains the three standard equations: money demand, which depends positively on income and negatively on the interest rate; output demand, which depends positively upon the other country's output, and negatively on the real rate of interest and the real exchange rate; a Lucas supply function, which postulates that deviations of output from its natural rate are a positive function of unanticipated movements in the price level. The stochastic shocks hitting each equation are assumed to be independently distributed with zero means and finite variances.

The two country blocks are connected by two relationships. The first one is the uncovered interest parity condition which assumes the perfect substitutability between the bonds of the two countries. However, this hypothesis is not strictly necessary, as the key results hold even if a constant risk premium is added to the interest parity condition so as to express imperfect bond substitutability, possibly stemming from the imperfect credibility of the exchange rate commitment.

The second relationship which connects the two country blocks is a stochastic version of PPP (see for instance Gros and Lane 1992) which assumes perfect substitutability in the output market, except for a random disturbance creating a wedge between the prices of the goods produced in the two countries. Rather than the result of market imperfections which prevent the law of one price from holding, such a random disturbance should be interpreted as an analytical short-cut to model the determination of the real exchange rate. This assumption is adopted to simplify the analysis but, as shown in Monticelli and Papi (1995), the key results of the analysis hold even when this assumption is relaxed and the real exchange rate is endogenously determined.

The money supply process is assumed to follow a general rule corresponding to the combination policy put forward in the classic paper by Poole (1970). This formulation – which encompasses the pure policies of money targeting and interest rate pegging as special cases – takes the money stock and the interest rate to be deterministically related even in the presence of stochastic disturbances. The authorities are in fact assumed to change the money stock in response to observed movements in the interest rate, as these embody information on the nature and size of the shocks hitting the economies. The optimal monetary instrument is defined by the intensity of the changes in money supply to movements in the interest rate which optimises the stabilisation objectives of the authorities. In general, the optimal monetary instrument will not be a pure policy, but rather a feed-back rule from interest rate movements to money stock changes, defining the extent to which monetary authorities should "lean with the wind" according to the structure of both economies and the relative size of the variance of all the disturbances.

Against the background of the model just sketched, this paper considers two different schemes of monetary co-ordination under an exchange rate agreement. In the first scheme, exchange rate stability is ensured by only one country, which will be indicated as non-anchor (NA) country: the NA-country relinquishes its monetary autonomy and adjusts its money supply to maintain exchange rate stability in the presence of shocks. The other country, the anchor country (A-country), retains full control of its money supply. Although this distribution of tasks mirrors the features of the perfectly asymmetric scheme of monetary co-ordination in which the anchor country pursues merely domestic objectives, the arrangement considered in the next section is different in a fundamental aspect. The degree of monetary freedom within the system is not necessarily used to pursue the domestic objectives of the A-country only; rather, the degree of symmetry – i.e. the importance attached to the objectives of the NA-country – is not established a priori but is liable to take different values.

The second co-ordination scheme, discussed in the Section 5, instead provides for monetary control to be exercised by an area-wide monetary instrument. In this case, the total money supply of the system is under the control of the authorities, while its distribution between the two countries is endogenous. In this case too, the degree of symmetry of the objectives pursued by monetary policy is not set a priori, but is taken to be a parameter.

4. Monetary Co-ordination with an Anchor

This section is devoted to the first co-ordination scheme which provides for the A-country to play the role of anchor. The money supply of NA-country is thus taken to be endogenous so as to maintain exchange rate stability, while the money supply process of the A-country is given by a general feed-back rule from interest rate movements to money supply changes. As discussed in what follows, the intensity of this feedback depends on the objectives pursued by monetary policy.

Assuming that the money supply rule of the A-country is constant over time, and that the random shocks hitting both economies are not serially correlated, the deviations of the log of the price levels from their trend levels can be expressed as a function of the random shocks and of the structural parameters of the model (details of the solution are shown in Monticelli and Papi 1995), as follows:

$$p_t^{NA} = \Gamma_0(m_t^A - v_t^A) + \sum \Gamma_j u_{jt} + \Gamma_\mu^{NA}\mu_t \qquad \Gamma_\mu^{NA} > 0$$

$$p_t^A = \Gamma_0(m_t^A - v_t^A) + \sum \Gamma_j u_{jt} + \Gamma_\mu^A\mu_t \qquad \Gamma_\mu^A < 0$$

where

p_t^A, p_t^{NA}	deviations of the price levels of the A- and NA-country, respectively, from their trends;
m_t^A	money supply of the A-country;
v_t^A	shock to the money demand of the A-country;
u_{jt}'s	shocks to the demand for and the supply of goods in both the A- and the NA-country;
μ_t	shock to PPP, interpreted as a shock to the real exchange rate;
Γ_i's	coefficients which are functions of the structural parameters including the one in the money supply rule that defines the intensity of the feed-back from interest rate movements to money stock changes.

The above equations provide two key insights on the interaction between the two economies under an exchange rate agreement complemented with the understanding that only the NA-country ensures exchange rate stability through appropriate changes in its money supply.

First, financial shocks hitting the NA-country do not influence the price level in either country. Through the commitment to exchange rate stability, NA-country's monetary authorities automatically accommodate domestic monetary shocks, thereby preventing them from affecting real or nominal variables in either country. Thus, if monetary shocks in one country represent the major source of instability in the area, it is to the benefit of both countries (irrespective of the stabilisation objective pursued by monetary policy) if the country with an unstable money demand ensures exchange rate stability. By putting forward the stability of money demand as the criterion for the choice of the country to play the role of nominal anchor in an exchange rate arrangement, this result provides an additional rationale, besides the difference in anti-inflationary credibility, for the common agreement on the central role played by Germany in the ERM (see also Bini Smaghi and Vori 1991).

Second, all shocks affect the price level of both countries in the same direction and with the same intensity, except for the disturbance to PPP, which, it has been recalled, can be interpreted as a shock to the real exchange rate. Thus, when this source of instability is negligible, the stabilisation objectives of the monetary authorities of both countries coincide exactly. Therefore, the asymmetric allocation of the burden of maintaining exchange rate stability does not provide any ground for contrasting interests between the two countries. Even if the A-country pursues purely domestic objectives in the choice of its monetary instrument, the NA-country benefits from the actions of the A-country as if its own stabilisation objectives were given priority. This is no longer the case when shocks to PPP are important: the degree of symmetry of the system comes to have a bearing on the choice of the optimal monetary instrument.

In addition to the degree of symmetry of the system, the choice of the optimal monetary instrument is affected by the objective function which describes the stabilisation objectives pursued by the authorities. In line with the prescriptions for the European Central Bank enshrined in the Maastricht Treaty, both countries are assumed to aim at stabilising the price level, which is equivalent to stabilising inflation in the simple model adopted here, where variables are expressed as deviations from their trend levels and disturbances are serially independent. The objective function is thus defined as follows:

$$\Phi = -\left[Var(p^{A}) + \theta Var(p^{NA})\right] \qquad 0 \leq \theta \leq 1.$$

This function encompasses the whole spectrum of the degrees of symmetry which can characterise the stabilisation objectives pursued by monetary policy while maintaining stable exchange rates. If $\theta = 0$, the co-ordination scheme becomes fully asymmetric: in setting its monetary policy (and hence the monetary conditions of the whole area given that the NA-country is an exchange rate pegger), the A-country only cares about domestic objectives and completely disregards the external implications of its choices. If $\theta = 1$, notwithstanding the asymmetry in the adjustment duties, the system is perfectly symmetric as monetary policy aims at minimising the fluctuations of the area-wide price level.[2] Between the two extremes, intermediate situations are possible, where the A-country places its domestic objectives before area-wide considerations, which are nonetheless taken into account.

Making use of the solutions for the price level in the two countries and rearranging Φ, it can be shown (for the analytical treatment the reader is referred to Monticelli and Papi 1995) that when the degree of symmetry in the exchange rate arrangement increases, the optimal monetary instrument of the A-country moves towards interest rate pegging. In other words, targets for the money supply are to be interpreted more flexibly, with a higher degree of accommodation of shifts in money demand. The intuition behind this result can be appreciated by focusing on the way μ, the disturbance to the real exchange rate, affects the two economies, given that, as shown by the solutions for the price level in the two countries, only this kind of shocks has a different impact on the price level of the two countries.

Consider the case when the A-country pursues a pure policy of money targeting and the realised value of μ is negative (that is, the real exchange rate of the A-country depreciates), exerting an expansionary impulse on the A-country and a contractionary one on the NA-country. The rise in the A-country's exports leads to an increase in money demand which is not accommodated in order to meet the target. The interest rate increases and cools down domestic demand, offsetting the expansion in foreign demand and thus stabilising both aggregate income and inflation. The situation is quite different for the NA-country. The appreciation of the real exchange rate exerts a deflationary impact on activity and so does the increase in the interest rate which the NA-country must adopt to maintain exchange rate stability. Monetary policy does not help stabilise the A-country's economy, but rather has pro cyclical effects. Stabilising the A-country results in "exporting" instability to the NA-country.

The international transmission of shocks through this mechanism is dampened if the A-country interprets its money supply target more flexibly, i.e. if it accommodates a higher share of the increase in money demand. The increase in the interest rate in the system is thus smaller, resulting, on the one hand, in a less effective stabilisation performance for the A-country and, on the other, in less instability exported to the NA-country. This explains why an increase in the degree of symmetry in the system, that is in the weight attached to the stabilisation objectives of the NA-country, implies a higher degree of accommodation of money demand changes.[3]

Turning to the other properties of the optimal monetary instrument, it can be shown that the classic findings by Poole (1970) are confirmed in the more general two-country setting: money demand instability calls for interest rate pegging and goods demand instability for money supply targeting. An increase in the variance of the shocks to the real exchange rate, instead, leads the A-country to move its optimal monetary instrument in a direction which depends on the importance attached to area-wide objectives. The reason for this ambiguity is that, as discussed above, the choice of the monetary instrument affects the allocation of this kind of disturbances between the two countries: the response of the monetary instrument to this kind of shocks can only reduce the instability in the price level of one country at the expense of increasing the instability in the price level of the other.

5. Monetary Co-ordination with Area-Wide Monetary Control

This section investigates the second scheme of monetary co-ordination within the exchange rate agreement. In this case too, only one country, the NA-country, carries out the task of ensuring exchange rate stability. The management of the degree of monetary freedom, however, is not assigned to the A-country, but is jointly seen to by both countries through the control of the total money supply in the area, leaving its currency composition endogenous. The implementation of this scheme of monetary co-ordination presumably requires an adequately developed institutional framework, which is not explored here. A preliminary discussion of the problems involved by area-wide monetary control is contained in Sardelis (1993), Kenen (1992), Monticelli and Viñals (1993).

Before discussing its properties, it should be noted that the co-ordination scheme based on the joint control of the monetary conditions of the entire area is different from monetary union. Even if exchange rate stability is perfectly credible, economic agents have precise preferences over the holding of the two currencies and therefore two distinct demands for money can be defined. Conversely, in a monetary union such a distinction is no longer possible and *only* one demand for money can be defined for the area (as in the model by Klein 1991). The difference in the transaction services supplied by the two currencies or the presence of legal restrictions which provide for the use of national currencies are two plausible reasons for the existence of well-defined demands for national currencies. If such demands exist, the maintenance of exchange rate stability requires the accommodation of shifts in the currency composition of the area-wide money supply, the total of which is however controlled by the authorities in the pursuit of the macroeconomic objectives of the system.

In the co-ordination scheme based on the joint control of the monetary conditions of the entire area, the money supply rule is given by an area-wide combination policy. The latter is a relationship between the area-wide money supply and the average[4] interest rate in the area, which encompasses a money stock target for the whole area and an interest rate pegging strategy at the area level as special cases. The supply of money of the NA-country is determined so as to maintain exchange rate stability by accommodating the shifts in the desired composition of the area-wide money stock which stem from the random disturbances hitting the two economies.

Under this second scheme of monetary co-ordination, the solution for the price level of the two countries is given by:

$$p_t^{NA} = \Gamma_0(m_t^A + m_t^{NA} - v_t^A - v_t^{NA}) + \sum \Gamma_j u_{jt} + \tfrac{1}{2}\mu_t$$

$$p_t^A = \Gamma_0(m_t^A + m_t^{NA} - v_t^A - v_t^{NA}) + \sum \Gamma_j u_{jt} - \tfrac{1}{2}\mu_t$$

where, in addition to the symbols already defined:

m_t^{NA}	money supply of the NA-country;
v_t^{NA}	shock to the money demand of the NA-country.

The first noteworthy implication of these equations is that shocks to the money demand of the NA-country enter the solution for both price levels, while they were absent in the solution of the model for the first scheme of monetary co-ordination. As the monetary instrument is defined at the area level, the endogeneity of the money supply of the NA-country, although necessary to ensure exchange rate stability, is no longer sufficient to absorb the financial shocks hitting the NA-country fully. In order to retain control over the area-wide money supply, changes in the demand for money in the NA-country are not fully accommodated and thus have a spill-over effect on the monetary conditions in the area.

Financial shocks affecting the two economies enter the price solution in additive form. Consequently, if the assumption that financial shocks are independent is maintained, monetary co-ordination based on an area-wide instrument will always be inferior to a co-ordination scheme which entrusts one country with the task of managing the degree of monetary freedom through a national instrument.[5] In the latter case, financial shocks hitting the NA-country are automatically absorbed, while the resort to an area-wide monetary instrument implies that financial shocks hitting *both* countries have destabilising effects.

However, area-wide monetary instrument is preferable to a national monetary instrument if the variance of the shocks to the area-wide money demand is smaller than the variance of the shocks hitting the most stable national money demand. To be satisfied within a simple analytical framework, this condition requires the presence of a (sufficiently large) negative correlation between the financial shocks which affect the two countries, as is the case, for example, if currency substitution is an important feature of the economic environment.

More generally, this condition can also be met as a result of the factors, which make the area-wide money demand more stable than national demands. Single-country equations typically omit foreign variables, partly as a consequence of the high degree of correlation between European interest rates and partly as a result of the difficulties in identifying the relevant variables. In contrast, the increasing degree of economic and financial integration within the EU has been associated with an intensification of international portfolio diversification and with growing currency substitution. These developments call for a re-examination of the role of foreign variables on the residents' demand for monetary assets. Cross-country spill-over effects can be captured in a simple way by aggregating money demand equations across countries which have strong economic and financial inter linkages. The specification bias affecting traditional single-country equations is thus reduced, although an aggregation bias may be introduced in the area-wide equation to the extent that there are different money demand relationships at the national level (Pesaran et al. 1989, Kremers and Lane 1992). Recent econometric evidence shows that an area-wide money demand performs at least as well as the best national equations, suggesting that the aggregation bias is relatively small (see Van Riet 1992, 1993, Monticelli and Papi 1995).

Moving to the coefficients for the disturbances to the real exchange rate – which, as shown in the previous section, underpin the relation between the degree of symmetry of the system and the optimal monetary instrument – the solution for the price levels under the second co-ordination scheme show that the coefficients in the two countries are equal in absolute value and are independent of the choice of the monetary instrument.

To appreciate the intuition underlying this result, it has to be recalled that, under an exchange rate arrangement, monetary policy is unable to reduce the *total* impact of asymmetric shocks, whatever their origin, which alter the real exchange rate. Only the relinquishment of nominal exchange rate stability can dampen the effects of this kind of shocks for the area as a whole. When one country is the anchor, its monetary policy can absorb the impact of these shocks but only at the expense of amplifying their effects in the other countries of the system. Conversely, if monetary co-ordination hinges on monetary control at the area level, monetary policy is unable to control the monetary conditions in any single country, irrespective of the monetary instrument adopted. As a result, monetary policy cannot distribute the impact of shocks to the real exchange rate, which thus affect all countries with the same strength (as a result of the assumption that the two countries have equal size) but with opposite direction.

The inability of monetary policy to distribute the impact of real exchange rate shocks among countries implies that, under the co-ordination scheme based on area-wide monetary control, the choice of the optimal monetary instrument is independent of the degree of symmetry in the system. In fact, there is no longer the possibility that national stabilisation objectives push in opposite directions in the choice of the area-wide monetary instrument. The thorny issue of the degree of symmetry of an exchange rate agreement is automatically solved by the resort to area-wide monetary control.

6. Policy Implications

A convenient way to discuss the policy implications of the analytical findings discussed in the previous sections is to consider, in sequence, the combinations of the presence of money demand (in)stability at the national and area-wide level.

It may be reassuring to start with the bliss point of money demand fans: *money demand functions are found by econometric analysis to be stable and predictable both for each country and for the area as a whole.* In this case, monetary aggregates are reliable indicators of the developments in the final variables, thereby also providing the opportunity to adopt a monetary policy strategy based on an intermediate target set in terms of money supply. Monetary co-ordination between countries participating into an exchange rate agreement can exploit the environment characterised by negligible financial shocks either by assigning to one country the role of anchor of the system (with the others behaving as exchange rate peggers) or by resorting to an area-wide monetary target which is then translated into national targets for domestic credit expansion according to the scheme made popular by Russo and Tullio (1988). The choice between the two solutions hinges on factors, such as credibility of the monetary authorities and existence of appropriate institutional arrangements, which are outside the framework of analysis put forward in the previous sections. However, two remarks are in order.

First, if each and every country has a stable money demand function, this can no longer be a discriminating criterion to select the anchor country in an asymmetric co-ordination arrangement and other considerations (size, credibility, political judgements, etc.) must be invoked. Second, if a symmetric co-ordination arrangement à la Russo and Tullio is chosen, the stability of both national and area-wide money demand functions, although necessary, is not sufficient for the successful implementation of the scheme. The stability and identity of national money multipliers – which in turn depends on the stability of bank behaviour and on sufficiently similar financial structures and regulations (most notably as regards provisions on compulsory reserves) – is also required. Otherwise, shifts in the monetary base within the area will give rise to changes in the area-wide money supply even if the total supply of base money is held constant.

This requirement can be appreciated considering the relationship between the change in the money supply of the whole area and the variation in the monetary base of the participating countries, denominated in a common currency, which is given by:

$$\Delta M^{area} = \sum_i \Delta M_i = \sum \kappa_i \Delta MB_i$$

where M is the nominal money supply; MB the monetary base; k the money multiplier; and the subscript i denotes national variables.

In each country, variations in the monetary base can be divided according to the creation channel: the domestic credit channel (ΔDC) and the foreign channel (ΔOR). The latter can be further split into changes in official reserves denominated in area currencies (ΔOR^{in}) and in third currencies (ΔOR^{ex}), i.e.

$$\Delta MB_i = \Delta DC_i + \Delta OR_i = \Delta DC_i + \Delta OR_i^{in} + \Delta OR_i^{ex}.$$

If the system adopts a flexible exchange rate regime with the rest of the world, there is no official intervention in third currencies and hence $\Delta OR_i^{ex} = 0$. The above relationships therefore imply that:

$$\Delta M^{area} = \sum_i \kappa_i (\Delta DC_i + \Delta OR_i^{in}).$$

Since official intervention in area currencies involves opposite variations in the official reserves of the countries involved, it follows that $\sum_i \Delta OR_i^{in} = 0$. However, this relationship is not sufficient to ensure that foreign exchange intervention does not entail changes in the monetary stance of the system as a whole, even if intervention is never sterilised so as to hold the total monetary base of the system constant. In addition, the monetary multipliers of all countries must be equal, viz., $\kappa_i = \overline{\kappa} \; \forall i$. This condition is necessary for $\sum_i \Delta OR_i^{in} = 0$ to *always* imply $\sum_i \kappa_i \Delta OR_i^{in}$. In other words, only if shifts in monetary base between countries do not give rise to changes in the total money supply because of a different relationship between monetary base and money supply within each country, $\Delta M^{area} = \overline{\kappa} \sum_i \Delta DC_i$ *always* holds.

Let us now turn to the case where *money demand is stable at the country level but not for the area as a whole*. Implicit in this scenario is the assumption that money demand is stable in some countries but not in others, otherwise the instability of the area-wide money demand function would be quite difficult to account for: the sum of negatively correlated national shocks can bring about area-wide stability despite instability at the national level, but the sum of "the absence of disturbances" cannot be expected to yield instability. The policy response to this constellation of money demand (in)stabilities is straightforward: any idea of adopting monetary control at the area level is to be forsaken since it is to the benefit of *all* countries, exchange rate peggers included, to select the country with the most stable money demand as the anchor of the system. This arrangement, in fact, makes it possible to enhance the stabilisation performance of monetary policy to the benefit of all countries and not only of the anchor. Pegging the exchange rate enables countries with an unstable money demand to accommodate financial shocks automatically thereby importing the stabilising effects of the anchor country's monetary policy.

When *money demand is unstable both in each country and in the area as a whole*, it may be hell for money demand fans and central bankers but it is certainly fun, if not heaven, for econometricians who are given a good chance to try their best efforts to look for the notorious black cat in the dark room. The prescription for monetary policy is clear: forsake monetary targets and beware of signals from developments in money supply, as they are likely to be misleading. Fortunately enough, there are plenty of indicators around; some are obvious, some esoteric, but all are capable of conveying useful information about the variables of interest. "Look at (nearly) everything" becomes the motto; making a consistent story of what you have looked at becomes the hard task.

More interesting is the policy implication when *(all) national money demands are unstable and the area-wide demand is instead stable*. In this case, it is to the advantage of *all* countries to perform monetary control at the area level and not with reference to the monetary conditions of a single country. In fact, the resort to an area-wide monetary instrument enables the exploitation of the stability of the demand for money for the area as a whole, enhancing the stabilisation performance of monetary policy to the benefit of *all* countries, including the country which would have performed the role of anchor. The latter, in the face of monetary shocks, would otherwise adopt the strategy of pegging the interest rate, which, although effective in coping with financial disturbances, would have the effect of amplifying the instability brought about by real shocks. This would impair the stabilisation performance of monetary policy both for the anchor country and for the other participants in the exchange rate agreement.

Nor is this all. If, as is likely, countries share the macroeconomic objective to be assigned to monetary policy, the choice of the co-ordination scheme based on area-wide monetary control entails the *automatic solution of the issue of the symmetry* of the ERM, which has plagued the system since its inception and is arguably one of the main causes of the 1992–93 exchange rate crisis. The reason for this additional implication is that, under an area-wide monetary control, monetary policy is unable to allocate the impact of shocks between the countries and hence there is no longer the possibility that national stabilisation objectives push towards opposite directions in the choice of the optimal monetary instrument.

The policy prescriptions discussed above are, as usual, subject to the caveats stemming from the resort to simplifying assumptions in the theoretical analysis as well as in the econometric exercises which underlie the evaluation of which scenario, among the four described in this section, actually holds true. Moreover, the prescriptions are contingent on the implicit hypothesis that asymmetric real shocks, which alter the real exchange rate and hence require differentiated national monetary stances, are of minor importance. However, if this condition is not met, it is not the case for monetary co-ordination based on area-wide monetary control, or for any other policy prescription, which no longer stands. Rather, it is real exchange rate stability which has to be forsaken. With sticky wages and prices, changes in the nominal exchange rate are the only instrument capable of reducing the total impact in the area of shocks to the real exchange rate. But this is another story; it is the EMU business.

NOTES

1. Within some central banks, the same questions may be phrased as: should interest rates be changed? If so, by how much? This variation, however, does not alter the gist of the matter.
2. Simple algebra can show that the optimal monetary policy is the same whether the objective function is defined as $-Var(p^A) - Var(p^{NA})$ or as $-Var(p^{NA} + p^A)$.
3. In the limit case when the A-country pursues a pure policy of interest rate pegging, the difference in the strength of the impact of real exchange rate shocks in the two countries disappears, since the A-country fully accommodates the increase in money demand stemming from a depreciation of the real exchange rate.
4. Since both countries are assumed to have the same size, the average needs no weighting.
5. The only exception occurs when financial shocks are the only source of disturbance for the two economies and, therefore, interest pegging is the optimal monetary strategy. In this case, under an exchange rate agreement, the national and the area-wide monetary instruments coincide.

REFERENCES

Arnold, I.J.M. (1994), "The Myth of a Stable European Money Demand", *Open Economic Review*, 5, 249–259.

Barro, R. and D. Gordon (1983a), "Rules, Discretion and Reputation in a Model of Monetary Policy",

Journal of Monetary Economics, 12, 101–121.

Barro, R. and D. Gordon (1983b), "A Positive Theory of Monetary Policy in a Natural-Rate Model", *Journal of Political Economy*, 91, 589–610.

Bekx, P. and G. Tullio (1989), "A Note on the European Monetary System, and the Determination of the DM-Dollar Exchange Rate", *Cahiers Economiques de Bruxelles*, 123, 329–343.

Bernanke, B. and F. Mishkin (1992), "Central Bank Behaviour and the Strategy of Monetary Policy: Observations from Six Industrialised Countries", in O.J. Blanchard, and S. Fischer (eds.), *NBER Macroeconomics Annual*, Cambridge (MA), The MIT Press, 183–228.

Bini Smaghi, L. and S. Vori (1991), "Currency Substitution, Monetary Stability and European Monetary Unification", *Rivista Internazionale di Scienze Sociali*, 37, 45–68.

Blackburn, K. and M. Christiansen (1989), "Monetary Policy and Policy Credibility: Theories and Evidence", *Journal of Economic Literature*, 27, 1–45.

Boyer, R.S. (1978), "Optimal Foreign Exchange Market Intervention", *Journal of Political Economy*, 86, 1045–1055.

Brunner, K. (1980), "The Control of Monetary Aggregates, in Controlling Monetary Aggregates III", *Federal Reserve Bank of Boston, proceedings of a conference at Melvin Village, New Hampshire*, October (1980), 1–65.

Bryant, R.C. (1983), *Controlling Money. The Federal Reserve and its Critics*, Washington D.C., The Brookings Institution.

Canzoneri, M.B., D.W. Henderson and K. Rogoff (1983), "The Information Content of the Interest Rate and the Price Level", *Quarterly Journal of Economics*, 98, 545–566.

Courakis, A.S. (1981), "Monetary Targets: Conceptual Antecedents and Recent Policies in the US, UK and West Germany", in A.S. Courakis (ed.), *Inflation, Depression and Economic Policy in the West*, London, Mansell, 259–357.

Cukierman, A. (1992), *Central Bank Strategy, Credibility and Independence*, Cambridge (MA), MIT Press.

Fase, M.M.G. (1993) "The Stability of the Demand for Money in the G7 and EC Countries: A Survey", *CEPS Working Papers*, 81.

Friedman, B.M. (1975), "Targets, Instruments and Indicators of Monetary Policy", *Journal of Monetary Economics*, 1, 443–473.

Friedman, B.M. (1977), "The Inefficiency of Short-Run Monetary Targets for Monetary Policy", *Brookings Papers on Economic Activity*, 2, 293–335.

Friedman, B.M. (1990) "Targets and Instruments of Monetary Policy", in B.M. Friedman and F.H. Hahn (eds.) *Handbook of Monetary Economics*, Amsterdam, North-Holland, 1185–1230.

Giavazzi F., S. Micossi and M. Miller (eds.) (1988), *The European Monetary System*, Cambridge, Cambridge University Press.

Giovannini, A. (1991), "Money Demand and Monetary Control in an Integrated European Economy", *European Economy*, special edition n. 1, chapter 5.

Gray, J.A. (1976), "Wage Indexation: A Macroeconomic Approach", *Journal of Monetary Economics*, 2, 221–235.

Gros, D. and T. Lane (1992), "Monetary Policy Integration within or without an Exchange Rate Agreement", *Open Economic Review*, 3, 61–82.

Kenen, P.B. (1992), *EMU after Maastricht*, Washington D.C., Group of Thirty.

Klein, M. (1991), "Bargaining for the Choice of Monetary Policy Instruments in a Simple Stochastic Macro Model", *CEPR Discussion Papers*, 553.

Kremers, J.J.M. and T.D. Lane (1990), "Economic and Monetary Integration and the Aggregate Demand for Money in the EMS", *IMF Staff Papers*, 37, 777–805.

Kremers, J.J.M. and T.D. Lane (1992), "The Implications of Cross-Border Monetary Aggregation", *IMF Working Papers*, 71.

LeRoy, S.F. and Waud, R.N. (1977), "Applications of the Kalman Filter in Short-Run Monetary Control", *International Economic Review*, 18, 195–207.

Monticelli, C. and L. Papi (1995), *European Integration, Monetary Co-ordination and the Demand for Money*, Oxford University Press, Oxford (forthcoming).

Monticelli, C. and J. Viñals (1993), "European Monetary Policy in Stage Three: What Are the Issues?", *CEPR Occasional Papers*, 12.

Papademos, L. and F. Modigliani (1983), "Inflation, Financial and Fiscal Structure and the Monetary Mechanism", *European Economic Review*, 21, 203–250.

Parkin, M. (1978), "A Comparison of Alternative Techniques of Monetary Control under Rational Expectations", *The Manchester School*, 46, 252–287.

Pesaran, M.H., R.G. Pierse and M.S. Kumar (1989), "Econometric Analysis of Aggregation in the Context of Linear Prediction Models", *Econometrica*, 57, 861–88.

Poole, W. (1970), "Optimal Choice of Monetary Instruments in a Simple Stochastic Macro Model", *Quarterly Journal of Economics*, 84, 197–216.

Riet, A.G. van (1992), "European Integration and the Demand for Money in the EC", *De Nederlandsche Bank Quarterly Bulletin*, 3, 33–43.

Riet, A.G. van (1993) "Studies of EC Money Demand: Survey and Assessment", *De Nederlandsche Bank Quarterly Bulletin*, 4, 63–75.

Rogoff, K. (1985), "The Optimal Degree of Commitment to an Intermediate Monetary Target", *Quarterly Journal of Economics*, 100, 1169–1190.

Russo, M. and G. Tullio (1988), "Monetary Policy Co-Ordination within the European Monetary System: Is there a Rule?", in F. Giavazzi, S. Micossi, S. and M. Miller (eds.), *The European Monetary System*, Cambridge University Press, 292–355.

Sardelis, C. (1993), "Targeting a European Monetary Aggregate: Review and Current Issues, Commission of the European Communities", *Economic Papers*, 102.

Sargent, T.J. and N. Wallace (1975), "'Rational' Expectations, the Optimal Monetary Instrument, and the Optimal Money Supply Rule", *Journal of Political Economy*, 83, 241–254.

Tinbergen, J. (1952), *On the Theory of Economic Policy*, Amsterdam, North-Holland.

Turnovsky, S.J. (1984), "Exchange Market Intervention Under Alternative Forms of Exogenous Disturbances", *Journal of International Economics*, 20, 279–297.

Woolley, J.T. (1987), "The Political Uses of Monetary Targets", in D.R. Hodgman and G. Wood (eds.), *Monetary and Exchange Policy*, London, MacMillan Press, 69–98.

Credit Characteristics and the Monetary Policy Transmission Mechanism in Fourteen Industrial Countries: Facts, Conjectures and Some Econometric Evidence*

CLAUDIO E.V. BORIO
Bank for International Settlements

ABSTRACT

This paper examines in detail the characteristics of credit to the non-government sector, including both interest and non-interest terms, in fourteen industrial countries and considers its potential implications for the transmission mechanism of monetary policy. Three findings merit particular attention. First, the share of securities in total credit is comparatively high in Anglo-Saxon countries. Second, most Anglo-Saxon countries are characterised by a relatively high share of adjustable rate credit. This is due primarily to the widespread use of adjustable rate mortgages by households. Outside the Anglo-Saxon group, the main exception is Italy; inside it, the United States. Third, the share of loans backed by real estate collateral appears to be comparatively high in most Anglo-Saxon countries. Elsewhere, it is very high in Sweden and Switzerland. There are also indications that the share is relatively high in Japan. To varying degrees, the above characteristics should be expected to amplify the impact of monetary policy on economic activity. Their relevance is broadly consistent with the cross-country pattern of results of simulations of national central bank models.

1. INTRODUCTION

In recent years academics, market observers and policy-makers alike have paid increasing attention to the process of internationalisation and globalisation of financial markets. This focus has inevitably highlighted the forces working for uniformity in financial structures and behaviour. By the same token, it has fostered the impression that remaining differences are minor or of little interest for most policy issues. The transmission mechanism of monetary policy is one important case in point.

This impression, however, may be quite misleading. In particular, the autumn 1992

*This paper is closely based on Borio (1995). The views expressed are those of the author and do not necessarily reflect those of the BIS. I would like to thank Philippe Hainaut and also Gerd Schnabel for invaluable statistical assistance and the staff of the national central banks contributing to this work for their kind cooperation.

Koos Alders, Kees Koedijk, Clemens Kool and Carlo Winder (eds.), Monetary Policy in a Converging Europe, pp. 77–115.

ERM crisis uncovered hitherto largely unnoticed cross-country differences in the speed, intensity and compass of the transmission of changes in policy interest rates to other interest rates in the economy. Together with differences in the health of the balance sheets of financial and non-financial agents, these implied a marked divergence in the ability of the authorities to sustain exchange rate commitments. More generally, they could be expected to affect the pattern of response of economic activity to monetary policy impulses.

There are clearly several elements of financial arrangements that may be relevant for the transmission mechanism.[1] The present paper documents one of them, viz. the structure of credit to the non-government sector. The paper covers fourteen industrial countries and considers several aspects of interest: who provides the credit; who receives it; its currency composition; whether it takes the form of loans or securities; its maturity breakdown; the adjustability of the contractual interest rates charged; and collateral.

There are good reasons for believing that the aforementioned features should contribute to shaping the impact of monetary policy on economic activity. To see this, a stylised characterisation of the transmission mechanism may be helpful. According to this, the central bank gears its instruments to influencing quite closely very short-term interest rates. Changes in such "policy-controlled" rates ultimately affect economic activity through four main channels. First, they induce changes in interest rates and yields on new financing and portfolio investments (*"marginal rates"*), thereby affecting the opportunity cost of real expenditure decisions (e.g. through the cost of capital). Second, they lead to changes in *average rates* on outstanding contracts, modifying incomes and cash flows and hence constraints on spending. Third, they affect *asset values*, impinging not only on wealth perceptions but also on the ability to borrow and willingness to lend ("credit availability"). Finally, they have an impact on the *exchange rate*, and hence on the relative price of assets and goods and services denominated in different currencies.

Within this framework, the structure of credit has a bearing on the channels of transmission in several ways. The strength of income effects associated with changes in interest rates will depend on the size of the indebtedness, on the maturity of the outstanding contracts and, above all, on the mix between fixed and adjustable rates. The speed with which policy rates affect interest rates on borrowed money is at least partly a function of the mix between intermediated and disintermediated credit. The significance of "credit availability" effects reflects to some extent the same mix; more importantly, it is potentially affected by specific contract terms, such as the use of collateral. Real estate is especially relevant in this context because of its widespread use as collateral and the interest rate sensitivity of its valuation. The strength of valuation effects connected with exchange rate changes will vary with the extent to which debt is denominated in foreign currencies. Finally, the sectoral incidence of monetary policy impulses will depend on the distribution and contractual characteristics of indebtedness.

Despite such strong priors, we still know very little about international differences in the structure and characteristics of credit impinging on the transmission mechanism. Admittedly, credit, while important, is but one element of the whole story. The findings of this study should therefore be assessed in conjunction with complementary work carried out at the BIS dealing with the complete balance sheets of non-financial agents and issues such as the responsiveness of lending rates to policy rates, part of a broader BIS-central banks project on the relevance of financial structure for cross-country differences in transmission mechanisms (BIS (1995)).

This inquiry is largely based on the central banks' responses to a questionnaire on financial structure and on subsequent contacts. It also relies on estimates based on other sources of information.[2] The main focus is on the stock of credit outstanding at the most recent comparable date available. Where possible, the situation in the early 1980s is also considered so as to identify any major changes over time.

The structure of the paper is straightforward. In the main section the empirical findings relating to the various characteristics of credit are discussed sequentially in some detail. Each of them is preceded by conjectures about their potential relevance for the transmission mechanism. The concluding section provides an overview of the main arguments and findings. It is written so as to be self-contained and relates the findings of this paper to the broader results of the joint BIS-central banks project on the transmission mechanism.

Table 1. Credit to the non-government sector[a] (as a percentage of GDP).

	1993[b]	1983[c]		1993[b]	1983[c]
Australia	98	102	Japan	202	158
Austria	88	73	Netherlands	115	93
Belgium	86	77	Spain	79	80
Canada	108	87	Sweden	143	94
France	90	71	Switzerland[d]	179	139[e]
Germany	125	97	United Kingdom	117	58
Italy	64	57	United States	114	96

[a]Loans from banks and other financial institutions as well as securities outstanding; excluding trade credit.

[b]Sweden and Switzerland: 1992.

[c]Australia: 1988; Belgium and Sweden: 1982; Italy: 1989.

[d]Pension fund and life assurance company loans partly estimated.

[e]Excluding securities.

2. Credit Characteristics: What They Are and Why They Matter

2.1. The Scale of Total Credit to the Non-Government Sector

The basic credit aggregate examined in this study covers the credit obtained by domestic households and businesses from domestic financial institutions plus any securities outstanding (not held by those institutions). It thus generally excludes trade credit and loans from abroad and from the government.[3] For simplicity, it will henceforth be referred to as "total credit to the non-government sector" or "total credit" for short.

The ratio of total credit to the non-government sector to GDP typically ranges from around 80 percent to 130 percent in the countries considered (Table 1). It is by far the highest in Japan, at around 200 percent, and the lowest in Italy, at less than 70 percent. The ratio is also comparatively high in Switzerland, Sweden and Germany; in Anglo-Saxon countries (the United States, the United Kingdom, Canada and Australia)[4] it is somewhat higher than in several continental European economies.

Generally speaking, the countries with relatively higher ratios and in the Anglo-Saxon group have experienced the faster increases during the past decade.[5, 6] The United States does not seem to fit this pattern clearly; the size of the rise, however, is somewhat underestimated, as by end-1993 a considerable downward adjustment in indebtedness had already taken place.

2.2. Breakdown by Recipients: Households and Businesses

The breakdown of total credit into the amounts received by households and businesses may help to cast light on the relative incidence of monetary policy on the two sectors. Both the level and, above all, the structure of indebtedness of the two categories of borrower are generally quite different, not least in terms of contract characteristics such as maturity, adjustability of interest rates, marketability of the claims, collateral and control over the timing and size of disbursements.[7] Several factors underlie such differences: the use of the funds (primarily housing expenditure and consumer credit for households vs. short-term and long-term capital needs for businesses), the size of the borrowing units, the sources of repayment, the information available about reimbursement capabilities, the ease of access to alternative funding sources, the sophistication of cash-flow management and targeted government policy in the pursuit of economic and social objectives. The differences in contract terms can affect the responsiveness of spending decisions to changes in monetary conditions as well as the specific channels of transmission.[8] Housing expenditure, for instance, is typically a component of aggregate demand found to be comparatively sensitive to interest rate changes; mortgage debt accounts for the bulk of credit to the household sector in all countries.

A breakdown of credit between households and businesses is available for all countries. International comparisons, however, should take into account the lack of uniformity in the definition of the sectors. The main problem relates to the treatment of unincorporated businesses, sometimes included in the household sector[9] and for which data are not always separately available (Table 2).[10] The unincorporated sector will generally include a wide spectrum of borrowers, ranging from self-employed individuals to possibly comparatively sizable business units.[11] Given the heterogeneity of the grouping, the terms on which credit is obtained will differ considerably, in some cases being relatively close to households regarded as consumer units, in others to those of larger production units. In order to facilitate comparisons, in the following paragraphs separate figures for alternative definitions of the household and business sectors will be provided whenever possible.

The available information indicates that, narrowly defined ("consumers"), the household sector accounts for less than half of total credit outstanding in almost all countries (Table 2). The main exceptions are the United Kingdom (well over 50 percent), the United States and Canada (not much over 50 percent).[12] At the other end of the spectrum, the share of credit to the household sector is lowest in Italy and Japan, the two countries with the highest saving ratios, in the region of 15 percent. On average, the share appears to be higher in Anglo-Saxon countries than elsewhere.

The amount of credit absorbed by the unincorporated sector varies considerably across countries. It ranges from less than 10 percent in the United Kingdom, France and, probably, Sweden to almost 20 percent in the United States.[13]

As regards movements over time in the share of the various sectors, credit to households appears to have grown faster than that to the business sector in a majority of countries. Its share has tended to rise in those belonging to the Anglo-Saxon group; no clear pattern emerges elsewhere. The increase has been especially pronounced in Australia (broad definition).[14] By contrast, marked declines have taken place only in Germany and Sweden. A sharp fall in the share of credit to the unincorporated sector is apparent in the United States.

2.3. Breakdown by Suppliers: Credit Intermediaries Versus Markets

A stylised distinction is often made between credit provided through credit intermediaries, such as banks and other financial institutions, and through the money and capital markets. This distinction would be of no relevance to the transmission mechanism if borrowers were indifferent between the two sources of funds. Several factors, however, limit the substitutability between them. Some of these are of a legal and regulatory nature. For example, at least until recently, several countries have tended to impose restrictions on the development of firms' access to money and capital market financing. One reason is that it was felt that their expansion could either undermine the "effectiveness" of monetary policy, especially if exercised through direct controls on credit intermediaries, or interfere with credit allocation objectives.[15] Other factors are of a more fundamental character. In particular, the greater the need

Table 2. Breakdown by recipients: households and businesses (as a percentage of total credit).

	AU	AT	BE	CA	FR	DE	IT	JP	NL	ES	SE	CH	UK	US
						1993								
Households[a]	53	32	48	52	38	53	29	28	43	41	37	51[b]	59	53
Consumers	. .	32	. .	52	29	38	16	16[b]	43	31[b]	. .	51[b]	54[b]	53
Unincorporated	. .	—	. .	—	9	15[b]	13	12[b]	—	10[b]	. .[c]	—	5[b]	—
Businesses	47	68	52	48	62	47	71	72	57	59	63	49[b]	41	47
Unincorporated	—	. .	—	10	—	—	—	—	. .	—	—	. .	—	18
Total	100	100	100	100	100	100	100	100	100	100	100	100	100	100
						1983								
Households	42	27	40	44	41	60	30	23	44	32	49	56[b]	65	48
Consumers	. .	27	. .	44	. .	47	. .	13	44	15[b]	. .	56[b]	54[b]	48
Unincorporated	. .	—	. .	—	. .	13[b]	. .	10	—	17[b]	. .	—	11[b]	—
Businesses	58	73	60	56	59	40	70	77	56	68	51	44[b]	35	52
Unincorporated	—	. .	—	13	—	—	—	—	. .	—	—	. .	—	26
Total	100	100	100	100	100	100	100	100	100	100	100	100	100	100

Key to symbols (this and following tables): — = not applicable (given definition used in reply to the questionnaire) or non-existent; . . = not available. AU = Australia; AT = Austria; BE = Belgium; CA = Canada; FR = France; DE = Germany; IT = Italy; JP = Japan; NL = Netherlands; ES = Spain; SE = Sweden; CH = Switzerland; UK = United Kingdom; US = United States.

[a]Generally including non-profit-making institutions.

[b]Estimate.

[c]Some 7 percent of bank lending to households and businesses.

for ex ante screening and ex post monitoring on the part of the lender because of the nature of the borrower or the use of the funds, the greater is the likelihood that the finance will be provided by a credit intermediary and take the form of a non-marketable loan rather than tradable securities. The main reason is that it is difficult credibly to transfer the information on which the transaction is based to other potential lenders, which limits the marketability and liquidity of the claim.

Given these possible limitations on substitutability, regardless of their origin, supply conditions impinging on the provision of the two basic forms of finance cannot be disregarded. And to the extent that monetary policy instruments have a differential impact on the two, they will also be of relevance to the transmission mechanism. For example, ceteris paribus, the poor state of banks' balance sheets in the United States in the late 1980s–early 1990s is widely believed to have blunted the expansionary impact of cuts in policy rates; but the problem would presumably have been more severe in the absence of well-developed securities markets, through which other, less constrained lenders could directly meet the higher demand for funds.

It is not straightforward to make propositions of general validity regarding the relationship between the degree of development of disintermediated finance across countries and the likely strength of the response of the economy to monetary policy impulses. Much will depend on the factors explaining the comparative size of the markets in specific cases. Nevertheless, on balance, compared with loan ("customer") markets, in securities ("auction") markets interest rates typically adjust faster[16] and investors are less willing to temporarily insulate borrowers from adverse changes in economic conditions. This is especially so when loan markets are characterised by close relationships between lenders and borrowers. On both grounds, therefore, securities markets would ceteris paribus tend to strengthen the impact of monetary policy.

Table 3. Breakdown by instruments: loans and securities[a] (as a percentage of total credit).

	1993[b]		1983[c]			1993[b]		1983[c]	
	Loans	Securities	Loans	Securities		Loans	Securities	Loans	Securities
AU	88	12[d]	84	16	JP	90	10	96	4
AT	98	2	97	3	NL	97	3	96	4
BE	93	7	88	12	ES	91	9	90	10
CA	83	17	83	17	SE	96	4	95	5
FR	85	15	92	8	CH	95	5	..	..
DE	94	6	98	2	UK	81	19	97	3
IT	95	5	93	7	US	80	20	83	17

In this and subsequent tables figures may not add up to 100 percent because of rounding.
[a]Excluding trade credit.
[b]Sweden and Switzerland: 1992.
[c]Italy: 1989; Australia: 1988; Belgium and Sweden: 1982.
[d]Including short-term securities (bank bills) held by OFIs (17 percent); including also those held by banks (21 percent).

Confirming widely held views, the available data indicate that securities generally make up a larger share of overall credit in Anglo-Saxon countries than elsewhere (Table 3). The quantitative significance of securities is highest in the United States and, surprisingly, the United Kingdom,[17] where they account for close to one-fifth of overall credit.[18] It is lowest in Austria, where less than 2 percent of overall credit takes this form. In addition, the above statistics probably underestimate the gap between the two groups of countries, since in several non-Anglo-Saxon economies the main issuers tend to be public sector enterprises, whose behaviour is likely to be less responsive to economic incentives and constraints.

As regards changes over time, the picture is mixed. In some countries there has been a considerable rise in the share of securities, most notably in the United Kingdom, Japan, France, Germany and the United States. Elsewhere, the share has mostly remained broadly unchanged or has even declined. At this level of aggregation at least, the figures suggest that often-heard claims of a pronounced *generalised* trend towards disintermediation of credit institutions do not appear to be justified.[19] Nor do the statistics point to any marked tendency towards convergence between Anglo-Saxon and other countries.[20]

2.4. Breakdown by Suppliers: Banks Versus Other Intermediaries

As regards the implications of the structure of credit for the transmission mechanism, it is not clear whether the distinction between banks and other financial intermediaries is of much interest. Conceptually, the specificity of "banks" has traditionally been regarded as deriving mainly from the liabilities side of the balance sheet, i.e. their ability to issue means of payment or short-term deposits. By contrast, the characteristics of credit contracts that may be relevant are captured only to a limited and varying extent by the dividing line between banks and other institutions. This is true, for example, for maturity, the adjustability of interest rates, the degree of reliance on private information and the illiquidity of the instruments. Nor can the incidence of direct controls be regarded any longer as a significant discriminating factor. And with the broader process of financial liberalisation, legal and regulatory differences between several types of loan-granting institution have been eroded, although long-standing distinctions are still easily traceable in the composition of their balance sheets, especially for those involved in the housing credit market. In fact, probably the main reason why the bank/non-bank division is of interest from the present perspective is essentially practical: the authorities often have more detailed information about whatever institutions they define as "banks", not least because of the special attention paid to them is the context of prudential regulation and supervision.

These ambiguities are clearly reflected in Table 4, which reports the breakdown of total loans between banks and other institutions found in the replies to the questionnaire. In countries with a long-standing universal banking tradition (Germany, Switzerland, Austria and the Netherlands), or in those that have recently enacted the

Table 4. Loans from banks and other financial intermediaries.

	Banks	OFIs	Banks	OFIs	Banks	OFIs	Banks	OFIs
	1993[a]		1983[b]		1993[a]		1983[b]	
	percent of total loans				percent of total credit			
AU	65	35	48	52	57	31	41	43
AT	99	1	97	3	97	1	94	3
BE	90	10	84	16	84	10	74	14
CA	60	40	58	42	50	33	49	35
FR	74/85[c]	26/15[c]	70/88[c]	30/12[c]	63/72[c]	22/13[c]	64/80[c]	27/11[c]
DE	89	11	84	16	84	10	82	16
IT	89	11	89	11	85	10	83	10
JP	54	46	45	55	49	42	44	53
NL	73	27	66	34	71	26	64	32
ES	91	9	98	2	82	8	88	2
SE	39	61	57	43	37	58	54	41
CH	81	19	81	19	77	18	81	19
UK	56/92[d]	44/8[d]	56/95[d]	44/5[d]	45/75[d]	36/6[d]	54/93[d]	43/5[d]
US	50	50	66	34	40	40	54	28

[a]Sweden and Switzerland: 1992.
[b]Australia: 1988; Belgium and Sweden: 1982; Italy: 1989.
[c]If specialised credit institutions are classified as banks.
[d]If building societies are classified as banks.

EC legislation setting out the contours of the single market in financial services, "banks" account for the bulk of lending; the main institutions excluded are certain specialised lenders (e.g. "Bausparkassen" in Germany), life assurance companies and pension funds. These are particularly important in Switzerland, where they account for one-fifth of total credit. In the Anglo-Saxon countries, Japan and Sweden the banks' share is considerably smaller, but even then there is a degree of arbitrariness in the classification.[21] In the case of the United Kingdom, for example, the share would not be much different from that in continental European countries if building societies were classified as "banks".

2.5. Breakdown by Maturity: Short-Term Versus Medium and Long-Term

The term to maturity is one of the key characteristics of a debt contract. Ceteris paribus, the shorter the maturity of an instrument, the greater is the scope for lenders and borrowers to alter the terms on which they transact funds, ranging from pricing to availability: at maturity new contracts must be entered into. As a result, ceteris paribus, the shorter the maturity of the contract, the higher is the speed with which the terms on which credit is granted can respond to monetary policy impulses. This is especially significant when policy changes have not been anticipated and hence have not been taken into account when entering into the transactions.

Two important qualifications, however, are in order. First, strictly speaking the term to maturity determines the *maximum* interval between the setting of contract terms: contracts may be renegotiated and often contain clauses that allow for the revision of certain terms either at the discretion of one of the parties or according to predefined rules. Early repayment and interest rate adjustment clauses are obvious examples. A correct picture of the room for response to monetary policy must also take such aspects into account (see below). Second, at any given point in time it is the *residual* rather than the *original* maturity of debt contracts that best captures the longest re-setting interval. Except for ad hoc surveys, the available information relates to original maturity.

Table 5. Breakdown by maturity: short-term versus medium and long-term[a] (as a percentage of total credit).

	1993[b]		1983[c]			1993[b]		1983[c]	
	s-t	m&l-t	s-t	m&l-t		s-t	m&l-t	s-t	m&l-t
AU[d]	40	60	38	62	JP	30	70	39	61
AT	27	73	25	75	NL	17	83	21	79
BE	23	77	. .	. .	ES[e]	40	60	. .	. .
CA	19	81	24	76	SE	29	71	38	62
FR	17	83	20	80	CH[d]	22	78	24	76
DE	16	84	19	81	UK	31	69	46	54
IT	51	49	53	47	US	15	85	18	82

Key to symbols (in this and following tables): s-t = short-term; m&l-t = medium and long-term.
[a]Short-term: up to one year (Italy: up to 18 months; Netherlands: up to two years).
[b]Sweden and Switzerland: 1992.
[c]Australia: 1988; Sweden: 1982; Italy: 1989.
[d]Excluding certain non-bank financial institutions (Australia: 11 percent of total credit in 1993).
[e]Excluding foreign currency loans.

Table 5 shows the breakdown of credit into short-term and medium and long-term. In almost all cases short-term is defined as credit with an original maturity of up to and including one year; the exceptions are Italy (eighteen months) and the Netherlands (two years). With the partial exception of Canada, it also includes various forms of revolving credit, such as advances on credit accounts and overdraft facilities. The breakdown is generally more accurate for continental European countries;[22] estimates play a greater role elsewhere, especially for non-bank financial intermediaries.

The figures suggest that medium and long-term credit accounts for well over half of total credit almost everywhere. The only exception is Italy, where it is just about half. The share is especially high in most of the countries with a long-standing universal banking tradition (typically around 80 percent or higher), which are also those that have enjoyed historically lower inflation rates. Elsewhere, it is also relatively high in France, Canada and the United States, although in Canada the medium-term component appears to be comparatively large, partly owing to the treatment of revolving credits. In no small measure the relatively high US figure reflects the breadth and depth of the corporate bond market.

Medium and long-term securities in fact account for the bulk of debt securities in

Table 6. Breakdown by maturity according to type of instrument[a] (as a percentage of each category of instrument).

	Loans				Securities			
	s-t	m&l-t	s-t	m&l-t	s-t	m&l-t	s-t	m&l-t
	1993[b]		1983[c]		1993[b]		1983[c]	
AU	38	62	36	64	52	48	47	53
AT	27	73	26	74	—	100	—	100
BE	23	77	. .	. .	12	88	—	100
CA	16	84	22	78	32	68	29	71
FR	17	83	21	79	16	84	—	100
DE	16	84	20	80	5	95	—	100
IT	54	46	57	43	—	100	—	100
JP	32	68	41	59	11	89	—	100
NL	17	83	22	78	5	95	. .	. .
ES	41	59	. .	. .	40	60	14	86
SE	29	71	40	60	22	78	4	96
CH	23	77	24	76	—	100	. .	. .
UK	38	62	47	53	3	97	—	100
US	17	83	20	80	8	92	6	94

[a]Short-term: up to one year (Italy: up to 18 months; Netherlands: up to two years). See also the footnotes to Table 5.

[b]Sweden and Switzerland: 1992.

[c]Italy: 1989; Australia: 1988; Belgium and Sweden: 1982.

Table 7. Breakdown by maturity according to borrowing sector,[a] 1993[b] (as a percentage of each sector's borrowing).

	Households[c]		Businesses			Households[c]		Businesses	
	s-t	m&l-t	s-t	m&l-t		s-t	m&l-t	s-t	m&l-t
BE	7	93	37	63	JP	3	97	35	65
CA	4	96	35	65	NL	8	92	23	77
FR	4/8	96/92	22/27	78/73	CH	21	79	24	76
DE	6/10	94/90	21/22	79/78	UK	18	82	50	50
IT	22/41	78/59	57/56	43/44	US	9	91	19	81

No data available for Australia, Austria, Spain and Sweden.

[a]Short-term: up to one year (Italy: up to 18 months; Netherlands: up to two years). See also footnotes to Table 5.

[b]Switzerland: 1992.

[c]Belgium and the United Kingdom: broadly defined; France, Germany and Italy: narrowly/broadly defined respectively.

virtually all countries. The only exceptions are Australia (if bank bills are included) and Spain, where the commercial paper market is quite developed (Table 6).

Household debt is predominantly medium and long-term everywhere: mortgage debt is by far the largest component and consumer debt, with the exception of credit card and other personal credit line borrowing, is typically medium-term (Table 7). The maturity of business credit is comparatively shorter. Italy again stands out as the country with the highest share of short-term credit for both households and businesses. The United Kingdom follows close behind.

Since the early 1980s the share of medium and long-term debt has generally either remained broadly stable or risen slightly (Table 5). The increase appears to have been pronounced only in the United Kingdom and Sweden. In both cases, however, shortcomings in the assumptions underlying the estimates may be partly responsible. The broad, albeit mild, trend is probably associated with lower inflation and, in several cases, higher shares for real estate and household credit.

Box 1: Summary of replies on early repayment of medium and long-term loans*.

Australia:	Possible; penalties in some cases.
Austria:	Possible, but very difficult.
Belgium:	Possible but discouraged; penalties (e.g. 3–6 months' interest).
Canada:	Most business loans under credit lines repayable at no cost; residential mortgages at significant cost except at repricing intervals. Corporate bonds usually callable.
Germany:	Generally possible; plays little role; expensive penalties.
Italy:	Mortgage loans: possible; penalties. Consumer credit: possible; no penalties.
Japan:	Possible but not significant; penalties.
Spain:	Possible; fixed rate loans generally subject to penalties.
Sweden:	Possible; penalties.
Switzerland:	Generally possible; not common; penalties.
United Kingdom:	Possible; penalties (e.g. 6 months' interest for fixed rate mortgages).
United States:	Generally possible without penalty (home mortgage, consumer and bank business loans). No information about non-bank business loans. Corporate bonds usually callable.

*No available information for France and the Netherlands.

Available information on early repayment clauses and conditions is limited (Box 1). On the whole, however, it suggests that the above picture needs to be modified only slightly. In most countries advance repayment of fixed-term loans is possible but not common. Although this may partly result from the range of interest rate movements observed and repricing clauses (see below), it would appear that penalties and other administrative costs associated with early repayment typically make it uneconomical. In Austria advance repayment of fixed rate debt is very difficult or virtually impossible in practice. The main exception to this general pattern is the United States. Most business and consumer loans as well as home mortgages can be repaid early at par without incurring any penalty at the time of the switch;[23] refinancing of mortgages has been very common. This suggests that the relatively high share of long-term financing in the United States overstates the effective maturity of the contracts and understates the freedom to adjust terms. Comparatively high room for manoeuvre also appears to exist in Australia and Canada, where penalties apply only in some cases.[24]

2.6. Adjustability of Interest Rates

The extent to which interest rates are free to adjust to changing economic conditions is probably the most important dimension of the transmission mechanism. These movements translate into changes not only in the *marginal* cost of funding, but also, and perhaps more significantly, in the *cash flow and income* of agents. At least three aspects of credit contracts have a bearing on this issue: the (residual) maturity; explicit or implicit clauses allowing for the revision of interest charges; and the basis on which those revisions take place, notably any reference rates. A fourth aspect, viz. the actual frequency, intensity and speed of the adjustment of rates on new and existing contracts is of course of interest but less amenable to descriptive analysis; these aspects are discussed in Borio and Fritz (1995) with reference to short-term bank loan rates.

Conceptually, two polar cases may be distinguished. At one extreme, maturities are very short or, if long, interest rates are revisable at very frequent intervals and tend to move together with other short-term rates. At the other extreme, maturities are long and interest rates are fixed until maturity. Ceteris paribus, in the flexible, short-term interest rate economy the response of interest rates to changes in policy controlled rates is likely to be faster and more intense; the variations in the short-run marginal cost of funding, income and cash flows would be correspondingly larger. This tends to front-load or accelerate the impact of monetary policy. Admittedly, the response to the change in the *marginal* cost of funds may arguably not be very different in the two economies to the extent that it depends on views about the *persistence* of the change. Nevertheless, cash flows would respond more quickly and intensely, reacting directly to the interest rate change rather than indirectly to any induced effect of policy on output and prices. The difference in the pattern of responses between the two stylised cases increases with the size of outstanding indebtedness and, at least for a policy tightening, with the skewness in its distribution: owing to the risk of default, the effect on highly indebted agents may be disproportionate. It may also depend on the extent to which indebtedness is concentrated among agents who, by their nature, are likely to face greater limitations on their access to external funding. Households and small firms are typical examples.

Building on the previous information on maturities and given other data limitations, it seems reasonable to adopt two complementary measures of the adjustability of interest rates on outstanding contracts. The first defines as adjustable rate all

Table 8. Adjustability of interest rates in the mortgage market[a] (approximate percentage shares/existence).

	AU	AT	BE	CA	FR	DE	IT	JP	NL	ES	SE	CH	UK	US
Adjustable[b]	>90	25	maj. of free	100	5[c]	90	75	60	>90	80	10	70	90	15
Indexed[d]	—	. .	—	—	5[c]	—	75	} 60	—	80	—	—	small	15
Reviewable[e]	>90	. .	—	—	—	>45[f]	—		. .	—	10	70	>80	—
Renegotiable[g]	—	. .	maj. of free	100	—	<45	—	—	. .	—	—	—	small	—
Fully fixed	<10	75[h]	rest[i]	0	95	10[j]	25	40[k]	<10	20[l]	90	30	10	85
Memorandum items:														
Percent adjust. ≤ 1 year	*>90*	*≤25*	*0*	*60*	*95*	*>45*	*75*	*60*	. .	*80*	*10*	*70*	*90*	*15*
Percent s-t rate related	*>90*	*0*	*0*	*60*	*0*	*<30*	*≤75*	*0*	*≈0*	*<10*	*10*	*0*	*90*	*15*
Main s-t rate	*3-mth*	—	—	*1-year*	—	. .	*6-mth*	—	—	. .	*6-mth*	—	*3-mth*	*1-year*

[a]Rough estimates based on various sources of information.

[b]In contrast with the remaining tables, adjustable rate debt is here defined as debt with rates that are not *fully* fixed, regardless of the length of the adjustment intervals.

[c]Only loans granted by some specialised private lenders (since 1988) and certain subsidised loans.

[d]The contract specifies the rate for the adjustments.

[e]The lender retains discretion over the timing and size of the adjustments (possibly between certain limits).

[f]'Commercial', savings and cooperative banks only.

[g]Adjustment of rates at fixed intervals specified in the contract.

[h]The whole of the subsidised sector.

[i]Including all the subsidised sector.

[j]Bausparkassen; mortgage banks also have some small amounts outstanding.

[k]A fraction of the lending by the House Loan Corporation.

[l]Almost all the subsidised sector, including the Banco Hipotecario de España and a fraction of the lending by deposit-taking institutions.

Sources: Central banks and European Community Mortgage Federation.

those debt instruments that are short-term or medium and long-term with rates *adjustable at no longer than one-year intervals*. The second adds to short-term instruments those which are medium and long-term with rates which tend to behave like *short-term rates*. In general, the interval of adjustment is likely to be a good guide to the flexibility of the interest rate charged: if, say, the interest rate is reviewed at yearly intervals, the setter need not take into account expected changes in reference rates over longer horizons. In some cases, however, this is not true: interest rates may be revisable at any time at the discretion of the lender but be de facto set in relation to rates or combinations of rates that themselves behave like longer-term ones.[25]

Despite the comparatively broad categories chosen, the available information on the adjustability of interest rates is very limited. What follows is largely based on estimates made on the basis of the nature of the business and samples of institutions. Care should therefore be taken when comparing the results: even if point estimates are given, in most cases there is significant uncertainty surrounding them.[26] The possibility of making comparisons over time is extremely limited.

A useful starting-point is the mortgage market: it accounts for a sizable share of medium and long-term lending, especially for the household sector; available information is somewhat greater; and it is there that the distinction between the two measures of adjustable rate contracts is most important. Several points emerge from a brief overview of the characteristics of mortgage contracts summarised in Table 8.

First, rates fixed *for the whole duration of the contract* are generally not common. The exceptions are Austria, France, Sweden and the United States, where the share ranges from 75 to over 90 percent. The option of refinancing without incurring penalties in the United States, however, qualifies the extent to which debt charges are truly fixed, i.e. unresponsive to broader interest rate changes. Elsewhere, the provision of fixed rate financing appears to derive from a combination of state involvement (subsidies), stable long-term funding sources and penalties for early repayment.

Second, there exist three types of variable rate loan depending on the nature of the contract.[27] With *reviewable rate* loans the lender retains the discretion to adjust the rate at any time and is not tied to any particular formula. Such loans are the norm in Australia, the United Kingdom and Switzerland, and seem to be common in Germany.[28] With *renegotiable rate* loans, standard in Canada and actively used in Belgium and Germany, rates are subject to renegotiation at contractually fixed intervals.[29] With *reference rate* or *index-linked* loans, widespread in Italy and Spain, the rate varies in relation to some other rate according to an explicit formula specified in the contract.

Third, the share of loans whose rate is adjustable *at no longer than one-year intervals* (the first measure) is very high (at least 70 percent but even 90 percent or more) in countries where reviewable rate loans are standard (Australia, the United Kingdom and Switzerland) and only somewhat lower (70–80 percent) where index-linked ones are the norm (Spain and Italy). It is also comparatively high in Canada (around 60 percent of residential mortgages), the only country where the periodicity of the adjustment for renegotiable rate loans is short, and in Japan.

Table 9. Breakdown by type of interest rate: adjustable and fixed,[a] 1993[b] (as a percentage of total credit).

	Short-term	Adjustable medium and long-term		Predominantly fixed		Total[c]
		(a) ≤ one year	(b) at s-t rate	(a) > one year	(b) at m. and l-t rate	
Australia	40	26	26	34	34	100
Austria	27	47	> 0	26	<73	100
Belgium	23	21	21	56	56	100
Canada	19	40	40	41	41	100
France	17	27	27	57	57	100
Germany	16	>23	23	<62	62	100
Italy	51	22	≤22	26	≥26	100
Japan	. .	>35[d]	35[d]	<65	65	100
Netherlands	17	> 8	8	<75	75	100
Spain	40	24	3	36	57	100
Sweden	29	6	6	65	65	100
Switzerland	22	52	8	25	69	100
United Kingdom	. .	73[e]	73[e]	27	27	100
United States	14	20	20	66	66	100

[a]See Table 5 for maturity definitions and sectoral coverage.

[b]Sweden and Switzerland: 1992.

[c]Short-term plus adjustable and predominantly fixed in categories (a) and (b) respectively.

[d]Short-term plus corresponding adjustable rate medium and long-term component. Since the source of information is different from that of the maturity table, maturity is shown as not available.

[e]Short-term plus adjustable rate medium and long-term.

Fourth, in a number of countries the share of loans at a rate that moves in line mainly with short-term rates (the second measure) is considerably lower than might be inferred from the periodicity of adjustments. This is especially true of Switzerland, Spain and Japan; it also applies to a lesser extent to Germany and Austria. In Switzerland and Germany this reflects the stable long-term sources of funding. In Spain it results from the choice of reference rate, typically itself the rate on medium-term mortgages applied by a group of institutions. This suggests that the purpose of indexation in Spain is not primarily protecting lenders against adverse movements in funding costs. The situation is similar in Japan, where a large proportion of total mortgages have rates which are adjusted generally twice a year, but are linked to long-term rates.[30]

Finally, the short-term interest rate to which the adjustments in mortgage rates are predominantly related varies across countries. Its maturity is especially short in the United Kingdom and Australia (three-month); it appears to be considerably longer-term in the majority of other countries (often a one-year rate).

Table 10. Breakdown by type of interest rate according to borrowing sector[a], 1993[b] (as a percentage of each sector's borrowing).

	AU	BE	CA	FR	DE	IT	JP	NL	CH	UK	US
Households:[3]											
Short-term adjust. m & l-t:		7	4	4	6	22/41	. .	8	21		9
(a) ≤ one year	77	11	49	9	>30	37/28	69[d]	>0	56	90	25
(b) at s-t rates		11	49	9	30	≤37/28	17[d]	0	8		25
Predominantly fixed:											
(a) > one year	23	82	48	87	<64	41/31	31	<92	23	10	66
(b) at m & l-t rates	23	82	48	87	64	≥41/31	83	92	71	10	66
Total[c]	100	100	100	100	100	100	100	100	100	100	100
Businesses:											
Short-term adjust m&l-t		37	35	22	21	57/56	. .	23	24		19
(a) ≤ one year	40	30	31	34	>19	20/20	>38[d]	>14	48	48	15
(b) at s-t rates		30	31	34	19	≤20/20	38[d]	14	8		15
Predominantly fixed:											
(a) > one year	60	33	34	44	<60	23/24	<62	<62	28	52	66
(b) at m & l-t rates	60	33	34	44	60	≥23/24	62	62	68	52	66
Total[5]	100	100	100	100	100	100	100	100	100	100	100

No data available for Austria, Sweden and Spain. There are indications, however, that the pattern in Spain is probably similar to those in France and Belgium.

[a]See Table 5 for maturity definitions and coverage.

[b]Switzerland: 1992.

[c]Australia, Belgium and the United Kingdom: broadly defined. Italy: households narrowly and broadly defined respectively.

[d]Short-term plus corresponding adjustable rate medium and long-term component. Since the source of information is different from that of the maturity table, maturity is shown as not available.

[e]Short-term plus adjustable and predominantly fixed in categories (a) and (b) respectively.

Turning next to total credit, Table 9 provides some very rough estimates of its breakdown between adjustable and fixed rates. The table provides estimates for the two definitions of variable rate debt; for simplicity, however, what follows focuses only on variable rate debt at short-term rates, i.e. short-term maturity plus medium and long-term at short-term rates (i.e. short-term plus adjustable medium and long-term on definition (b) in the table).

Subject to the qualifications outlined above, the share of variable rate credit appears to be especially high in the United Kingdom and Italy, at close to 75 percent. It is also relatively high in Australia (about two-thirds). At the other end of the spectrum, variable rate debt related to short-term rates appears to be lowest in the Netherlands (around one-quarter), Switzerland and Germany (around one-third). It is of a similar order of magnitude in the United States and, possibly, Sweden and Japan.

A rough, still very preliminary breakdown between households and businesses is available for fewer countries. Given the assumptions required to obtain it, it should be treated with even greater caution than the estimates relating to total credit.

In Anglo-Saxon economies the share of predominantly fixed rate debt of the household sector appears to be of a similar order of magnitude (United States and Canada), or even lower (Australia and the United Kingdom) than for the business sector (Table 10). This results mainly from the conjunction of the characteristics of the mortgage market and a sizable stock of outstanding fixed rate long-term securities. By contrast, and for much the same reasons, in continental European countries the household share of predominantly fixed rate debt is typically considerably larger than for the business sector. Germany and Switzerland seem to be two exceptions, in that the orders of magnitude appear to be similar. This may partly be due to the inaccuracy of the estimates made.[31]

Despite the considerable variation across countries, the share of medium and long-term debt at predominantly fixed rates of the household sector is generally around 50 percent or higher. It is significantly lower only in the United Kingdom and Australia.

The equivalent share for the business sector generally ranges between one and two-thirds. As might be expected, the share tends to be comparatively high where it is so also in the aggregate. Some exceptions exist, however, mirror-imaging the polarisation of the composition of household debt. The share is quite low in Belgium and, to a lesser extent, in France; it appears to be relatively high in Australia.[32, 33]

A rough estimate of the breakdown of total loans between banks and other lending institutions according to the flexibility of interest rates charged is presented in Table 11. Confirming a priori stylised views, it indicates that the share of predominantly fixed rate medium and long-term lending is comparatively high (around 50 percent or more) in several countries with a long-standing tradition of universal banking, such as Germany, the Netherlands and Switzerland.[34] It is also of a similar order of magnitude in Belgium and, interestingly, the United States. Elsewhere, it is generally lower.

The breakdown of credit between fixed and adjustable rate may give an incom-

Table 11. Breakdown by type of interest rate according to loan-granting institutions[a], 1993[b] (as a percentage of total lending by each category of institution).

	AU	AT	BE	CA	DE	IT	JP	NL	ES	SE	CH	UK	US
Banks:													
Short-term adjust. m & l-t:	43	28	26	26	18	57	. .	24	42	70	29		20
(a) ≤ one year	28	48	25	44	27	22	>57[c]	>11	28	0	51	85	15
(b) at s-t rates	28	>0	25	44	27	≤22	57[c]	11	5	0	11		15
Predominantly fixed:													
(a) > one year	29	24	49	30	55	21	<43	<65	29	30	20	15	64
(b) at m & l-t rates	29	<72	49	30	55	≥21	43	65	33	30	60	15	64
Total[d]	100	100	100	100	100	100	100	100	100	100	100	100	100
OFIs:													
Short-term adjust. m & l-t:	24	0	0	0	0	27	. .	0	24	3	0		14
(a) ≤ one year	37	0	0	56	>0	40	>14[c]	>0	0	10	70	≥90	30
(b) at s-t rates	37	0	0	56	0	≤40	14[c]	0	0	10	0		30
Predominantly fixed:													
(a) > one year	39	100	100	44	<100	33	<86	<100	76	87	30	≤10	56
(b) at m & l-t rates	39	100	100	44	100	≥33	86	100	76	87	100	10	56
Total[4]	100	100	100	100	100	100	100	100	100	100	100	100	100

No data available for France.

[a]See Table 5 for maturity definitions and coverage.

[b]Sweden and Switzerland: 1992.

[c]Short-term plus corresponding adjustable rate medium and long-term component. Since the source of information is different from that of the maturity table, maturity is shown as not available.

[d]Short-term plus adjustable and predominantly fixed in categories (a) and (b) respectively.

Box 2: Procedures to alleviate the burden of interest rate adjustments[a]

Australia:	Maturity adjustment for housing loans common. No information on other loans.
Austria:	Floors and caps for loans related to money market rates.
Belgium:	*Generally none; some cases of interest ceilings.
Canada:	Maturity adjustment in the case of some mortgages.
France:	*Duration adjustment in some cases (e.g. new formulae by specialised mortgage companies).
Germany:	*Some smoothing possible; recently loans with interest rate caps on offer.
Italy:	*Maturity adjusted only exceptionally.
Japan:	Not significant.
Netherlands:	*Maturity adjusted only in some cases.
Spain:	Maturity adjustments not normal practice.
Sweden:	Maturity adjustments used very sparingly.
United Kingdom:	Building societies may adjust maturity if the borrower is in difficulty.

[a]No available information for Switzerland and the United States. Responses to the questionnaire and additional information on the mortgage market obtained from the EC Mortgage Federation (denoted by an asterisk).

plete picture of the sensitivity of borrowers' cash flow to interest rate changes in at least three cases. First, as already discussed, where agents have the option to repay early without incurring penalties. Secondly, when lenders offer mechanisms to help insulate their customers from "excessive" interest rate movements, a typical example being maturity adjustments aimed at smoothing total servicing payments. The information available suggests that these are especially common in Australia, of some quantitative significance in Canada but of less relevance elsewhere, including the United Kingdom;[35] in general, where present, they tend to apply mainly to housing loans (Box 2). Finally, borrowers may actively use derivatives to alter the characteristics of their interest rate risk profile. Derivatives are primarily employed by large companies, routinely by those with access to the international markets. They have long been a significant risk-management tool especially in the United States and other Anglo-Saxon countries. Because of the dearth of data, however, it is difficult to determine their impact on the aforementioned stylised findings.

2.7. Non-Price Restrictions on Credit Extension: Collateral

The extent to which lenders can influence the timing and amount of credit extensions other than through the interest rate (and related fees) is another dimension of the transmission mechanism of monetary policy, sometimes discussed under the umbrella term of "credit availability". One possibility is setting non-price terms in the contracts; the most common of these is collateral. A second, complementary one is simply to retain discretion over the timing and amount of credit supplied on any given interest and non-interest terms and to ration credit. Rationing can easily result from regulatory controls on interest rates or quantities.[36] but it can also occur in their absence: given limited information about the characteristics of individual borrowers and insufficient control over their behaviour, restricting the amount supplied may be necessary to provide the lender with an adequate ex ante return on the funds granted.

Straightforward statistical information on non-interest rate terms is very hard, and in some cases impossible, to obtain. As regards the quantitative significance of rationing, it may be reasonable to presume that regulation-induced rationing is unlikely to play a significant role nowadays following the general relaxation of restrictions on credit institutions' balance sheets and interest rates. It may have survived in the housing sector in some countries; even so, the general expansion of the unconstrained finance segment limits further its macroeconomic significance. Rationing which is not due to regulation is even harder to measure.[37] By contrast, collateral terms are somewhat more amenable to statistical documentation.

Collateral may matter in the context of the transmission mechanism for at least two reasons. First, for a *given set of characteristics of the borrowers*, changes in monetary policy may have an impact on the collateral terms required by lenders at any given interest rate. Tougher/easier collateral requirements can be one way of helping to restrict/encourage credit growth. Second, and more importantly, for any *given set of terms called for by lenders*, monetary policy may have an effect on the characteristics of borrowers. Directly, via changes in the interest rates, and indirectly, via induced changes in output and prices, it can have a significant influence not only on the likelihood of default of borrowers but also on the value of the collateral at their disposal. In general, the collateral channel would tend to reinforce the impact of policy. Higher policy rates, for instance, would lead ceteris paribus to a deterioration in the creditworthiness of lenders and a decline in the value of collateral taking the form of financial and real assets. This in turn would reduce the availability of credit at any given interest rate.

On a priori grounds, the first channel, felt through altered conditions in the supply of credit, may be expected to be effective primarily when banks' freedom to adjust interest rates is constrained or when monetary policy results in changes in banks' balance sheets that alter their incentive or ability to take on risks. A possible example would be the interaction of a policy tightening with a weak capital position of the institutions and a competitive or political environment hostile to sizable increases in interest rates. Elements of such a scenario have clearly been present in those countries where there have been concerns about a credit crunch, notably Anglo-Saxon ones. More generally, however, unless the balance sheet of lenders is especially vulnerable or policy is implemented through direct controls, this channel is unlikely to be important.[38]

By contrast, the second channel, that operating via induced changes in the characteristics of borrowers, is likely to be more important. Ceteris paribus, those features of the financial structure that raise the sensitivity of the borrowers' probability of default to changing monetary conditions should also tend to heighten the quantitative significance of this channel; the level and skewness of indebtedness is but one ex-

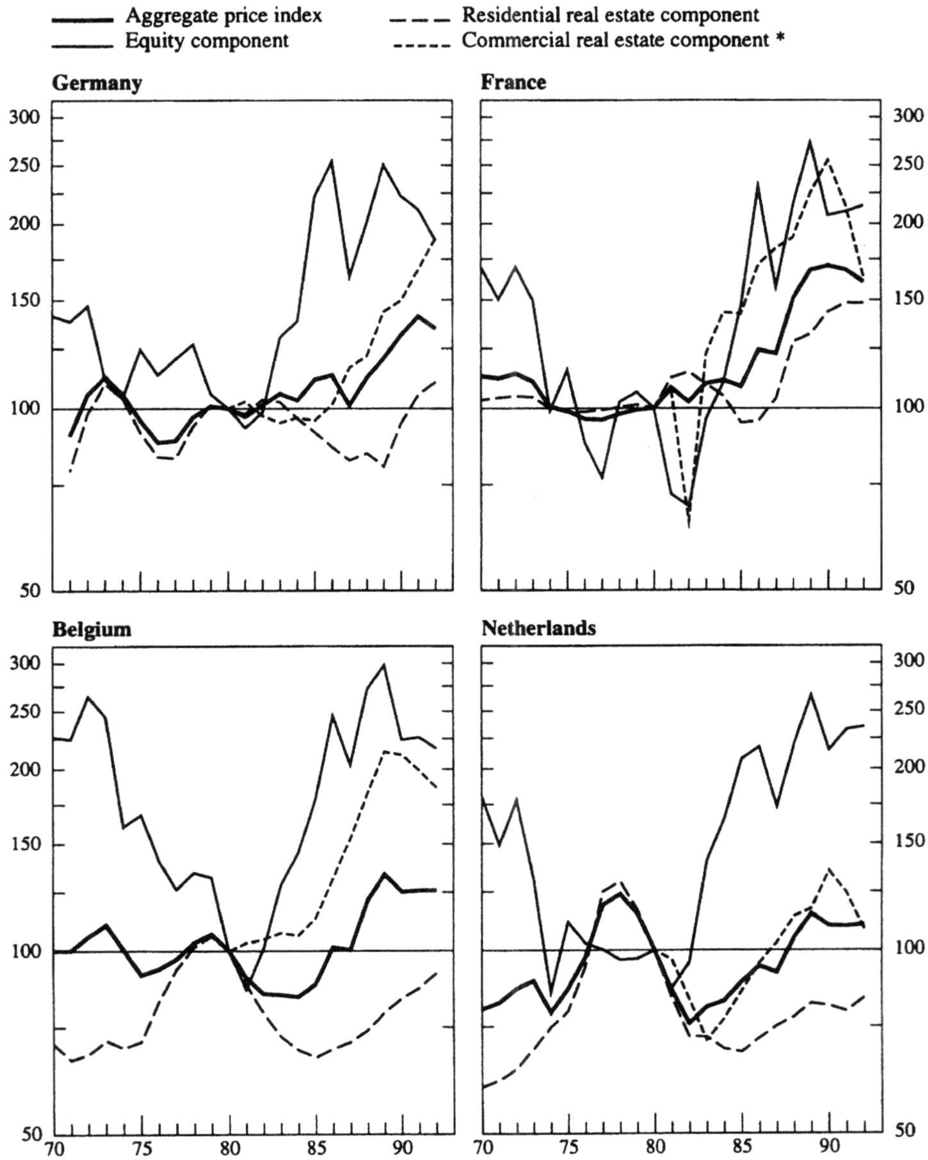

Note: The real aggregate asset price index is a weighted average of equity and residential and commercial real estate price indices deflated by consumer prices. The weights are based on the composition of private sector wealth.

* Index not shown for the above countries and Norway in the 1970s as it is proprietary information.

Source: Borio et al. (1994).

Figure 1. Real asset prices: aggregate and components.(1980 = 100; semi-logarithmic scales.)

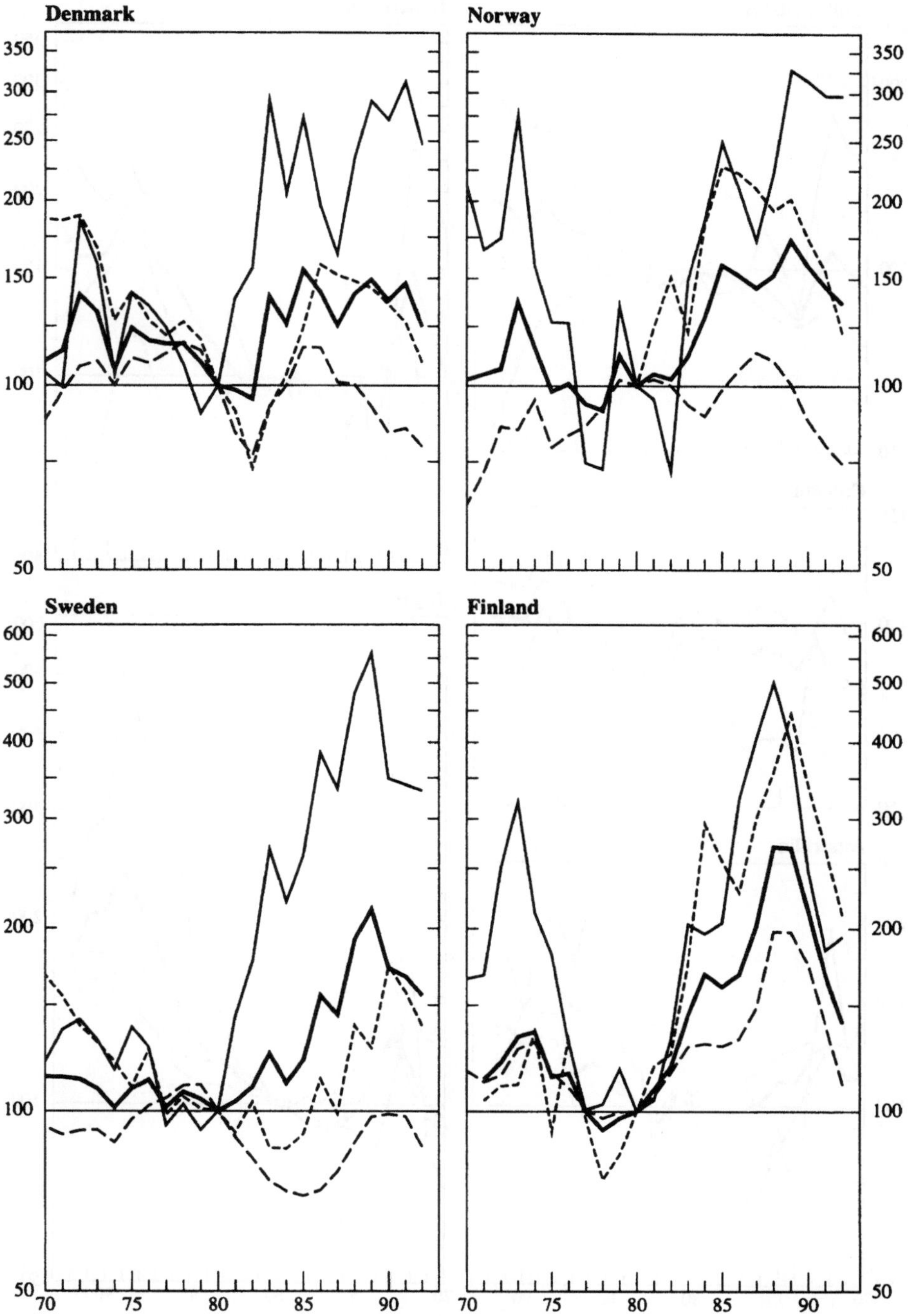

Figure 1. (Continued.)

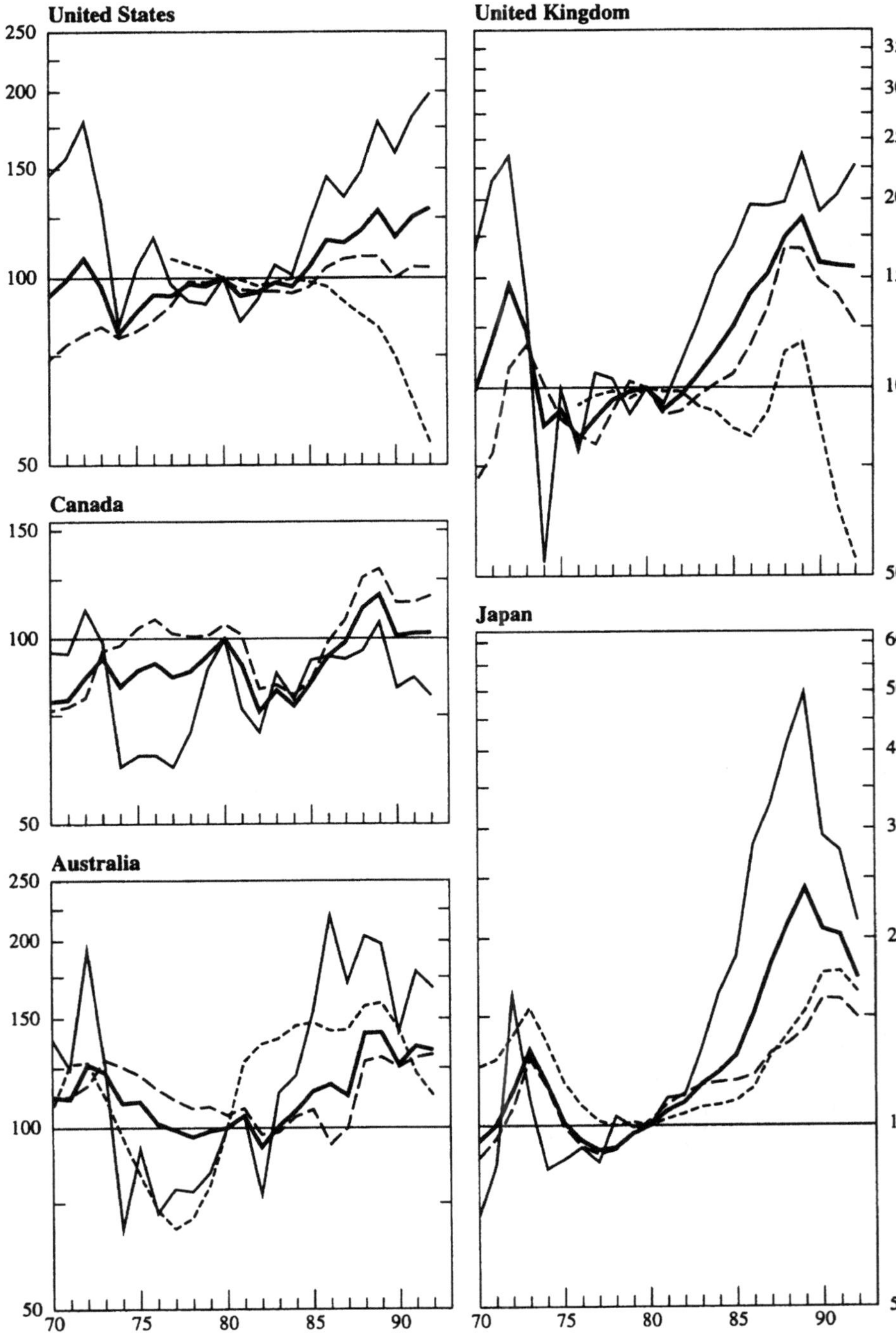

Figure 1. (Continued.)

Table 12. Collateralisation of loans (as a percentage of each category of institution's lending).

	AU	AT	BE	CA	FR	DE	IT	JP	NL	ES	SE	CH	UK	US
							1993[a]							
Banks	. .	70	. .	90	. .	v. high	66	68[c]	. .	33[d]	. .	86	. .	63
Real estate	48	31	26	43	44	30	45[b]	28[c]	36	32[d]	. .	81	32	56
Other	. .	39	. .	47	. .	. .	21[b]	40[c]	. .	1[d]	. .	6	. .	7
OFIs	. .	. .	. .	90	. .	v. high	. .	. .	. .	37	100	42	. .	92
Real estate	9	. .	100	75	33	90	. .	. .	37	37	100	41	92	76
Other	. .	. .	. .	15	. .	. .	. .	. .	. .	. .	. .	1	. .	16
Total	. .	69	. .	90	. .	v. high	. .	. .	. .	34	. .	78	. .	78
Real estate	34	31	34	56	41	36	40	. .	36	33	>61	73	59	66
Memorandum item: *Real estate backing bank loans to businesses (percent)*	. .	*28*	. .	*4*[e]	. .	*27*	. .	*25*	*4*	*25*	. .	*73*	. .	*43*
							1983[f]							
Banks	. .	73	. .	. .	. .	v. high	61	61	. .	16[d]	. .	88	. .	60
Real estate	14	34	28	20	41	37	. .	24	38	. .[d]	. .	81	15	54
Other	. .	39	. .	. .	. .	. .	. .	37	. .	. .[d]	. .	7	. .	6
OFIs	. .	. .	. .	. .	. .	v. high	. .	. .	. .	48	100	44	. .	86
Real estate	9	. .	100	77	42	90	. .	. .	30	48	100	42	93	66
Other	. .	. .	. .	. .	. .	. .	. .	. .	. .	. .	. .	2	. .	20
Total	. .	71	. .	. .	. .	v. high	. .	. .	. .	21	. .	79	. .	69
Real estate	12	33	39	44	42	45	. .	. .	35	. .	>43	73	50	58
Memorandum item: *Real estate backing bank loans to business (percent)*	. .	*26*	. .	*1*	. .	. .	. .	*18*	. .	. .	. .	*73*	. .	*37*

[a]Sweden and Switzerland: 1992.

[b]For short-term credit banks (66 percent of total bank loans in 1993), for which accurate figures exist, the shares of real estate and other collateralised loans are 19 and 31 percent respectively. Rough estimate for long-term credit banks.

[c]Excluding trust accounts.

[d]Excluding official credit institutions, included among OFIs for present purposes (6 and 11 percent of total bank loans in 1993 and 1986 respectively).

[d]For all financial institutions, 10 and 7 percent in 1993 and 1983 respectively.

[e]Australia: 1988; Belgium and Sweden: 1982; Italy: 1989; Spain: 1986.

ample of this (see above and Kneeshaw 1995). The same is true of those features that magnify the valuation effect of monetary policy on collateral; an obvious candidate is the share of total credit backed by assets whose price is in principle quite responsive to interest rate changes, most notably real estate.

That this channel may indeed be quantitatively significant seems to be confirmed by the experience of several countries since the early 1980s. Major increases in asset prices, especially real estate prices (Figure 1), have typically gone hand in hand with a rapid expansion in credit, especially in several Anglo-Saxon and Nordic countries and also in Japan. This has at times appeared to generate a vicious circle. Higher asset prices relax credit conditions, which in turn pushes up prices further, an analogous process occurring in the downward direction but possibly amplified by defaults and bankruptcies.[39] Admittedly, collateral is only part of the story. Asset prices may simply be correlated with expectations regarding the prospects of the economy and contribute to the formation of views regarding returns on investments, factors which would normally affect lending decisions. Similarly, changes in the stance of monetary policy are only one possible reason for the observed credit expansion; deregulation has had a major independent effect. Nevertheless, it is equally difficult to argue that the valuation of collateral has played a minor role or that monetary policy has not been in part responsible for these developments, at least in those countries experiencing the largest movements.[40]

The very limited and preliminary information available on collateral is summarised in Table 12. Again, the figures should be treated with caution. In particular, it has as yet not been possible to establish the extent to which the information is comparable across countries owing to possible differences in definition and coverage.

For the countries for which information is available, the share of total loans backed by collateral is in the region of 70 percent or over. The only exception appears to be Spain, for which it is only one-third. The difference is such that it raises doubts about the comparability of the figures. As regards banks, the share is especially high in countries with a long-standing universal banking tradition and also in Japan and Canada; it is considerably lower in Italy and Spain.

Loans collateralised with *real estate* make up a least one-third of total loans in all countries. The share is exceptionally high in Switzerland, at around three-quarters; it is around 60 percent or over in most Anglo-Saxon countries and Sweden. Indications suggest that it may also be quite high in Japan. The pattern is similar as regards the banking sector. The extent to which these results owe to limitations in the coverage of the underlying statistics and methodology of estimation is unclear.[41]

Over time, the share of real estate backed loans has tended to rise, at times markedly, precisely in those countries where it is now comparatively high; it has remained broadly stable or fallen elsewhere. In most cases, these are also the countries where the interaction between asset prices and credit has caused greater concern. This finding lends some support to the hypothesis that collateral may have had a significant role to play in these developments.

Table 13. Credit denominated in foreign currencies.[a]

	Foreign currency loans				Foreign currency credit			
	1993		1983[b]		1993		1983[b]	
	Percent of total	Percent of business	Percent of total	Percent of business	Percent of total	Percent of business	Percent of total	Percent of business
AU	3	8	4	7	3	6	3	5
AT	6	8	. .	. .	5	8	. .	. .
BE	8	17	6	11	8	14	5	9
CA	5	13	8	17	10	21	12	22
FR	4	7	4	7	6	9	6	10
DE	1	1	0	1	1	1	0	1
IT	14	19	11	17	14	20	12	17
JP	4	. .	6	. .	8	. .	. .	. .
NL	4	6	2	4	3	6	2	4
ES	5	8	. .	. .	4	7	. .	. .
SE	9	15	11	23	10	16	13	25
CH	3	6	2	5	3	5	2	5
UK	5	19	9	26	4	11	8	24

No data available for the United States.

[a]The figures are only approximate because the coverage is not always complete. For more information, see Borio (1995).

[b]Australia: 1988; Austria: 1987; Belgium: 1982; Italy: 1989; Japan: 1988.

2.8. Credit Denominated in Foreign Currency

When borrowers obtain funds in foreign currency, the domestic currency equivalent of their average funding costs and debt burdens will subsequently depend on the actual path of the exchange rate and, if the borrowing is at variable rates, of foreign interest rates. If these variables do not follow their anticipated paths, the ex post cash flow, income and balance-sheet positions could differ substantially from the anticipated ones, thereby exerting a significant influence on lending, borrowing and spending decisions.[42] Thus, changes in domestic interest rates no longer have a *direct* effect on part of the indebtedness of residents, which comes to depend on foreign monetary conditions.[43] On the other hand, the importance of the exchange rate in the transmission mechanism is heightened.

The quantitative significance of this channel will depend, inter alia, on the size and distribution of the net positions of agents in foreign currency. At the aggregate level, a rather crude indicator is the share of foreign currency denominated credit in the total.[44] Though incomplete, the available information suggests that this share was typically of the order of 5 percent or less at the end of 1993 (Table 13). It was considerably higher, however, in Italy, Sweden and Canada.[45] In the two European countries, a significant rise took place in the years preceding the ERM crisis of

Table 14. Summary of findings[a] (scores on cardinal scale).

	AU	CA	UK	US	AT	BE	FR	DE	IT	JP	NL	ES	SE	CH
Total credit	2	2	3	3	1	1	1	3	1	4	3	1	4	4
Credit to households[b]	3	4	4	4	2	3	2	2	1	1	3	2	2	3
Securitised credit	3	4	4	4	1	2	3	2	1	2	1	2	1	1
Non-bank credit	3	4	4/2[c]	4	1	1	3/2[d]	1	1	4	2	1	4	2
OFI loans	4	4	4/1[c]	4	1	1	3/1[d]	1	1	4	3	1	4	2
Short-term credit	4	1	3	1	2	2	1	1	4	3	1	4	2	2
Adjustable rate credit[e]	4	3	4	1	1	2	2	1	4	1	1	2	1	1
households	4	3	4	2	. .	1	1	2	2–3	1	1	. .[f]	. .	2
businesses	2	4	3	1	. .	4	4	2	4	2	2	. .[f]	. .	1
Real estate collateral[g]	2	4	4	4	2	2	3	2	2	. .	2	2	4	4
Foreign currency credit[g]	1–2	3	1–2	. .	1	2	1	1	4	2	1	1	3	1

[a]Scores on a cardinal scale ranging from 1 ("comparatively very low") to 4 ("comparatively very high"). The key shares together with the corresponding ranges are shown in Box 1.

[b]Narrowly defined; where not available, based on likely size of the unincorporated sector.

[c]Excluding/including building societies from/in the definition of banks.

[d]Excluding/including specialised financial institutions from/in the definition of banks.

[e]Related to short-term rates.

[f]Probably similar to France and Belgium.

[g]Where no precise figures are available, the classification is only approximate.

autumn 1992,[46] as companies borrowed abroad to avoid high nominal interest rates at home and the exchange rate was under persistent upward pressure.

Box 3: Background information to Table 1.*

Total credit:	measure:	percentage of GDP.
	ranges:	≤ 90; 91–110; 111–130; > 130.
Credit to households:	measure:	share of credit to households (narrowly defined) in total credit.
	ranges:	≤ 25; 26–40; 41–50; > 50.
Securitised credit:	measure:	share of securities in total credit.
	ranges:	≤ 5; 6–10; 11–15; > 15.
Non-bank credit:	measure:	share of OFI loans plus securities in total credit.
	ranges:	≤ 20; 21–34; 35–49; > 49.
OFI loans:	measure:	share of OFI loans in total loans.
	ranges:	≤ 15; 16–25; 26–35; > 35.
Short-term credit:	measure:	share of short-term credit in total credit.
	ranges:	≤ 20; 21–29; 30–39; > 39.
Adjustable rate credit:	measure:	share of adjustable rate credit related to short-term rates (up to and including one-year maturity) in total credit.
	ranges:	≤ 40; 41–50; 51–60; > 60.
– Households:	measure:	share of that type of credit in total credit to households.
	ranges:	≤ 20; 21–40; 41–60; > 60.
– Businesses:	measure:	share of that type of credit in total credit to businesses.
	ranges:	≤ 35; 36–45; 46–55; > 55.
Real estate collateral:	measure:	share of loans backed by real estate collateral in total lending.
	ranges:	≤ 30; 31–40; 41–50; > 50.
Foreign currency credit:	measure:	share of foreign currency financing in total credit.
	ranges:	≤ 6; 7–9; 10–12; > 12.

*The ranges have partly been chosen with a view to avoiding bunching around thresholds.

3. Conclusion

Some of the main findings of this inquiry may be more easily summarised with the help of Table 14. The table highlights certain key characteristics of credit to the non-government sector. For any given characteristic, it assigns to each country a score ranging from 1 ("comparatively very low") to 4 ("comparatively very high"); [47] details on the measures and percentage brackets are shown in Box 3. As a heuristic device, Anglo-Saxon countries (the United States, the United Kingdom, Canada and Australia) are grouped together.

The corresponding groupings are useful in a number of respects. This is not so much true for the ratio of total credit to GDP:[48] Anglo-Saxon economies do all fall in the mid-range, but by implication other countries are either ranked above (notably Japan, Switzerland, Sweden and Germany) or below. It applies, however, to three ratios, all comparatively high in Anglo-Saxon countries, viz. the shares of credit to households, in the form of securities and granted by non-banks. The United Kingdom is the member of the group that fits least well, mainly because of the ambiguity in the definition of a "bank".[49] Similar definitional problems cloud the position of Sweden and Japan, otherwise more akin to that of countries in the non-Anglo-Saxon group.

As regards changes over time, a preliminary inspection hardly reveals a tendency towards convergence with respect to the aforementioned characteristics. The ratio of total credit to GDP has tended to grow comparatively fast in both Anglo-Saxon and other high-ratio countries. The polarisation of the share of credit going to the household sector has, if anything, increased. The share of securities in total credit has tended to rise in Anglo-Saxon countries;[50] with the exception of Japan, France and Germany, little growth can be detected elsewhere. That of "banks" has either remained broadly stable or fallen in the Anglo-Saxon group, and has risen or changed little in a majority of other countries; a sharp increase, though, can be observed in Australia, partly as a result of changes in the legal status of certain institutions.

The findings concerning convergence, in particular, should be treated with caution. The use of estimates at only two points in time may be misleading, not least because of the different cyclical positions of the economies. Similarly, comparing stock figures at ten-year intervals tends to understate the impact of more recent changes, which would be reflected primarily in flows. Nevertheless, the findings do suggest that convergence has primarily occurred in other dimensions. The most important one is the relaxation of direct controls and constraints on the balance sheets of financial institutions. This dimension, of great significance for the transmission of monetary policy, cannot be captured by the above statistics.

In fact, from the perspective of the transmission mechanism, most of the above findings, taken in isolation, are of moderate significance. The comparatively high share of credit to households in Anglo-Saxon and a few other countries suggests that the analysis of the impact of monetary policy should pay particular attention to this sector. At least for the Anglo-Saxon countries, this conclusion is reinforced by considering household sector debt in relation to income and assets (Kneeshaw 1995). A high share of disintermediated finance indicates that the relative characteristics of the supply of credit are likely to play a significant role. Although precise generalisations are difficult, on balance in securities markets interest rates typically adjust faster and investors are less willing to temporarily insulate borrowers from adverse changes in economic conditions. This suggests that, ceteris paribus, monetary policy may be more powerful in Anglo-Saxon countries.

Of greater interest is the maturity breakdown and, complementary to it, the degree of adjustability of interest rates on debt contracts. For present purposes, "variable" or "adjustable" rate debt has been defined to comprise debt on which interest rates are reviewable within one year (including, therefore, all short-term credit) *and* move primarily in relation to short-term rates. The second criterion is important because in a number of countries rates may be adjustable at any time or at short intervals but, mainly because of the sources of financing of institutions, they tend to behave more like long-term rates. This is the case, for example, in Switzerland, Spain, Japan and, to a lesser extent, Germany, especially in the mortgage market. On a priori grounds, one would expect that, the larger the share of variable rate financing, the stronger will be the cash-flow and income effects associated with monetary impulses. Moreover, as highlighted by the ERM crisis of 1992, the widespread use of variable rate financing can complicate the pursuit of exchange rate targets in the short run: it can speed up and amplify the transmission of higher short-term rates geared to defending the external value of the currency, a rather uncomfortable situation, especially in the presence of weaknesses in the balance sheets of both non-financial and financial sectors.

The available estimates are still rather tentative, at least with regard to adjustable rate financing. They suggest that the basic criterion chosen for classifying countries performs rather well in this case too, although subject to qualifications. Anglo-Saxon countries appear on average to exhibit comparatively high shares of short-term and variable rate credit. This is especially true for households. Indeed, in sharp contrast to most other countries, in all of them the share of household credit at variable rates appears to be at least roughly as high as that of the business sector, and considerably higher in the United Kingdom and Canada. The specificities of housing finance and the comparatively high share of fixed rate long-term securities are primarily responsible for this result.

A major exception to the aforementioned pattern is the United States. In terms of the share of both short-term and adjustable rate financing the country ranks very low, its characteristics apparently being considerably closer to those of, say, Germany and Switzerland. One important qualification is the ease with which agents can switch between variable and fixed rate debt. In contrast to most other countries, the *marginal* cost of switching is very low. Although agents may and often do pay up front for this flexibility, no pecuniary penalties attach to the early repayment of much of the debt at the time of the switch. This is true at least in the mortgage sector and for a sizable fraction of corporate bond financing, which is usually in the form of callable securities. The evidence indicates that early repayment is indeed quite common. A second qualification is that the use of off-balance-sheet instruments, notably swaps, for the management of interest rate risk exposures appears to be considerably more widespread than elsewhere. The quantitative significance of this factor, however, is much harder to assess.

Among non-Anglo-Saxon countries, one significant exception to the general pattern is Italy: its financial system exhibits the highest share of variable rate credit, possibly as high as around three-quarters. Admittedly, the definition of short-term credit for Italy extends to eighteen months. But the main reasons for this finding appear to be the exceptionally high share of current account, reviewable rate credit from banks and the size of the adjustable rate sector in the mortgage market.

Information on changes in the share of variable rate financing over time is extremely limited. Countries were able to provide estimates only for the present situation, and even then only very rough ones. Better data are available, however, on the maturity breakdown, a key element for calculating total adjustable rate debt. The share of short-term credit appears to have remained remarkably stable compared with the early 1980s, generally falling only slightly, by around 2–5 percentage points. The only two countries where a marked fall has been observed are Sweden and the United Kingdom; even so, this fall may be overstated by the assumptions underlying the breakdown. Far less is known about the evolution of the share of medium and long-term debt at adjustable rates. There are some indications that it has risen in certain segments, notably in the mortgage sector in those countries where variable rate lending was introduced only during the 1980s, typically as a result of deregulation. Sweden and Belgium are two such examples. By contrast, it appears to have fallen in the same sector in other countries, especially the United Kingdom and the United States. These few pointers, taken in isolation, would suggest a certain degree of convergence. They are not, however, sufficient to form an overall view of developments.

Interest rates, the "price" of credit, are but one, albeit the most important, factor influencing the response of agents to changing supply and demand conditions. A second dimension concerns those elements that affect, broadly speaking, the "availability" of credit.

Collateral is one of them. Changes in the value of collateral can affect the availability of credit for two reasons. Ex ante, they change the expected pay-off to lenders in the event that the borrower defaults. Ex post, they affect lenders' actual loss experience, influencing the terms on which they can in turn obtain funds and their perceptions of risk. The positive relationship between the value of collateral and credit availability can generate a self-reinforcing process, in both the upward and downward direction. Clear signs of this process were evident in several countries during the 1980s and early 1990s, especially in some Anglo-Saxon and Nordic countries and also in Japan: asset prices, notably real estate prices, went through a boom-bust cycle; easy access to credit gave way to concerns about a potential credit crunch. Ample credit availability was due in no small measure to structural developments, namely deregulation and heightening competitive pressures. But at least in those countries experiencing the largest asset price movements, it was also connected in part with comparatively easy monetary conditions. In general, the collateral channel would tend to reinforce monetary impulses: a tightening/easing of policy would be associated with downward/upward pressure on the value of collateral. The quantitative significance of this channel increases with the sensitivity of collateral values to interest rates and with the use of collateral in debt contracts.

Information on collateral is very limited. Fortunately, some data are available for the real estate component, a key one in the present context. Barring definitional problems, the evidence suggests that even here the distinction between Anglo-Saxon and other countries is quite useful. More importantly, it points to a considerable overlap between the set of countries where the interaction between asset prices and credit has been most pronounced and those where the share of real estate collateralised loans is highest or has risen most sharply. Three out of the four Anglo-Saxon countries exhibit comparatively high shares of total loans backed by real estate collateral; Australia appears to be an exception, being broadly in line with the rest. Outside this group, the share is very high in Switzerland and Sweden. No precise figures are available for Japan, but there are indications that the country may rank relatively high. Data for the early 1980s suggest that these countries and Australia are also the ones that have experienced the largest increase in the share over time,[51] whereas it has mostly remained broadly stable or fallen elsewhere. On the whole, the evidence lends some support to the view that the interaction between credit availability and collateral may have had a significant role in the aforementioned developments during the recent business cycle.

Explicit consideration of the currency composition of credit discloses an additional dimension of the transmission mechanism. Changes in domestic interest rates do not have a *direct* effect on the part of the indebtedness of residents denominated in foreign currency, which depends on foreign monetary conditions. On the other hand, the relevance of the exchange rate in the transmission mechanism is heightened, through its effect on the domestic currency value of outstanding debt. Proper assessment of the significance of this channel would call for a consideration of both assets and liabilities together with on and off-balance-sheet exposures. The data collected here look at only one, though important, side of the story but exclude credit received directly from non-residents unless it is in the form of securities (where available). Here, the basic criterion for classifying countries is of little help. Foreign currency denominated credit is typically of the order of 5 percent or less of total credit in most countries. It is considerably higher only in Italy and, to a lesser extent, Sweden and Canada.

In sum, three findings of this study merit particular attention. First, the share of securities in total credit is comparatively high in Anglo-Saxon countries. Second, most Anglo-Saxon countries are characterised by a relatively high share of adjustable rate credit. This is due primarily to the widespread use of adjustable rate mortgages by households. Outside the Anglo-Saxon group, the main exception is Italy; inside it, the United States. Third, the share of loans backed by real estate collateral appears to be comparatively high in most Anglo-Saxon countries. Elsewhere, it is very high in Sweden and Switzerland. There are also indications that the share is relatively high in Japan.

To varying degrees, the above characteristics tend to amplify the impact of monetary policy; they can therefore serve as a basis for a classification of countries in terms of the likely strength of the response of economic activity to changes in policy rates. Before doing so, however, it is worth considering certain additional findings of the other papers included in the broader joint BIS-central banks project.

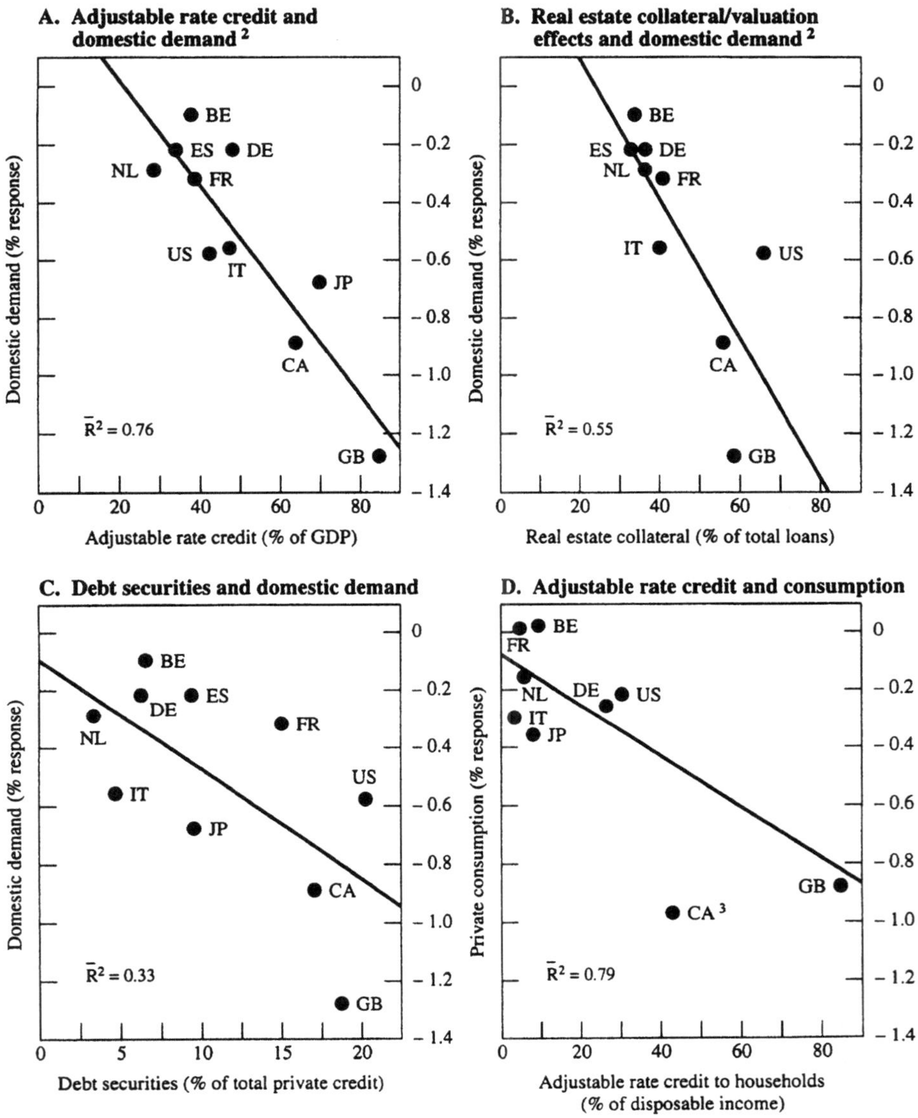

[1] Percentage point deviations from baseline in domestic demand and private consumption according to the simulations of national central bank models (100 basis points increase in policy rates maintained for two years). The deviations are measured in the second year following the tightening. For domestic demand, domestic channels only; the results are similar if real GDP or total domestic demand is used.

[2] Adjustable rate credit (percent of GDP) and real estate collateral (percent of total loans) jointly "explain" 86 percent of the cross-country variation in domestic demand.

[3] A dummy is added for Canada: consumption also includes residential construction and inventories.

Source: BIS (1995).

Figure 2. Financial structure and economic activity.[1]

On the basis of an examination of the whole balance sheets of households and businesses, Kneeshaw (1995) argues that valuation, income and cash-flow effects may be typically more powerful in Anglo-Saxon countries, Japan and Sweden. In particular, households in these countries are more heavily indebted and/or hold a larger proportion of their wealth in the form of assets whose price is highly interest rate sensitive and subject to large fluctuations, such as equity and real estate.[52] In addition, Borio and Fritz (1995) conclude that the adjustment of short-term bank loan rates to policy rates is faster in Anglo-Saxon countries, taken as a group, than elsewhere, although systematic differences largely disappear after one year. At one end of the spectrum, adjustment is full and immediate in the United Kingdom. By contrast, it is considerably slower in Germany and France.[53]

On balance, the foregoing evidence suggests that at one end of the scale the impact of monetary policy might be expected to be stronger in the United Kingdom, Canada and, to a lesser extent perhaps, Australia. In these countries the structure tends to speed up the adjustment of interest rates and amplify income/cash-flow and valuation effects. The United States could also belong to the same group, with question marks owing to the different degree of adjustability of rates on existing contracts. Outside this group, the impact might be expected to be comparatively high in Japan, reflecting mainly gross indebtedness levels and potential valuation effects. The position of Sweden appears to be similar. At the other end of the spectrum, most other continental European countries should rank comparatively low. Because of the exceptionally high share of adjustable rate debt, however, the response of economic activity could be stronger in Italy.

Interestingly, this ranking is broadly borne out by a simulation of national central bank econometric models (BIS 1995). Moreover, simple statistical exercises appear to confirm the relevance of financial structure (Figure 2). The reductions in economic activity following a standardised temporary tightening are greater in countries where adjustable rate credit is more important and where the share of lending backed by real estate[54] is higher. A similar, albeit weaker, relationship is also discernible with respect to the share of debt securities in total private sector credit. At the sectoral level, variable rate debt helps to explain differences in the behaviour of consumption.

The above findings hardly amount to conclusive evidence of the significance of financial structure. The elements of financial structure embedded in the models are rather crude.[55] Furthermore, econometric exercises based on common identifying assumptions failed to detect significant cross-country differences in the impact of monetary policy (Smets 1995), Gerlach and Smets 1995, and Tryon 1995).[56] Nevertheless, they do indicate that certain often neglected aspects of financial structure deserve considerably more attention than received hitherto.

Turning next to more general conclusions, this inquiry has revealed a significant gap in existing information about the characteristics of debt contracts. Some of these characteristics, such as the degree of adjustability of interest rates, are probably at the heart of the transmission mechanism of monetary policy. For the narrow purposes of this study, this dearth of information complicates an assessment of the margin of error surrounding the findings, especially as regards international comparisons. From a longer-term perspective, it raises the question of whether some effort on the part of the relevant national authorities to upgrade statistics in this area may not be justified.

As regards policy, two issues appear to merit further analysis. One is the extent to which differences in financial structure can complicate the pursuit of coordinated monetary policies internationally. Events in 1992 during the ERM turbulence are just the most conspicuous example of this. Looking ahead, structural differences also have potentially significant implications for the operation of monetary policy in the prospective EMU. A second issue pertains to the ultimate determinants of financial structure. Neither the present study nor the other contributions to the broader project make much of an attempt to explain the reasons for existing cross-country differences. An understanding of what lies behind them would clearly be of interest. It would cast light on the extent to which certain characteristics are likely to persist over time as well as on their probable future evolution. Above all, it would help to identify the extent to which certain features are, directly or indirectly, shaped by the course of monetary policy itself, most notably the average maturity and degree of interest rate variability of debt contracts.[57] This may not matter so much in the short run. It is, however, of considerable relevance in the long run to the extent that the monetary authorities have some preference for one set of financial arrangements over another.

Notes

1. That financial structure should affect the transmission mechanism of monetary policy in the first place is hardly a controversial claim. Financial structure would be irrelevant only in a world of perfectly competitive markets and perfect information; but then in such a world it would not be meaningful to talk about monetary policy at all: notions of "liquidity" and "money" would simply be artificial constructs devoid of any useful function. The harder empirical question which lies behind disagreements about the significance of financial structure is how far the theoretical paradigm can be pushed as a guide to actual behaviour, at least as a first approximation.
2. Borio (1995) contains considerably more information about the data used and lists the main assumptions underlying the estimates made.
3. In some cases the aggregate may not fully meet these criteria. The discrepancies would in any case be small.
4. The denomination "Anglo-Saxon" is simply used for want of a better term.
5. Unfortunately, the figures for Australia cannot illustrate the increase as the earliest observation relates to 1988.
6. The large increase in Germany is partly due to reunification.
7. What follows focuses exclusively on the characteristics of contract terms. Other factors are of course relevant to the assessment of the responsiveness of the two sectors to monetary policy impulses. Gearing ratios and the assets side of balance sheets are considered in Kneeshaw (1995).

8. A rapidly expanding literature on the relevance of liquidity constraints to expenditure and production decisions, for instance, is beginning to document these.
9. The sector comprising households narrowly defined and unincorporated businesses is sometimes referred to as the "personal" sector.
10. See Borio (1995) for more details.
11. Moreover, the size and composition of this sector will vary significantly across countries depending on the structure of production, legal, regulatory and tax factors impinging on the decision to incorporate, the precise statistical criteria adopted and the accuracy of reporting systems.
12. The very high Swiss figure may in part reflect the extensive use of housing credit at relatively attractive amortisation conditions: capital is never repaid while the borrower retains the benefits of the capital gain. Nevertheless, in relation to household income, indebtedness remains suspiciously high. See Kneeshaw (1995).
13. A second source of lack of uniformity in the breakdown of credit between households and businesses arises from the treatment of public sector enterprises. The available information appears to indicate that they are included in the business sector in most countries; the United Kingdom and Japan are two notable exceptions. Given the share of credit absorbed by these companies, the main impact is likely to be on the relative size of the stock of debt securities outstanding (see below).
14. It also appears to have been very large in Spain (narrow definition), but the underlying estimates are very rough.
15. The former argument applies mainly to the development of money markets such as the commercial paper market, and the latter to that of longer-term capital markets.
16. On these issues, see Borio and Fritz (1995).
17. In the United Kingdom, this results from a recent sizable upward revision in total securities, accompanied by a more moderate downward revision in bank lending. Before the revision, the share of securities was less than 10 percent.
18. Securitised mortgages are not included in the above figures.
19. The picture may of course be somewhat different if specific sub-sectors, maturity brackets or periods are considered.
20. Certain caveats should be borne in mind when interpreting the above data. There is a grey area surrounding the stylised distinction between intermediated credit/loans, on the one hand, and market financing/securities, on the other. This in some instances affects the comparability of national statistics and may have a bearing on the transmission mechanism more generally. Two significant examples relate, respectively, to the treatment of private placements and the characteristics of commercial paper. For a detailed analysis of these, see Borio (1995), Alworth and Borio (1993) and Carey et al. (1993).
21. Borio (1995) contains the details on the classification used.
22. Except for Sweden and Switzerland.
23. In addition, most corporate bonds are callable.
24. A more complete picture should also take into account additional refinancing costs in all countries.
25. Similarly, and regardless of loan maturity, rates may be revisable but very unresponsive to other rates generally. This appears to be the case, for example, with rates on credit card lending in the United States and also elsewhere. No such adjustment, however, has been made in the estimates shown below.
26. See Borio (1995) for details on the methodology adopted in the various countries.
27. These definitions follow those adopted by the European Community Mortgage Federation.
28. The freedom to adjust rates may, however, be constrained. For example, in Germany, legal provisions require that any change be objectively fair in accordance with commercial practice, pursuant to the relevant case law.
29. In Germany, where it is widespread, this type of loan is assimilated to a fixed rate loan.
30. The rate on adjustable rate loans of the Housing Loan Corporation is based on the funding rate set by the Government, in turn moving in line with the coupon rate on new issues of ten-year govern-

ment bonds. These rates have a cap of 5.5 percent. The adjustable rate on bank housing loans is set in relation to the long-term prime rate, itself linked to the five-year interest-bearing debenture issued by three long-term credit banks. Since early 1994 a new type of bank housing loan, related to the short-term prime, appears to have been allowed.

31. In the case of Germany, the result is driven by the assumption that three-quarters of consumer credit is at variable rates.
32. The share also appears to be comparatively high in the United Kingdom upon the upward revision in the stock of debt securities.
33. There are indications that the overall pattern in Spain may be quite similar to those in France and Belgium.
34. No comparable results are available for France. However, some indications can be drawn from a 1992 central bank survey of nine large banks, accounting, respectively, for half and around one-third of bank and total loans to households and businesses. The survey indicated that 52 percent of total French franc denominated loans to these sectors were at predominantly fixed rates. The definition of variable rate used covered two sets of contracts: (i) those with a residual maturity of at most three months; (ii) those at rates adjusted with a periodicity not exceeding one year. Class (ii) corresponds to one of the definitions used in the text.
35. In the United Kingdom, however, it has been estimated that around 40 percent of all mortgage borrowers are on an annual review scheme, whereby the interest charges are changed only once a year. Any underpayment arising from differences in the timing of the review of interest rates and interest charges is capitalised and added to the interest payments in the following periods.
36. Or, indeed, other non-interest terms such as collateral requirements.
37. Borio (1995), however, provides information on the share of credit supplied under credit lines, taken as a sign of the *absence* of rationing.
38. The replies to the questionnaire, couched more broadly in terms of non-interest conditions, were not inconsistent with this view. They did acknowledge, however, a widespread lack of information, in part due to problems in identifying the direct impact of policy.
39. The process can of course interact with the supply factors discussed in the context of the first channel.
40. For a detailed cross-country analysis of these issues, see Borio et al. (1994).
41. See Borio (1995) for details on the series used and estimates made.
42. If the financial intermediaries themselves take open foreign currency positions, there may also be an independent effect on the supply of credit through unexpected deteriorations or improvements in the intermediaries' profit and loss accounts and balance sheets.
43. Of course, the *ability* to invest and borrow freely in foreign currencies raises also the usual questions about the autonomy of national monetary policies even if the *actual size* of the positions is not large.
44. Note that since the present aggregate excludes credit obtained abroad unless it is in the form of securities, it tends to *underestimate* overall foreign currency credit. For complementary indicators, see Kneeshaw (1995).
45. However, some other countries could fall within this category, depending on the share of foreign-denominated securities, for which figures are sometimes not available.
46. Because of the dates chosen, this is only partly reflected in the above figures.
47. The terms "comparatively high/low" should be interpreted loosely. The ranges were not chosen so as to necessarily split the set of countries in the sample into two groupings of equal size.
48. Total credit is defined to exclude any direct credit from non-residents (unless in the form of securities) as well as trade credit and direct lending from the government sector.
49. It would have been true also for the share of securities in total credit (score = 2) had it not been for the very large recent upward revision. See below.
50. The short sample period makes it difficult to compare Australia, where it has fallen, with the rest.
51. The exception is Switzerland, where the share has remained broadly stable.
52. Similarly, Kneeshaw finds little evidence on convergence over time between the two groups in

terms of the above characteristics. Since the early 1980s, some convergence seems to have taken place with respect to the gearing of the gearing sector, which has grown faster in Anglo-Saxon countries, where it was lower.

53. The estimation is carried out on monthly data. The broad picture does not appear to have changed substantially over time.
54. This variable can act in part as a proxy for more general valuation effects.
55. The most significant correspondence is that short-term rates are allowed to affect expenditures in those countries where adjustable rate credit is predominant, notably in the United Kingdom, Canada and Italy.
56. Gerlach and Smets (1995) adopt a Structural VAR approach; Tryon (1995) simulates the Multi-country Model of the Federal Reserve. See the introduction to BIS (1995) for reasons why, on balance, the results on national central bank models may be the more appropriate benchmark.
57. For instance, a preliminary analysis confirms that the share of adjustable rate debt tends to be higher in countries with a track record of comparatively high inflation.

References

Alworth, J.S. and C.E.V. Borio (1993), "Commercial Paper Markets: A Survey", *BIS Economic Papers*, 37, Basle, April.

Bank for International Settlements (1995), "Financial Structure and the Monetary Policy Transmission Mechanism", *C.B. 394*, Basle, March.

Borio, C.E.V., N. Kennedy and S.D. Prowse (1994), "Exploring Aggregate Asset Price Fluctuations Across Countries", *BIS Economic Papers*, 40, Basle, April.

Borio, C.E.V. and W. Fritz (1995), "The Response of Short-Term Bank Lending Rates to Policy Rates: A Cross-Country Perspective", *C.B. 394*, Bank for International Settlements, Basle, March.

Borio, C.E.V. (1995), "The Structure of Credit to the Non-Government Sector and the Transmission Mechanism of Monetary Policy: A Cross-Country Comparison", in *Financial Structure and the Monetary Policy Transmission Mechanism, C.B. 394*, Bank for International Settlements, Basle, March (Reprinted as *BIS Working Paper*, 24, April 1995).

Carey, M., S. Prowse, J. Rea and G. Udell (1993), "The Economics of the Private Placement Market". *Staff Study*, 166, Board of Governors of the Federal Reserve System, Washington D.C.

Gerlach, S. and F. Smets (1995), "The Monetary Transmission Mechanism: Evidence from the G-7 Countries", in *Financial Structure and the Monetary Policy Transmission Mechanism, C.B. 394*, Bank for International Settlements, Basle, March (forthcoming *Working Paper*, BIS).

Kneeshaw, J.T. (1995), "Non-Financial Sector Balance Sheets in the Monetary Policy Transmission Mechanism", in *Financial Structure and the Monetary Policy Transmission Mechanism, C.B. 394*, Bank for International Settlements, Basle, March (Reprinted as BIS *Working Paper, 25*, April 1995).

Radecki, L.J. and V. Reinhart (1994), "The Financial Linkages in the Transmission of Monetary Policy in the United States", in *National Differences in Interest Rate Transmission, C.B. 393*, Bank for International Settlements, Basle.

Smets, F. (1995), "Central Bank Macroeconometric Models and the Monetary Policy Transmission Mechanism", in *Financial Structure and the Monetary Policy Transmission Mechanism, C.B. 394*, Bank for International Settlements, Basle, March (forthcoming *Working Paper*, BIS).

Swank, J. (1993), "A Survey of Bank Behaviour in the Netherlands", *Domestic Research Department Series*, 71, De Nederlandsche Bank, June.

Tsatsaronis, C. (1995): "Is there a Credit Channel in the Transmission of Monetary Policy? Evidence from Four Countries", in *Financial Structure and the Monetary Policy Transmission Mechanism, C.B. 394*, Bank for International Settlements, Basle, March (forthcoming *Working Paper*, BIS).

Who Needs Bands? Exchange Rate Policy before EMU*

TAMIM BAYOUMI
International Monetary Fund

ABSTRACT

Two issues are discussed. The first is which countries might benefit from entry into EMU before the millennium. Germany and her immediate neighbors appear the most likely to benefit; however, our knowledge is too uncertain to say whether all, some, or no countries would reap economic benefits. The second issue is how to avoid exchange rate instability in the transition to EMU. Experience from earlier exchange rate regimes suggests that an early announcement the parities at which different currencies would enter EMU could reduce such instability if governments were willing to accept the required limitations on domestic policies.

1. INTRODUCTION

The signing of the Treaty on European Union (the Maastricht Treaty) on 7 February, 1992 marked an important shift in European monetary arrangements. While discussion of a single currency in western Europe was certainly not new even in official circles (the Werner report in 1970 also presented a path for moving to a single currency), none of the earlier plans had been agreed by the relevant national governments. By providing a specific path to European monetary union (EMU), the Maastricht Treaty moved the discussion of a single European currency from the theoretical to the practical. Events since the signing of the Treaty, however, in particular the exchange rate problems experienced by a number of countries in 1992 and 1993, have made the exchange rate path to EMU envisioned in the Maastricht Treaty less tenable. At the same time, many of the deadlines in the Treaty are fast approaching, making this an opportune time to reconsider issues associated with the transition to EMU.

*The author would like to thank, without implication, the participants in the workshop and in particular the two discussants Messrs. Gros and Icard, for useful comments. Thanks are also due to Barry Eichengreen, Donogh MacDonald, and Peter Clark for their comments. This paper does not necessarily reflect the views of the IMF.

Koos Alders, Kees Koedijk, Clemens Kool and Carlo Winder (eds.), Monetary Policy in a Converging Europe, pp. 117–129.

This paper focuses on two such issues. First, which countries might benefit from entry into EMU before the millennium, and second, which exchange rate policies are best designed to move countries with individual national currencies to currency union. There is a considerable amount of empirical work assessing the suitability of EU members for joining EMU, looking at both the potential benefits and costs. The benefits include the gains from lower transactions costs, greater competition, and more integrated markets. The costs come from the loss of monetary independence, and largely depend upon the size and correlation of underlying disturbances and the availability of mechanisms other than the exchange rate for alleviating country-specific disturbances. Rather than adding to this already extensive literature, this section of the paper will provide a brief personal interpretation of the existing evidence. The basic message is that while we know a significant amount about the relative suitability of different countries for EMU, we know relatively little about whether all, some, or no countries would benefit economically from joining a single currency before the millennium. The reason for this is that our knowledge of the benefits from EMU, which are an essential part of any assessment of the economic value of membership, is too uncertain to provide the required level of precision.

The second issue that is discussed is the exchange rate path to EMU. A path to EMU was initially provided by the Maastricht Treaty. As far as monetary policy and exchange rates were concerned, the Treaty outlined a gradual evolution from a system of limiting exchange rate fluctuations between member countries to the permanent and fixed exchange rates implied by a single currency using the existing Exchange Rate Mechanism (ERM). In the autumn of 1992 and 1993, however, the ERM came under market pressures which forced the United Kingdom and Italy to suspend membership, the Nordic currencies to abandon their unilateral pegs against the ECU, Portugal, Spain, and Ireland to devalue their parities, and the remaining participants to widen the bands of fluctuation of their currencies from 2¼ percent to 15 percent.

These developments are inconsistent with the gradual evolution of the exchange rate regime from one of narrow exchange rate bands to a single currency, as envisioned in the Maastricht Treaty.[1] The second part of the paper is devoted to discussing possible exchange rate arrangements in the transition to EMU. The focus is on the experience of earlier exchange rate regimes, with particular emphasis on the pre-1914 gold standard. These experiences suggest that one potential way of moving to EMU whilst avoiding the financial instability of 1992 and 1993 would be to announce the rates at which different currencies would enter EMU. Such a policy would only work, however, if governments were willing to accept the limitations on domestic policies implied to validate such a commitment.

2. Who Should Join EMU Initially?

There has been a considerable empirical literature on the suitability of EMU for the potential participants.[2] Its guiding principle has been the theory of optimum currency areas, initiated by Mundell (1961). Mundell noted that membership in a currency union involved certain benefits and costs. The benefits involve reduced transaction costs between participants in a currency union, which provide direct benefits through the reduced level of resources required to provide such services and indirect benefits through more scope for economies of scale, greater competition, and more integrated markets.

The costs involve the loss of monetary sovereignty. A single currency implies that monetary and exchange rate policy can no longer be directed exclusively at domestic concerns, but must take account of the situation of all members of the union. As long as all regions face the similar disturbances, the costs will be relatively small. However, if members face dissimilar underlying disturbances, the potential costs will be higher. In addition to the nature of the underlying disturbances, the costs depend upon the effectiveness of non-monetary mechanisms such as labor mobility (as emphasized by Mundell 1961) or fiscal policy to alleviate the impact of these disturbances. They also depend upon the likely effectiveness of monetary and exchange rate policies in the same context.[3]

The empirical literature on the potential costs of EMU has come to some relatively consistent conclusions. In terms of underlying shocks, the current members of the EU appear to include a core of countries involving Germany and her close partners (the Netherlands, Belgium, Luxembourg, France, Denmark, Austria, and possibly Sweden) who face relatively similar underlying disturbances and are hence relatively good candidates for EMU. By contrast, there also appears to be a periphery of countries which have relatively idiosyncratic underlying disturbances, and who are probably less well suited for a single currency.[4] The United Kingdom, Greece, Finland, and Portugal are fairly clearly members of this group, while Italy and Spain are most probably also in this category.

To the extent that other factors have differing implications within the EU they tend to reinforce this distinction between the core and the periphery. Intra-regional trade is highest within the core countries, making them the better candidates for a monetary union using the McKinnon criterion. Labor mobility, which provides one mechanism for adjusting to idiosyncratic disturbances, appears to be generally lower within individual EU countries than it is in the United States, an economic area of similar size and wealth but with an already existing currency union. Labor mobility between EU countries is even lower, and appears likely to remain so given large linguistic and cultural differences. Federal fiscal transfers, which provide another way of adjusting to disturbances, are projected to remain relatively unimportant in the EU,[5] although domestic fiscal policy may accomplish the same role.

The literature on the potential benefits from EMU is somewhat less developed than that on the potential costs.[6] The direct benefits from lower transactions costs, which come from freeing the resources required for transactions between currencies (including customs inspections) are relatively small, less than 1 percent of GDP. Any major gains from EMU are therefore likely to come from the indirect benefits of economies of scale, greater competition, and more integrated markets.[7] It is also relatively clear that the benefits are going to be largest, at least in the short-run, for smaller economies and those which are most involved in inter-regional trade. Unfortunately, it is impossible to provide any accurate estimates of the size of these indirect benefits. Supporters of EMU, not surprisingly, believe the gains could be large, with EMU providing increasing benefits over time as greater competition and more integrated markets move the EU onto a higher growth path. Skeptics, equally predictably, are unconvinced. We simply do not have enough information to be able to differentiate between these very different analyses.

This uncertainty about the economic gains from EMU make it very difficult to assess which countries would benefit from membership before the millennium. The analysis of the costs makes it fairly clear that the Germany, France, the Benelux countries, and Austria are better placed to join a currency union than the remaining countries in the EU. These countries are also likely to receive relatively large benefits because of their high level of regional trade. However, whether entry into EMU would provide net economic benefits for all members of the EU, for only the core countries, or for no countries at all is still an open question.

The impact of EMU would not, of course, be limited to the economic sphere. The greater economic integration that would be generated by a single currency would also have profound social and political implications. Given the uncertainties involved in assessing the net economic benefits of a single currency, these non-economic considerations may well be play a relatively important role in the decision of whether or not to join the single currency. In any case, the rest of this paper puts aside the question of the initial composition of EMU, and moves on to the issue of what exchange rate policies might best be pursued to avoid financial instability in the transition from several national monies to a single currency.

3. From National Monies to Emu

The Maastricht Treaty envisaged a gradual transformation from the existing ERM arrangements to a single currency through a number of stages. Stage One involved an expansion of Structural Funds, greater surveillance of national policies by the Commission, and the participation of all currencies in the narrow bands of the ERM (which were, at that time, plus or minus 2¼ percent of the central parity). Stage Two, to start in 1994, involved a strengthening of EU surveillance over macroeconomic policies and the creation of the European Monetary Institute (EMI) as a precursor to the European Central Bank which would control the money supply in EMU. The EMI could "formulate opinions or recommendations on the overall orientation of monetary policy or exchange rate policy", however, national authorities would retain power over monetary decisions. Finally, Stage Three, which would start sometime between 1997 and 1999, would involve the creation of the European Central Bank (ECB) and the eventual replacement of national monies by the ECU.

Entry into Stage Three of EMU required a country to comply with a number of convergence criteria involving fiscal deficits, government debt, inflation, interest rates, and the exchange rate. The criteria were to be initially evaluated during 1996, at which point the initial membership of EMU could be decided. While all of these convergence requirements were important, this discussion will focus on the exchange rate requirements.

One exchange rate requirement was that the currency was a member of the ERM, and that in Stage Two its exchange rate was fluctuating within the normal exchange rate bands, which were universally interpreted at the time as being the "narrow" 2¼ percent bands used by long-term ERM members in 1991. Another requirement was that a country had not experienced "severe tensions" or devalued its ERM exchange rate parity against any other member on its own initiative within the last two years. Since this criterion was most likely to be to be considered in mid-1996 it significantly limited the ability of individual governments who wished to join EMU from devaluing their central parity after mid-1994. However, these arrangements did not exclude all realignments after this time. Countries could revalue during Stage Two, or could change their parities at the initiative of others. More importantly, nothing was said to prevent a "last realignment" on the eve of Stage Three, just prior to entering into EMU.

The first requirement, that currencies were to join the narrow bands of the ERM, did not appear particularly onerous at the time of the Maastricht Treaty. With the accession of the pound sterling, peseta, and escudo to the Mechanism in 1989–90, every currency except the Greek drachma was already participating in the System (although sterling, the peseta, and the escudo were using the wider 6 percent bands). In addition, there had been no realignments of parities since 1987.[8] Within two years, however, market pressures significantly loosened the ERM arrangements and, to all intents and purposes, invalidated the original plan of moving gradually from the narrow ERM bands to EMU.

The problems began in the early autumn of 1992, after the Danish electorate rejected the Maastricht Treaty in a referendum in June and when opinion polls indicated that the French electorate might also reject the Treaty in their referendum later in the year. These developments created considerable doubt as to the future of the EMU project. This uncertainty rapidly became evident in exchange rate markets, where market pressures quickly mounted on those countries whose exchange rates and monetary policies appeared most out of line with domestic economic conditions.[9] These sustained pressures resulted in significant changes in the ERM. Over the course of the next three months the pound sterling and lira suspended their membership in the ERM, the peseta and escudo devalued their central rates, and several other currencies, most notably the French franc, came under significant pressure.[10] Outside of the ERM itself, the Nordic currencies were also forced to abandon their unilateral pegs against the ECU.

The remaining currencies entered a period of calm through early 1993. However exchange rate pressures recurred later in the year. As in 1992, these pressures appear to have been triggered by perceived tensions between the monetary policies required to maintain the exchange rate peg and the domestic economic situation. While a number of currencies were involved in this second round of market pressure, the focus was on the French franc. As in 1992, these market pressures eventually resulted in significant changes in the ERM. However, in this case it took the form of a widening of the intervention bands from 2¼ to 15 percent.[11]

The very wide latitude in exchange rates afforded by the new bands has in essence moved the ERM back to a system in which exchange rates are determined by market forces. The ERM currencies have generally remained reasonably close to their central parities in spite of the new exchange rate flexibility afforded by the wider bands, presumably reflecting market perceptions about the policies of member governments.[12] However, this should not obscure the fact that the exchange rate system within which these countries are currently operating is significantly different from the earlier one, with market forces playing a much more important role in day-to-day determinant of exchange rates under the new bands than under the old.

The new bands appear large enough that exchange rates could move a considerable distance from their equilibrium values. The exchange rate parity chosen by Great Britain in her disastrous decision to rejoin the gold standard in 1925 is generally estimated to have been overvalued by around 10 percent, implying that both the correct and incorrect parities could have fallen within the existing 15 percent ERM bands. Nor do market signals necessarily give the correct information in such situations. The appreciation of sterling prior to rejoining the gold standard was believed by Keynes (amongst others) to have reflected anticipation of the new regime, not fundamentals, a supposition supported by modern theory.[13]

The exchange rate tensions of 1992 and 1993 reflected many factors, of which the most important was the interaction between the macroeconomic consequences of German reunification and cyclical conditions in other European countries. Reunification of the eastern and western halves of Germany led to a significant expansion in domestic Germany demand, reflecting both the new investment opportunities for German business and the expansion of the fiscal deficit. High demand led to price pressures, which in turn caused the monetary authorities to raise interest rates. This forced the other members of the ERM to raise interest rates in order to maintain the exchange rate peg. However, this rise in interest rates was incompatible with the domestic needs of other countries in which domestic demand was already weak.

As this inconsistency between the external and domestic requirements of monetary policy became clear, market participants began to expect an ERM realignment.

Since any such realignment would involve a significant losses to anyone holding the devaluing currencies, they switched assets out of the weak currencies, a move which undermined the market exchange rate. In short, perceived tension in policies led to overwhelming market pressures for a change in the exchange rate.

The problems of the ERM in 1992 and 1993 have close parallels with the collapse of the Bretton Woods fixed exchange rate system in the early 1970s.[14] In both cases there was a significant shift in the macroeconomic policy of the center country, caused by the pressures of economic reunification in the case of Germany within the ERM and by the effects of the Vietnam war on the United States at the end of Bretton Woods. In both cases the other participants in the system were unwilling to change their macroeconomic policies to conform to this shift by the center country, or to allow exchange rate parities to be altered for fear of undermining confidence in the system. Finally, both crises occurred after a period of liberalization of international capital markets.

The fact that both the ERM and Bretton Woods ran into severe problems after a period when capital markets were liberalized has led some to argue that the real culprit is highly open international capital markets. In particular, Barry Eichengreen and Charles Wyplosz have drawn the lesson from the experience of the ERM in 1992–93 that capital markets need to be curtailed through capital controls during the remainder of Stage Two.[15]

Their argument is based on a model in which, with high capital mobility, market participants' beliefs about the exchange rate become self-fulfilling. If markets decide that an exchange rate is wrong, then the pressure against the authorities become so strong that the peg cannot be held regardless of whether the peg is fundamentally sound or not. The result is a world with multiple equilibria, in which governments are unable in impose any order on exchange rates. Even if a government is prepared to defend an exchange rate peg, the markets can overwhelm the barricades and sack the citadel.

Although appealing in some respects, I do not find this analysis fully convincing. The exchange rates which came under most pressure in both 1992 and 1993 were clearly those where the resolve of the government to raise interest rates appeared weakest. Since monetary and exchange rate policies are, in the end, simply different sides of the same coin, this implied an unwillingness to defend the exchange rate peg. It is noticeable that in those countries where the authorities were clearly prepared to defend the peg, most noticeably the Netherlands, the exchange rate came under little or no pressure throughout 1992–93. It appears difficult to square this observation with the notion that speculators were choosing exchange rates to "knock off" their pegs without regard to economic fundamentals.

To be fair, Eichengreen and Wyplosz recognize this point. Their argument is that if the exchange rate crisis had not occurred, the peg could have been maintained, implying a world of multiple equilibria. In the absence of private market activity, however, almost any policy can be maintained. It is always private individuals who undo inadvisable government policies, since the governments who have embarked on the policies presumably remain committed to them. At this level the difference between the multiple equilibrium explanation and the conventional one comes close to one of semantics.

What remains difficult to explain is why the mood of market participants changes so rapidly from one month to the next. It is clear that at some point actions becomes self-reinforcing. As pressure on an exchange rate mounts it becomes prudent for market participants who have not yet started to "speculate" to hedge their bets by liquidating their own holdings of that currency. This makes it difficult to predict exactly when a currency will come under pressure. I suspect that the answer to this question lies more in the area of social psychology than economics. But the observation that market behavior involves elements of herd behavior, which makes it almost impossible to predict what will happen from one day to the next, is very different from saying that markets were wrong, or that the original doubts about policies which create such pressures are unfounded.

At the same time, history provides a striking example of a successful fixed exchange rate regime in an environment of high capital mobility, namely the pre-1914 gold standard. During the heyday of the regime, which lasted for 34 years from 1879–1913, exchange rates between the major participants were unchanged. At the same time international capital markets were extremely open and net capital flows were large. While there are many differences between the nineteenth century and the present day, particularly in the role of government policy over the cycle, the fact that governments at that time were able to maintain fixed exchange rates for such a long period must put into question the notion that private capital flows inevitably destabilize a fixed exchange rate regime.

Economists who study international monetary arrangements characterize the different regimes according to their different "rules of the game".[16] During the gold standard, the rule was that full convertibility of the currency into gold (ie a fixed exchange rate) would be maintained except in the face of certain well defined events which were not under the control of the authorities, principally wars. In the face of such events the government was allowed to suspend gold convertibility, however they were expected to come back to the system *at the original gold parity*. As a result, even in countries where gold convertibility had been temporarily suspended, investors retained a belief that the value of their investment was secure in the long-run. In the nomenclature of game theory, the gold standard as a fixed exchange rate regime with well defined escape clauses.

The U.S. Civil War provides a good illustration of how the system operated. Gold convertibility was suspended soon after the beginning of the war (in January 1862) due in part to a run on the banks caused by government demand for specie. From then until 1879 the value of the currency (nicknamed greenbacks) was determined in private markets. The gold value of these greenbacks depreciated significantly during the war, falling at one point to around 40 percent of the pre-war value. After the war, the government did not rejoin the gold standard at the new depreciated level of the currency. Rather, policies were directed towards restoring the pre-war value of the currency in terms of gold.

Some of these moves were discretionary, such as accumulating gold reserves in such a way as to vindicate the announced rate. These policies were reinforced by legislation, including the Contraction Act of 1866, which provided funds for a withdrawal of U.S. notes. The most important piece of legislation, however, was the Resumption Act of 1875. The Act laid down the date in 1879 on which gold convertibility was to be recommenced at the pre-civil war parity. This policy created significant political controversy, and between 1875 and 1879 there were several attempts to repeal the Act. However, all of these were unsuccessful, and the pre-war gold parity was reestablished on 1 January, 1879.[17]

The important point is that the parity at which the United States re-entered the gold standard was never in serious doubt. Even when gold convertibility was suspended and the currency was floating against other currencies, private investors had an expectation as to what the exchange rate would be in the long-run. As a result, private capital flows generally operated to stabilize the value of the currency, rather than destabilize it. This is particularly true in the period after the passage of the Resumption Act, when there was a clear date at which the pre-civil war parity was likely to be recommenced.

If transactions in private capital markets were generally stabilizing even when convertibility was suspended but predicted to be resumed, such centripetal forces were even stronger when gold convertibility was still in force. This explains why the gold standard system could last for such a long period of time. Because the future value of the currency was known with some certainty, there was no reason for market participants to put pressure on the currency today. Hence, the rules of the game in the pre-1914 gold standard tended to make private capital flows stabilizing.

The Bretton Woods system and the ERM were, by contrast, adjustable peg fixed exchange rate systems. In both cases the government agreed to limit exchange rate movements around a par value, but also retained the right to change the par value in the appropriate circumstances.[18] Since such changes in the par value involved a permanent change in the rate of exchange between one currency and another, revisions implied permanent losses for private investors. Furthermore, since these losses were incurred between one day and the next, they were too large to be easily compensated for through differences in interest rates across currencies. Even annualized interest rates in three figures do not imply very large returns overnight. Hence, if a devaluation appeared likely to occur, market participants tried to switch out of the currency, and private market "speculation" becomes destabilizing.

A formal version of this argument can be found in the literature on exchange rate target zones. If the exchange rate peg is credible, as it was under the pre-1914 gold standard, then the exchange rate responds less to changes in fundamentals under a fixed exchange rate system (a target zone) that it would under a free float. The target zone stabilizes the exchange rate because market participants realize that the necessary policies will be taken to keep the rate within the band.[19] However, if the exchange rate peg is thought likely to change, then opposite result can occur, with the exchange rate becoming more sensitive to changes in fundamentals with the zone than without it.[20] In this case, as the exchange rate moves towards the edge of the band, the probability of a revaluation of the central parity sets up a one way bet in which market participants can hope to gain significantly by speculating against the currency while the losses incurred if the parity is not revalued are relatively small.

This analysis has direct implications for exchange rate policy in the transition to EMU. The experience of the pre-1914 gold standard indicates that a fixed exchange rate regime is most stable when the par values in the system are expected to be maintained over long periods of time. From this perspective the exchange rate arrangements in the Maastricht Treaty were like a badly written book. There was a beginning and a middle, but no well defined end. With no guidance as to future parities, market participants' confidence in existing ERM parities began to erode after the Danes rejected the Maastricht Treaty in a referendum. Fundamentals made the direction of potential parity changes relatively clear—nobody was expecting a devaluation of the deutsche mark against the other currencies. As a result, the system was susceptible to destabilizing capital flows which, in the event, unwound the existing ERM arrangements relatively quickly.

The lessons from history are that one way of avoiding such market pressures would be to provide a credible commitment as to the future value of the currency, as illustrated by the U.S. Resumption Act of 1875. In the context of EMU this could be achieved by announcing the eventual exchange rate parities at which the different currencies will enter EMU.[21] If underlying economic policies are consistent with this parity, which is a big if, then the current exchange rate will remain reasonably close to the bilateral rates at which EMU will occur. Deviations from these exchange rate parities would then reflect such factors as interest rate differentials and expected time of entry into EMU. Indeed, the exchange rate becomes a measure of the confidence of market participants in the announced parity, and hence the confidence that they have about entry into EMU.[22] Such a commitment would therefore justify an exchange rate convergence criterion similar to the original one in the Maastricht Treaty.

Such a commitment also provides a simple and clear focus with which to justify directing macroeconomic policies towards EMU. During the 1980s a number of European countries used their exchange rate peg as a signal of their commitment to lowering the rate of domestic inflation. A preannounced EMU parity could provide a similar role with respect to monetary union, providing a public signal of a country's commitment to joining the currency union.[23]

To make any announcement of such future exchange rate parities credible the national governments involved would have to implement policies consistent with such an exchange rate commitment. As discussed earlier, the U.S. during the greenback period followed a number of policies to bolster their commitment to returning to the original gold parity in addition to the Resumption Act. European governments who wish to join EMU are already constrained by the convergence criteria in the Maastricht Treaty. However, it is possible that these obligations will not be sufficient to convince private markets of their commitments to the announced parities. The new exchange rate commitment and convergence criterion could therefore impose new constraints upon the governments concerned. In general, it does not appear unreasonable to expect a government which is committing to fixing its exchange rates against other currencies permanently by entering into a currency union to be able to maintain the policies required to validate a preannounced EMU parity.

The alternative is to allow the current system of wide bands and little or no guidance about future ERM parities to continue. Such a policy could produce difficulties. Continuing exchange rate instability might make it more and more difficult to define and agree on correct final parities for EMU, making entry into the single currency more difficult. At the same time, the behavior of private exchange rate markets may well be of very limited use in deciding the future parities as exchange rate changes in private markets may well reflect expectations about the future peg rather than fundamentals, as appears to have been the case for Great Britain prior to April 1925.

4. Conclusions

Moving to a single currency provides a number of challenges. This paper has discussed two such issues. On the question of which countries are likely to benefit economically from an early entry into EMU, it was suggested that Germany, France, and the Benelux countries are likely to experience relatively high levels of benefits and relatively low levels of costs. However, the uncertainties surrounding the estimates of the benefits are simply too large for one to say whether all EU members, the core countries alone, or no countries will benefit economically from EMU. Turning to the issue of exchange rate policies in the transition from separate monies to EMU, it was suggested that one method of avoiding exchange rate instability during the transition was to announce the rates at which separate currencies would enter EMU at a relatively early stage.

Notes

1. The consistency of the currency arrangements with the Maastricht criterion remains in doubt. The issue depends upon whether the 15 percent ERM bands can be described as "normal", as defined by the treaty. A protocol also stipulates that the currency participate in these bands without "severe tensions", a form of words which could be used to expand the criteria for EMU membership beyond simple maintenance of either the old 2¼ or new 15 percent ERM bands.

2. See Eichengreen (1992) and Bean (1992) for surveys.
3. McKinnon (1963) argued that more open economies were better candidates for a currency union since monetary policy became less effective in these circumstances, while Kenen (1969) emphasized the role of the composition of output in the efficacy of the exchange rate.
4. See Weber (1990) and Bayoumi and Eichengreen (1992, 1993). A more positive view of prospects for EMU is provided in Bini-Smaghi and Vori (1993), who find most disturbances in Europe to be industry-specific, and argue that exchange rate changes are not a useful way of alleviating such disturbances. However, using a similar methodology and a wider data set Bayoumi and Prasad (1995) find country-specific disturbances are important for Europe.
5. Structural Funds are important for certain poor countries, although not for the EU as a whole. However, they reflect long-term income differentials, not short-term disturbances.
6. A widely quoted set of estimates are contained in Commission of the European Communities (1990).
7. The distribution of these benefits could be significantly altered by fiscal transfers, such as Structural Funds, as such "side-payments" could be used to transfer some of the potential benefits between countries.
8. When the lira moved from wide to narrow bands in 1990, the central parity was devalued but the lower parity remained unchanged.
9. For a detailed chronology of the period and analysis of events, see IMF (1993).
10. The Irish pound devalued its central parity later in the year.
11. Except in the case of the Dutch guilder and the Deutsche mark, where the 2¼ percent bands were retained.
12. Although the renewed pressure on several currencies and the devaluation of the central parities of the peseta and escudo in early 1995 indicate that this situation may not last.
13. Miller and Sutherland (1994).
14. Bordo (1995). The collapse of the Bretton Woods system is described in more detail in Garber (1992).
15. Eichengreen and Wyplosz (1993).
16. Bordo and Kyland (1995) and McKinnon (1993).
17. See Bordo and Kyland (1995) for a longer discussion of this period.
18. In the Bretton Woods system changes in the par value were supposed to occur only in the case of a fundamental disequilibrium in the balance of payments, and theoretically generally required the agreement of the International Monetary Fund. In practice, however, such changes appear to have been made on a unilateral basis.
19. This is the essence of the original target zone model developed by Krugman (1992).
20. See Bertola and Cabalero (1992). This also helps to explain why the widening of the ERM bands in 1993 reduced exchange rate instability, as the excess sensitivity to fundamentals would disappear once the bands were widened.
21. These parities need not be set in stone. Even during the gold standard period countries could, and did, suspend convertibility in response to exceptional events. However, to operate as a reasonable commitment device it would be necessary to ensure that such a change in parities was only made in the face of shocks which were large, unexpected, and independent of government policies. There is also the so called end-game problem, that, once parities are chosen, national governments have an incentive to cheat in various ways. All I would mention in this context is that some level of trust would appear implicit in any agreement to join a common currency.
22. In the case of the United States after the Civil War, the passage of the Contraction Act in 1866 caused a significant strengthening of the greenback in terms of gold.
23. In addition, as with the ERM in the late 1980s, it is possible that such a commitment could actually lower the costs of achieving EMU through beneficial credibility effects. The existence of such credibility effects has been wifely debated in the literature.

References

Bayoumi, T. and B. Eichengreen (1992), "Is There a Conflict Between EC Enlargement and European Economic Unification?", CEPR Discussion Paper 646, forthcoming *Greek Economic Review*.

Bayoumi, T. and B. Eichengreen (1993), "Shocking Aspects of European Monetary Union", in F. Torres and F. Giavazzi (eds.), *The Transition to Economic and Monetary Union in Europe*, Cambridge, Cambridge University Press.

Bayoumi, T. and E. Prasad (1995), "Currency Unions, Fluctuations, and Adjustment: Some Empirical Evidence", *CEPR Discussion Paper*, 1172.

Bean, C. (1992), "The Economics of EMU", *Journal of Economic Perspectives*, 6, 31–52 (Fall).

Bertola, G. and R.J. Cabalero (1992), "Target Zones and Realignments", *American Economic Review* 82, 520–536 (June).

Bini-Smaghi, L. and S. Vori (1993), "Rating the EC as an Optimal Currency Area: Is it Worse than the U.S.?", *Banca d'Italia Temi de Discussione*, 187.

Bordo, M.D. (1995), "Is there a Case of a New Bretton Woods International Monetary System?", paper given at the American Economic Association Meetings held in Washington, DC January 6–8th 1995, forthcoming in the *American Economic Review*.

Bordo, M.D. and F.E. Kyland (1995), "The Gold Standard as a Commitment Mechanism", forthcoming in T. Bayoumi, B. Eichengreen and M. Taylor (eds.), *Modern Perspectives on the Gold Standard*, Cambridge, Cambridge University Press.

Commission of the European Communities (1990), "One Market, One Money: An Evaluation of the Potential Benefits and Costs of Forming an Economic and Monetary Union", *European Economy*, 44, (October 1990).

Eichengreen, B. (1992), *Should the Maastricht Treaty Be Saved?*, Princeton Studies in International Finance, 74 (Princeton: International Finance Section, December 1992).

Eichengreen, B. and C. Wyplosz (1993), "Unstable EMS", *Brookings Papers on Economic Activity*, 1, 51–143.

Garber, P.M. (1993), "The Collapse of the Bretton Woods Fixed Exchange Rate System", in M.D. Bordo and B. Eichengreen (eds.), *A Retrospective on the Bretton Woods System: Lessons for International Monetary Reform*, Chicago, University of Chicago Press.

International Monetary Fund (1993), *World Economic Outlook: October 1993*, Washington, International Monetary Fund.

Kenen, P.B. (1969), "The Theory of Optimum Currency Areas: An Eclectic View", in R.A. Mundell and A.K. Swaboda (eds.), *Monetary Problems of the International Economy*, Chicago, University of Chicago Press.

Krugman, P. (1992), "Target Zones and Exchange Rate Dynamics", *Quarterly Journal of Economics*, 106, 669–682 (August).

Miller, M. and A. Sutherland (1994), "Speculative Anticipations of Sterling's Return to Gold: Was Keynes Wrong", *Economic Journal*, 104, 804–812 (July).

McKinnon, R.I. (1963), "Optimum Currency Areas", *American Economic Review*, 53, 717–725.

McKinnon, R.I. (1993), "The Rules of the Game: International Money in Historical Perspective", *Journal of Economic Literature*, XXXI, 1–44.

Mundell, R.A. (1961), "A Theory of Optimum Currency Areas", *American Economic Review*, 51, 657–665.

Weber, A. (1990), "EMU and Asymmetries and Adjustment Problems in the EMS: Some Empirical Evidence", *CEPR Discussion Paper*, 448.

The Best Way to EMU: Summary of the Panel Discussion

KOOS ALDERS,[1] KEES KOEDIJK,[2] CLEMENS KOOL[2]
AND CARLO WINDER[1]
[1]*De Nederlandsche Bank, Amsterdam, The Netherlands*
[2]*Limburg Institute of Financial Economics, University of Limburg, Maastricht, The Netherlands*

The workshop was concluded by a panel discussion with the title "The Best Way to EMU". The objective was to place the issues that had come up in the presented papers in a broader policy perspective. The panel consisted of professor Thygesen from the University of Copenhagen, professor De Grauwe from the Catholic University of Leuven, professor Bakker from the Dutch central bank (DNB), and Mr. Hogeweg from the European Monetary Institute (EMI).

The panel discussion was centered around four provocative statements formulated by the workshop's organising committee. In turn each of these statements was covered according to the following structure. First, one of the members of the panel gave his view on the statement under consideration. Then, the other members could comment on the first speaker. Subsequently, the floor was opened for a short general discussion.

Statement 1: In the Run-up to Stage Three of Emu, it is Recommendable to Narrow the Current Formal Fluctuation Margins within the Ems

In a first reaction, De Grauwe answered with a resounding "no" to this statement. On the contrary, in order to have a smooth transition to EMU one should allow the wider margins to be used. There are several reasons for this. First, there will continue to be shocks hitting countries differently during the transition period, putting pressure on the exchange rates. It would be foolish to try to defend these. This will only invite speculative crises which cannot be contained. Second, there will be great uncertainty about the rates that will be "irrevocably fixed". Third, there will be great uncertainty about the membership issue. Two years before the start (i.e. in January 1997) it will be uncertain who will become a member. This uncertainty will have a great impact in the foreign exchange markets, making speculators very nervous. News (including political news) will be watched closely. Slight pieces of news will be blown up. Very turbulent financial markets should therefore be expected as we approach the Third Stage. Trying to narrow the margins is inviting disaster, and will almost surely lead to a postponement of EMU.

Koos Alders, Kees Koedijk, Clemens Kool and Carlo Winder (eds.), Monetary Policy in a Converging Europe, pp. 131–141.

The view that exchange rates should be kept fixed together with the other nominal convergence criteria, inflation convergence and interest rate convergence, is in De Grauwe's view based on a fundamental misconception of the step into a monetary union. The step into an EMU is a fundamental regime shift, in which the national currencies are eliminated and replaced by a new and single currency. There is no reason whatsoever why one needs to fix the exchange rates in advance. There is also no need to force national inflation rates to be (almost) equal prior to entry into the union. Inflation is the loss of purchasing power of national currencies. With EMU the national currencies are abolished and therefore also the inflation attached to these currencies. After the monetary reform there will be a single currency to which a new inflation rate will be attached. The inflation rates will automatically converge. So in a sense trying to have convergence in inflation rates before the union, is making life difficult, because with different currencies and central banks it will always be difficult to equalise inflation expectations. Once there is a single currency, however, it is easy to do so. Thus, the contradiction is that the Maastricht Treaty wants nominal convergence as a condition for EMU while nominal convergence occurs automatically once one is in the union.

As opposed to De Grauwe, Bakker replied with a soft-spoken "yes". Although he admitted that past experience made it difficult to defend a return to narrow margins, the current system provides too few disciplinary mechanisms as witnessed by recent events. Moreover, the instruments of the Basle-Nyborg agreement do not work well in the present wide-band arrangement. Intervention obligations are absent, so only interest rates and the band itself can be used. It is argued, however, that interest rate changes may be counterproductive in this wide band, while exchange rate movements can easily run out of hand as has been seen in the Spanish case. Narrow margins can function as a beacon and should be in place at least for the participating countries when the decision to go to Stage Three of EMU is taken.

Hogeweg stressed two points. First, regardless of the width of the margins, the essence of the end-game is the credibility of the exchange rate level at which countries will enter monetary union. Then, the question is which mechanism will maximize that credibility. Second, the end-game problem will never provide a solution for, for instance, the debt problem of Belgium, since the last-minute leeway can only be used after the decision that a country may enter is taken. So the need to conform to the Maastricht Treaty criteria remains.

Thygesen supported De Grauwe's scepticism about a return to narrow margins. Firstly, this issue is not discussed seriously at the present time. In general, countries are not interested in this option now, possibly because they want to retain some uncertainty with respect to the alternatives to go into monetary union. Secondly, one should delay discussion about narrowing the margins until Stage Three is just about to start. At that point, the countries that have decided to join may have an interest in somewhat tighter arrangements than the simple reference formulation in the Treaty that exchange rates should be a matter of common concern. Moreover, fluctuations in the exchange rates of countries that do not join, could undermine the strength of some that have joined.

In the general discussion, Neumann argued that at the start of the monetary union, private agents will be uncertain about the inflation path the new European Central Bank will generate. To reduce this uncertainty, convergence of inflation rates before the union may be beneficial. Second, he suggested that the current wide fluctuation margins should be maintained formally, but that individual countries should try to gradually stabilise their exchange rate on long-term equilibrium values and, thus, de facto use much more narrow margins. This will also prevent end-game incentives to a great extent. Viñals agreed with De Grauwe that narrowing the margins without further preconditions now would be an invitation to undesirable speculation. He disagreed with De Grauwe about the convergence conditions, though. One of the problems of a monetary union is whether the new European Central Bank will be prepared to follow a prudent non-inflationary policy. The main objective of the convergence criteria therefore is to reveal whether individual countries put enough priority on price stability to endure the cost of bringing inflation down before the union.

In conclusion, De Grauwe made it clear that one should distinguish between issues of low and stable inflation and issues of monetary unification. The purpose of a future European Central Bank should be to have low inflation. In the Maastricht Treaty institutions have been designed, namely central bank independence and non-monetisation of budget deficits, which in the long run should form a guarantee for low inflation. But that should be separated from the problems of a monetary union. A monetary union can be achieved in six months despite existing inflation differentials and economists do a disservice to society by pretending nominal convergence is an absolute precondition.

Statement 2: Is EMU Viable without a Strong Political Union?

Bakker stressed that the statement put forward by the organisers was topical indeed. In the run-up to the Intergovernmental Conference in 1996 the first skirmishes with respect to the setting of the agenda are already discernible. Should it be a substantial agenda, including significant steps towards political integration? Or should the objectives be set much lower and should the discussion be confined to mundane questions such as the number of Commissioners? The camps are clearly divided. In a much-canvassed speech on 9 February,[1] the British Chancellor of the Exchequer Kenneth Clarke said that "it is quite possible to have monetary union without political union." On the other hand, Bundesbank President Hans Tietmeyer has come out forcefully in favour of a solid political foundation for EMU in order to make it durable.[2]

In defining his own position, Bakker took as a starting point that there are two asymmetries in the Maastricht Treaty. First, there is an imbalance between Monetary

Union and Economic Union. Monetary Union is based on supranational decision-making and implies the complete rendering of sovereignty in the monetary sphere. Economic Union, on the other hand, is based on national decision-making and relies primarily on a non-binding obligation to co-ordinate. Although there are curbs on government borrowing and debt, it is questionable whether in practice the procedures to make the authorities comply, will be sufficiently robust and enforceable if a central authority is lacking. Second, there is an imbalance between EMU and Political Union. EMU is framed in the institutional context of the Treaty of Rome, whereas EPU, in the new pillar structure of the Treaty of Maastricht, is merely based on voluntary intergovernmental co-operation. These two asymmetries in the Treaty on European Union entail considerable risks, in both economic and political terms.

With respect to the economic risks, Bakker stressed that the switch-over to a single currency not only carries with it important benefits, but may also involve considerable costs. The latter are potentially most relevant for Germany because its participation in the monetary union can be regarded as a concession. Such a concession is only worthwhile if sufficient guarantees are built in to ensure that stability-oriented policies are pursued in the Third Stage. Without these guarantees, there is no certainty that market forces will suffice to bring about national fiscal and wage policies in line with the stability-oriented policy of the European Central Bank. If imbalances were to occur, the European Central Bank would be subject to enormous pressures. One might argue that the European Central Bank should just hold the line and assert its independence by taking unpopular measures. But it might find it difficult to explain its actions across the union and thus run the risk of losing the full backing of the general public which is necessary to validate its independent position. For the political risks, Bakker started from the presumption that Germany will demand the price of political integration for accepting monetary union. It has made this clear all along. But what is meant by political union? In Bakker's view, it should not involve creating new European powers in new policy areas. Rather, political integration should focus on remedying the asymmetries in the present Treaty by strengthening the E of EMU and the P of the existing EPU. As far as the E of EMU is concerned, in the long run there is a need for a supranational economic policy-making authority to complement monetary union. Such an authority may eventually have the task to co-ordinate fiscal and wage policies, and to act as a countervailing power to the independent European Central Bank. As far as the P of EPU is concerned, adequate common decision-making in the foreign policy and juridical pillars of the Maastricht Treaty should be introduced, combined with better democratic control at the European level.

Thygesen stated that in general it is accepted too readily that EMU is a concession made by Germany, for which it is entitled to ask for other things. It is overlooked that Germany has a major interest in stable exchange rates with its main trading partners as well. The German experience has been that the Deutsche Mark tends to become too strong and too volatile in the absence of tight monetary arrangements which is a great inconvenience to the real economy in Germany. Firstly, Thygesen claimed that we listen too much in this respect to the German financial sector and the Bundesbank. Secondly, the claim for political union may be helpful to the integration of Eastern Europe in the European Union. While the old members of the EU progressed from strictly economic arrangements towards the concept of political union, the perspective of East-European countries is necessarily different, putting more emphasis on the political aspects of a union. There is no harm for them in developing and participating in a political union ahead of time and not linking it to a membership of an Economic and Monetary Union, which may take some time for those countries.

De Grauwe conceded with the idea that without a political union, national fiscal authorities may implement policies that are inconsistent with the common monetary policy. With a political union, however, it is possible that a common centralised fiscal policy will be inconsistent with monetary policy as well, in which case the pressure on the European Central Bank to adjust monetary policy will weigh much heavier than in the case of individual national fiscal policies. In fact, for this reason one would not want to have a political union. However, De Grauwe was in favour of a political union, and stated that already now there is a considerable amount of political union. Half of current national legislation is in fact European legislation. The question is how much political union is desired and in what areas. The theory of optimum currency areas suggests that some degree of fiscal centralisation is desired, but it is simply not clear whether ten, twenty or forty per cent of the budget should be centralised. Saying yes to political union, therefore, provides no useful information, as it does not tell what kind of political union it will be, nor how much is needed to make the political union viable.

The general discussion started with Gros, who argued that conceptually there is an inherent asymmetry between monetary and economic union. For a monetary union, a supranational institution (European Central Bank) with a common policy is required, while for an economic union only some common policies to assure open and competitive markets are necessary. So the asymmetry is in the concept, not in the Treaty. Gros also asked how a centralised fiscal authority whose main objective it is to prevent excessive debt creation can achieve its goals without taking away much of national fiscal autonomy. Neumann maintained that Germany was not particularly interested in fixed exchange rates with its trading partners, and that the neighbouring countries are so much interested in fixed exchange rates with Germany that they will maintain them also without EMU. According to Neumann, the German wish for a European union is politically motivated, to avoid a new isolation of Germany and a German "Alleingang".

Statement 3: The Only Way to Establish a Solid Basis for Emu is to Start with a Core Emu Around the French-German Axis

According to Thygesen, the answer should be yes; if the final stage of EMU is launched it will comprise a limited group of participants and both Germany and France will have to take part for the decisive step to be taken.

In his view the idea of participation by all Member States had been given up at least by 1990. The Delors Report of 1989 already hinted that "a degree of flexibility concerning the date and conditions on which some member countries would join certain arrangements would have to be envisaged".[3] The prospect that at least one member state (Greece) would be unable to meet the qualification criteria within a foreseeable time span gave additional legitimacy to the idea of different speeds, since it was clearly unacceptable that the slowest country should determine the pace of monetary unification for all others. When the prospect of enlargement to Central and Eastern Europe emerged, the need to differentiate the speed of accession to the final stage of European Monetary Union became even more obvious. Thygesen recalled that the Maastricht Treaty is, for obvious reasons, silent as to which countries could participate, whether at the earliest date or at the final deadline of January 1999. The presumption in the Treaty is simply that all countries which are economically ready, i.e., which meet the convergence criteria with a sufficient degree of approximation, will also be politically obliged to join and not to block others who are ready. Two member states – Denmark and the United Kingdom – obtained by means of separate protocols the right to defer their decision to join. Nothing which happened during the ratification process has modified this basic fact – but the difficulties after the recession of 1991–1993 to achieve the criterium relating to the budget deficits diminished the number of likely participants. Although it might still be technically possible to find a majority of seven (or eight) countries ready to go ahead when the first effort to reach a decision in the European Council before the end of 1996 has to be made, it now seems more likely that the final stage will start only on 1 January 1999,[4] at which point there is no required minimum number of participants. In theory, therefore, full monetary union could start with an enlarged Deutsche Mark-bloc of Germany, Austria and the Netherlands. That would make only a limited difference to these participants, though it holds the attraction for the two smaller countries of giving them some limited influence on the joint monetary policy. Such a mini-union would only marginally protect Germany against the high degree of exchange rate volatility and the tendency towards excessive appreciation which is the fate of a strong currency floating individually. Germany has had a foretaste of that recently, though not to the same extent as Japan did during the last decade.

For both economic and political reasons, the German preference in the late 1990s is likely to be in a more broadly based monetary union. German politicians consider a monetary union as an essential step towards political union; without the former the latter is unlikely to materialise.[5] While Germany will certainly insist on a strict interpretation of the convergence criteria, it also wants monetary union to start with more than a few satellite currencies and notably with France. Thygesen disregarded the possibility that Germany will not meet the convergence criteria; it already does so in 1995 and there is little reason to think that will change over the two years which follow.

Thygesen said France was currently in a more ambiguous position. Since 1983 its policy has been aiming primarily at disinflation and a stable exchange rate vis-à-vis the Deutsche Mark. It has succeeded in nominal convergence, even to the point of having an inflation rate below Germany's for some years. Over the past two years France has, however, taken some budgetary steps which have significantly enlarged an otherwise modest budget deficit in order to encourage demand. It would need to reduce the deficit by a couple of percentage points to be sure of qualifying for the final stage of EMU. That is not, by international standards, an unusual adjustment over a period of 2–3 years, but by French standards it is. A high priority is moreover given in the French economic debate to reducing unemployment from the currently very high level of more than 12 percent. For France there is accordingly the perception of a conflict between the political decision to seize the opportunity of a monetary union which France has done more than any other country to advance and the difficulties of meeting the economic criteria. This perception makes it unlikely that France could seize the opportunity already in late 1996, but it remains by far the most likely scenario that it will have come sufficiently close to the required performance a year later, so that it could join a final stage which will start on 1 January 1999.

Like Germany, France also has a conception of what would be the ideal size of the core group. Many in France would consider a monetary union with Germany, Austria, the three Benelux countries and possibly a couple of other similar countries – Ireland and Finland would be the countries most likely to come next – a risky venture. Ideally, France would like at least one more major country to join in order to provide additional counterweight to Germany and thereby limit the risk of the European currency becoming excessively prone to appreciation against third currencies as well as against those European currencies that have not joined the final stage. With Italy unlikely to qualify for quite some time, the best prospects for additional candidates are Spain (with Portugal) and the United Kingdom. If Germany and France seem ready to go ahead that will in itself have a major impact on attitudes in these other countries. As regards the United Kingdom, the main objective of the government's policy has been to delay and, if possible, to prevent the formation of a monetary union. But if the monetary union will be established, the United Kingdom is in Thygesen's view likely to want to take part, not least if the 1996–97 election results in a Labour government.

Bakker agreed that Europe cannot afford to wait too long for all the lagging countries, so that EMU should be started with a core group, where it would be unthinkable that France and Germany would not be in. It would, moreover, provide a good incentive for the other countries to make policy adjustments in order to join also in the near future. It, thus, in that sense has the dynamic element mentioned by Hogeweg. It is a situation, though, that cannot last too long according to Bakker, because a multi-speed EMU is not framed into a good institutional setting. It has as a counterpart a European Council where all countries are sitting, and a European Parliament where all countries are represented.

De Grauwe agreed with the statement also but pointed out one problem with the strategy to start with a core group of countries to form an EMU. He labelled this the Belgian problem and deemed it a serious one. The current debt to GDP ratio is 140 percent for Belgium and the deficit is around 6 percent of GDP. Even if Belgium would succeed in bringing down its deficit to 3 percent in 1996/1997, its debt to GDP ratio would still be 125–130 percent in 1999. Then, a first possibility would be to close the eyes for the too high debt position and let Belgium participate, because an EMU without Belgium would be unthinkable. Clearly, this will create a political problem as other countries in the periphery may have a claim to say: "why them and not us?" Such an important political conflict and problem may split the union apart. If this strategy will be taken it will be clear for all to see that the Maastricht way of convergence was a script that was written in advance so as to keep the Southern countries outside the union. It will become obvious that this was the intention right from the beginning. Alternatively, of course, one may decide to leave Belgium out at the start, forcing the civil servants of the European Union to live with the Belgian franc.

Statement 4: What Should the Policy Strategy of the Ecb Be?

Hogeweg started by making clear that in the masterplan according to which the EMI organises its preparatory work the discussion on the strategy of monetary policy comes last. The EMI is currently much more focused on the instruments that would be available for the European Central Bank to choose from. The reason behind this timing order is, on the one hand, the idea that there is a relative degree of independence between the instruments used and the specific strategy pursued, and on the other hand that it takes a long lead time to implement any instrument after the decision to use it. It is of crucial importance that on day one of Stage Three a set of instruments is effectively available. At the moment, there are three types of strategies pursued in the countries of the European union. Germany is the prime case of clear intermediate monetary targeting, the United Kingdom directly targets inflation, while a large group of countries uses the exchange rate as its prime policy target. Clearly, for the case of the European Central Bank after the start of EMU, this last option is less relevant and less likely. Intermediate monetary targeting used to be fashionable not so very long ago and has been practised by a large number of countries. Gradually, more and more countries have abandoned such strategy, primarily because the demand for money broke down. It would be interesting to know whether these countries are happier now with the new strategy or would prefer to return to intermediate monetary targeting when suddenly their demand for money function became stable again.

Hogeweg ventured that a decision by the future European Central Bank on its strategy would not only depend on the empirical question of the stability of the demand for money at the time and in the area of the monetary union, but also on the preferences of policy makers, as developed over time in their experience in the individual countries. Hogeweg concluded by saying that it is premature for expressing a preference for intermediate monetary targeting or direct inflation targeting. That will have to wait until the arrival of Stage Three.

De Grauwe argued that at least initially, in the first few years of the operations of the European Central Bank, it should not use monetary targeting. Experience shows that there is a problem with monetary targeting when there are lot of financial innovations and institutional changes, because the money supply may become an unclear concept and, therefore, dangerous to use as a targeting device. When an Economic and Monetary Union will be established, the European Central Bank will be confronted with huge and unknown institutional changes and great uncertainties concerning the money stock. Thus, it would be a great mistake to start with monetary targeting by the European Central Bank initially. It would be advisable in such case to pursue inflation targeting, the more since several instruments, including – but not exclusively – the money stock, are available. Afterwards, it depends on how the dust settles in EMU.

Thygesen tended to agree with De Grauwe that it might even be more in continuity with policy in the transition if initially after the start of Stage Three emphasis was put on inflation targeting, because of the inevitable break in relationships that would arise as completely fixed exchange rates or the common currency would come about. It would provide continuity, but of course it is a new era. Thygesen, therefore, hoped that the EMI will take up the task of producing and publishing inflation reports for the total group of countries in the way some central banks – in the UK and Sweden, for example – are doing already, to gain some more experience on this point.

Bakker fully disagreed with previous speakers and stated a preference for monetary targeting for three reasons. First, it is the only approach which has been tested up till now in countries like Germany, France and – indirectly – in countries which have linked their currencies to the Deutsche Mark, like Austria, the Netherlands and Belgium. This policy has proven to be credible and to work out well for inflation. Second, a move to inflation targeting implies looking at a variety of indicators, as already indicated by De Grauwe and Thygesen. This will make decision making in the council of the European Central Bank extremely difficult, and prone to political interference because everybody can refer to the indicator that best suits his needs. Third, the fear for a structural break is over-emphasised. The important issue is having enough credibility at the start of the Third Stage.

Having heard the other panelists expand on his introduction, Hogeweg expressed a personal preference for intermediate monetary targeting. He stressed though that it may be difficult, because of the possibility of breaks in the expectations and behaviour of economic agents and structural changes in the money supply. A rigid policy of monetary targeting from day one has the risk of making big mistakes, which may hamper and damage the credibility and track record of the European Central Bank. Whatever the difficulties for decision making may be, looking at a broad range of indicators is mandatory in the first period of EMU. In that sense, he strongly supported the production of inflation reports by the EMI.

In support of monetary targeting, Gros noticed that a pure change in unit of account does not necessarily entail a large structural change in the relation between nominal income and monetary aggregates. The relation between inflation, inflationary expectations and interest rates – the instruments of monetary policy – may be much more affected, though, because of the different monetary policy environment in many countries. From an operational view, both monetary and inflation targeting appear to be feasible according to Fischer. However, monetary targeting may be an easier way simply because there are certain start-up costs involved with inflation targeting in general. Firstly, even though data would be available for all of Europe, there is no experience in interpreting this data. It takes time before one is comfortable with these various indicators. Secondly, there is less risk of manipulation when one focuses on one monetary aggregate than on a whole range of indicators under the checklist approach. Finally, although currently inflation reports are mostly associated with central banks targeting inflation, this is not a necessary link. Every central bank could and should publish inflation reports.

According to Briault, the Bank of England has tried inflation targets, has come to like it and intends to stick to it. Briault claimed that even the Bundesbank does not target money. Over the past years interest rates have not responded to changes in monetary aggregates and money has been running well above target. So, the Bundesbank has brought credibility to monetary targets, not the other way round. Because of the fortunate medium-term link between inflation and money growth, with implicit inflation targeting, ex post the money supply appears to be kept on track quite well in Germany. Unfortunately, it does not work in the UK. Finally, Briault stated he was willing to use all information available in money growth, but objects to throwing away all other information. He was worried about the idea that only monetary targeting is able to provide credibility. If monetary targeting does not work and the relations between money and prices break down, the European Central Bank will have to rely on other indicators.

Andersen took a position in favour of inflation targeting. He objected to Bakker's analysis that only money targeting has been tested. Even the Bundesbank uses a range of indicators. The Swedish experience is that, in terms of transparency, inflation targeting is easily explained to market participants and politicians. Also political interference is less under inflation targeting when the information can be transmitted clearly.

Notes

1. Speech by Kenneth Clarke to the European Movement on 9 February 1995.
2. See e.g. Hans Tietmeyer, Europäische Währungsunion und Politische Union – das Modell mehrerer Geschwindigkeiten, Europa Archiv, Folge 16, 1994, p. 457–460. In this article Tietmeyer states: "A common monetary policy and at the same time unco-ordinated national economic and financial policies is hardly compatible in the longer run. Hence, monetary union requires far-reaching and lasting political union in the sense of a viable economic and political framework with clear decision-making powers." (translation by editors)
3. Report on economic and monetary union in the European Community (the "Delors Report"), Office for Official Publications of the European Communities, Luxembourg, par 44.
4. The ECOFIN Council in Versailles in April 1995 agreed that one year will be required from the decision to start the final stage until the ECB can become operational. To meet the latest starting date in the Treaty of 1 January 1999 a decision would be required before the end of 1997.
5. See, in particular, the paper issued by the CDU/CSU party in September 1994 ("Schäuble-Lamers paper").

Authors, Discussants, Members of the Panel, Organisers and Other Workshop Participants

AUTHORS, DISCUSSANTS, MEMBERS OF THE PANEL AND ORGANISERS

Dr. J.A.J. Alders (Koos)
Organiser/editor
De Nederlandsche Bank

Drs. I.J.M. Arnold (Ivo)
Discussant
Nijenrode University

Prof. dr. A.F.P. Bakker (Age)
Panel
De Nederlandsche Bank

Dr. T. Bayoumi (Tamim)
Author
International Monetary Fund

Dr. W.C. Boeschoten (Willem)
Discussant
De Nederlandsche Bank

Dr. C. Borio (Claudio)
Author
Bank for International Settlements

Mr. C.B. Briault (Clive)
Discussant
Bank of England

Prof. dr. M.M.G. Fase (Martin)
Discussant
De Nederlandsche Bank

Dr. A. Fischer (Andreas)
Author
Swiss National Bank

Prof. dr. P. de Grauwe (Paul)
Panel
Catholic University of Leuven

Drs. J.M. Groeneveld (Hans)
Organiser/author
De Nederlandsche Bank

Dr. D. Gros (Daniel)
Discussant
Centre for European Policy Studies

Dr. H. Herrmann (Heinz)
Discussant
Deutsche Bundesbank

Drs. G.P.J. Hogeweg (Gert Jan)
Panel
European Monetary Institute

Dr. L.H. Hoogduin (Lex)
Organiser
De Nederlandsche Bank

Mr. A. Icard (André)
Discussant
Banque de France

Prof. dr. K.G. Koedijk (Kees)
Organiser/author/editor
LIFE, University of Limburg

Dr. C.J.M. Kool (Clemens)
Organiser/author/editor
LIFE, University of Limburg

Dr. C. Monticelli (Carlo)
Author
Banca d'Italia

Prof. dr. M.J.M. Neumann (Manfred)
Discussant
University of Bonn

Mr. P. Poret (Pierre)
Discussant
Organisation for Economic Co-operation and Development

Dr. J. Swank (Job)
Discussant
De Nederlandsche Bank

Prof. dr. N. Thygesen (Niels)
Panel
Copenhagen Business School

Mr. J. Viñals (José)
Discussant
Banco de España

Dr. C.C.M. Winder (Carlo)
Organiser/editor
De Nederlandsche Bank

Other Participants

Mr. K. Andersson (Krister)
Sveriges Riksbank

Drs. H. Benink (Harald)
LIFE, University of Limburg

Dr. J.A. Bikker (Jaap)
De Nederlandsche Bank

Prof. dr. E.J. Bomhoff (Eduard)
Nijenrode University

Ms. A.B. Christiansen (Anne Berit)
Norges Bank

Dr. M. Dombrecht (Michel)
National Bank of Belgium

Prof. dr. S.C.W. Eijffinger (Sylvester)
Tilburg University

Prof. dr. C. van Ewijk (Casper)
University of Amsterdam

Dr. J. de Haan (Jacob)
University of Groningen

Dr. E. Hochreiter (Eduard)
Oesterreichische Nationalbank

Prof. dr. J.J.M. Kremers (Jeroen)
Dutch Ministry of Finance

Prof. dr. J. Muysken (Joan)
University of Limburg

Dr. P. Pikkarainen (Pentti)
Bank of Finland

Ms. drs. H.M. Prast (Henriëtte)
University of Amsterdam

Prof. dr. P.C. Schotman (Peter)
LIFE, University of Limburg

Dr. A.A. Weber (Axel)
University of Bonn

Prof. dr. C.C.P. Wolff (Christian)
LIFE, University of Limburg

FINANCIAL AND MONETARY POLICY STUDIES

*1. J.S.G. Wilson and C.F. Scheffer (eds.): *Multinational Enterprises.* Financial and Monitary Aspects. 1974 ISBN 90-286-0124-4

*2. H. Fournier and J.E. Wadsworth (eds.): *Floating Exchange Rates.* The Lessons of Recent Experience. 1976 ISBN 90-286-0565-7

*3. J.E. Wadsworth, J.S.G. Wilson and H. Fournier (eds.): *The Development of Financial Institutions in Europe, 1956–1976.* 1977 ISBN 90-286-0337-9

*4. J.E. Wadsworth and F.L. de Juvigny (eds.): *New Approaches in Monetary Policy.* 1979 ISBN 90-286-0848-6

*5. J.R. Sargent (ed.), R. Bertrand, J.S.G. Wilson and T.M. Rybczynski (ass. eds.): *Europe and the Dollar in the World-Wide Disequilibrium.* 1981 ISBN 90-286-0700-5

*6. D.E. Fair and F.L. de Juvigny (eds.): *Bank Management in a Changing Domestic and International Environment.* The Challenges of the Eighties. 1982 ISBN 90-247-2606-9

*7. D.E. Fair (ed.) in cooperation with R. Bertrand: *International Lending in a Fragile World Economy.* 1983 ISBN 90-247-2809-6

8. P. Salin (ed.): *Currency Competition and Monetary Union.* 1984 ISBN 90-247-2817-7

*9. D.E. Fair (ed.) in cooperation with F.L. de Juvigny: *Government Policies and the Working of Financial Systems in Industrialized Countries.* 1984 ISBN 90-247-3076-7

10. C. Goedhart, G.A. Kessler, J. Kymmell and F. de Roos (eds.): *Jelle Zijlstra, A Central Banker's View.* Selected Speeches and Articles. 1985 ISBN 90-247-3184-4

11. C. van Ewijk and J.J. Klant (eds.): *Monetary Conditions for Economic Recovery.* 1985 ISBN 90-247-3219-0

*12. D.E. Fair (ed.): *Shifting Frontiers in Financial Markets.* 1986 ISBN 90-247-3225-5

13. E.F. Toma and M. Toma (eds.): *Central Bankers, Bureaucratic Incentives, and Monetary Policy.* 1986 ISBN 90-247-3366-9

*14. D.E. Fair and C. de Boissieu (eds.): *International Monetary and Financial Integration.* The European Dimension. 1988 ISBN 90-247-3563-7

15. J. Cohen: *The Flow of Funds in Theory and Practice.* A Flow-Constrained Approach to Monetary Theory and Policy. 1987 ISBN 90-247-3601-3

16. W. Eizenga, E.F. Limburg and J.J. Polak (eds.): *The Quest for National and Global Economic Stability.* In Honor of Hendrikus Johannes Witteveen. 1988 ISBN 90-247-3653-6

*17. D.E. Fair and C. de Boissieu (eds.): *The International Adjustment Process.* New Perspectives, Recent Experience and Future Challenges for the Financial System. 1989 ISBN 0-7923-0013-0

18. J.J. Sijben (ed.): *Financing the World Economy in the Nineties.* 1989 ISBN 0-7923-0090-4

FINANCIAL AND MONETARY POLICY STUDIES

19. I. Rizzo: *The 'Hidden' Debt.* With a Foreword by A.T. Peacock. 1990 ISBN 0-7923-0610-4
*20. D.E. Fair and C. de Boissieu (eds.): *Financial Institutions in Europe under New Competitive Conditions.* 1990 ISBN 0-7923-0673-2
21. R. Yazdipour (ed.): *Advances in Small Business Finance.* 1991 ISBN 0-7923-1135-3
*22. D.E. Fair and C. de Boissieu (eds.): *Fiscal Policy, Taxation and the Financial System in an Increasingly Integrated Europe.* 1992 ISBN 0-7923-1451-4
23. W.C. Boeschoten: *Currency Use and Payment Patterns.* 1992 ISBN 0-7923-1710-6
24. H.A. Benink: *Financial Integration in Europe.* 1993 ISBN 0-7923-1849-8
25. G. Galeotti and M. Marrelli (eds.): *Design and Reform of Taxation Policy.* 1992 ISBN 0-7923-2016-6
*26. D.E. Fair and R. Raymond (eds.): *The New Europe: Evolving Economic and Financial Systems in East and West.* 1993 ISBN 0-7923-2159-6
27. J.O. de Beaufort Wijnholds, S.C.W. Eijffinger and L.H. Hoogduin (eds.): *A Framework for Monetary Stability.* Papers and Proceedings of an International Conference (Amsterdam, The Netherlands, 1993). 1994 ISBN 0-7923-2667-9
*28. D.E. Fair and R. Raymond (eds.): *The Competitiveness of Financial Institutions and Centres in Europe.* 1994 ISBN 0-7923-3131-1
29. A.F.P. Bakker: *The Liberalization of Capital Movements in Europe.* The Monetary Committee and Financial Integration, 1958–1994. 1996 ISBN 0-7923-3591-0
30. H.A. Benink: *Coping with Financial Fragility and Systemic Risk.* 1995 ISBN 0-7923-9612-X
31. K. Alders, K. Koedijk, C. Kool and C. Winder (eds.): *Monetary Policy in a Converging Europe.* Papers and Proceeding of an International Workshop. 1996 ISBN 0-7923-3746-8

*Published on behalf of the *Société Universitaire Européenne de Recherches Financières* (SUERF), consisting the lectures given at Colloquia, organized and directed by SUERF.

Kluwer Academic Publishers – Dordrecht / Boston / London

MIX
Papier aus verantwortungsvollen Quellen
Paper from responsible sources
FSC® C105338

If you have any concerns about our products,
you can contact us on
ProductSafety@springernature.com

In case Publisher is established outside the EU,
the EU authorized representative is:
Springer Nature Customer Service Center GmbH
Europaplatz 3, 69115 Heidelberg, Germany

Printed by Libri Plureos GmbH
in Hamburg, Germany